I0477380

THE NEW AESTHETIC AND ART:

CONSTELLATIONS OF THE POSTDIGITAL

SCOTT CONTRERAS-KOTERBAY AND ŁUKASZ MIROCHA

Theory on Demand #20

**The New Aesthetic and Art:
Constellations of the Postdigital**

Authors: Scott Contreras-Koterbay and Łukasz Mirocha
Editorial support: Miriam Rasch, Nadine Roestenburg

Cover design: Katja van Stiphout
DTP: Léna Robin
EPUB development: Léna Robin

Printer: Print on Demand
Publisher: Institute of Network Cultures, Amsterdam, 2016
ISBN: 978-94-92302-08-3

Contact
Institute of Network Cultures
Phone: +31 20 5951865
Email: info@networkcultures.org
Web: http://www.networkcultures.org

This publication is available through various print on demand services.
EPUB and PDF editions of this publication are freely downloadable from
our website, http://www.networkcultures.org/publications/#tods

This publication is licensed under the Creative Commons
Attribution-NonCommercial-NoDerivatives 4.0 International (CC BY-NC-SA 4.0).

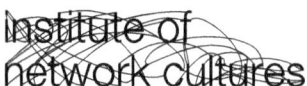

Contents

ACKNOWLEDGEMENTS

This book has been written by two authors who at first glance could not be more different, from different academic background, at a different moments of career development and from different generations. Scott is a full professor at East Tennessee State University, where he teaches art history in the Department of Art & Design and aesthetics in the Department of Philosophy & Humanities with a primary research focus in aesthetic ontology and Lacan. Łukasz is a an early-career researcher, currently afiliated with the University's of Warsaw Faculty of 'Artes Liberales' while collaborating with the newly founded Digital Economy Lab (DELab) at the University of Warsaw. He also works as a journalist and consultant covering emerging digital technologies, digital society and culture.

This book had its start at the International Congress of Aesthetics, a highly select and ambitious international conference devoted to aesthetics, art and media study, held in Kraków, Poland in the summer of 2013. Assigned to speak on the same panel because we were presenting on the same topic – digital autonomy and the New Aesthetic – we quickly realized that we had many more overlapping academic interests. As a result of our first meeting on the first day of the conference we decided to take a more creative approach to our presentations, splitting them up so that each could address the areas we planned on covering in a logical sequence and inadvertently taking over the dynamic of the successful session. Since our time in Kraków, we have been exchanging ideas and quickly realized that publishing a co-authored book would be a perfect opportunity to collaboratively produce an introduction to New Aesthetics incorporating not only an approach ensconced in a broad theoretical of digital technology's impact but also its impact on the contemporary art world.

We would like to thank: the Institute of Network Cultures at the Amsterdam University of Applied Sciences for giving us the possibility to publish our work with them, and particularly Miriam Rasch and Nadine Roestenburg for taking great care of us throughout the writing, editing and publishing process; East Tennessee State University's Office of Research & Sponsored Programs, Department of Art & Design and Honors College, all of whom provided specific financial support that made the project possible in its final stages; the Polish government, which financed Łukasz' work from the budget for science of the Republic of Poland as a research project within the 'Diamond Grant' programme in 2012-2016; and the artists included herein, many of whom supplied information and images about their work and were incredibly gracious in their responses to our inquiries.

For the last 4 years Łukasz has been a research director of a project funded by the Polish Ministry of Science and Higher Education. This early-career research grant allowed Łukasz to meet and share ideas with many distinguished scholars whose knowledge, insight and support were crucial for emergence of many ideas presented in the book. He is particularly grateful to the research community of the Digital Aesthetics Research Center/Participation Information Technologies Group at the University of Aarhus where he spent some time as a visiting researcher in 2014. He would like to also thank the research community of the Sussex Humanities Lab at the University of Sussex which he visited in 2015.

Scott would like to thank his many friends and colleagues across many disciplines in his university and his family and friends. He especially thanks his wife and son Karlota and Anton for their love and support; the book would never have been finished as soon as it was if Karlota didn't encourage him to go to Warsaw for a few days, and Anton appears in one of the images inside.

Łukasz would like to express particular thanks to Christian Ulrik Andersen (Aarhus University), David M. Berry (University of Sussex), Piotr Celiński (Maria Curie-Skłodowska-University), Damien Charrieras (City University of Hong Kong), Lev Manovich (CUNY), Søren Bro Pold (Aarhus University), Krzysztof Rutkowski (University of Warsaw), Winnie Soon (Aarhus University) and Piotr Wilczek (University of Warsaw). You have always been kind and very supportive. Your ongoing encouragement pushed me to work even harder to develop my ideas.

Scott Contreras-Koterbay
Łukasz Mirocha
Johnson City, TN, USA
Brighton, UK
Warsaw, Poland
2014-2016

INTRODUCTION

The increasing digitalization of our everyday lives has been marked by the appearances of new forms of visual manifestations that do more than simply provide information but have become autonomous objects that transform how we live. In a pervasive fashion, such phenomena – whether they appear on our smartphone, our computers, our enhanced televisions, billboards and advertisements and a myriad of other forms – have taken on their own lives becoming seemingly autonomous and out of our control. What is intriguing and, for some, troubling about these new digital objects is not just that they exist and function without human intervention and input but that we readily accept their presence in our lives. Cutting edge technologies and trends such as machine learning, adaptive algorithms, big data and Internet of Things rapidly foster emergence of stand-alone computational ecosystems and entities. Although they are of human design, most of their everyday interactions are not directly human-centered; therefore, while purportedly enriching our experiences the programs we use on our smartphones and other devices have begun to have lives outside of our control, acting for us without our knowledge; retaining information about our lives, our interactions with software today generates and constitutes the existence of the digital phenomena that start to take on lives of their own. Smartphones are the easiest example to use because the choices we make about what we want to know about the world through them and the choices we make when we act in the world are then stored, redefined, altered and represented to us in a manner which is seemingly natural and tailored to our own choices but which is also artificially created and manipulative. To put it another way, digital phenomena have become entities in their own right, functioning in a way that allows us to believe we are in control of our world when, in fact, the exact opposite is taking place as we respond to these entities. On an everyday basis, most of us are screen essentialists as the field of our human-machine interaction is limited to the information displayed on the screen. And what makes these entities even more difficult to comprehend is not so much the control they have over our lives but their independence from their original sources; interactive software very quickly takes on a life of its own far beyond its programmers' intentions when acquiring more data and allowing its algorithms to respond and reprogram itself in response to that data. Jean Baudrillard's notion of the simulacrum was insufficient; the world hasn't become a simulation of our own making but a simulation of our simulations' making, as we are increasingly living in their world not our own. Contemporary society and culture have become effectively data feed.

The New Aesthetic has been described as 'an attitude, a feeling, *a sensibility*'. In part a reflection of the expanding use of digital technology, it has increasingly become an indication at almost an essentialist level of specific artistic and design tendencies and practices. The concept of the New Aesthetic was initiated by James Bridle on his blog in 2011 where he started to gather images and things that seemed to identify a new aesthetic of the future. The term is used to describe the increasing presence in the physical world of such visual phenomena rooted in digital technology and the internet, in an effort to describe the increasing proliferation of visual languages dependent on self-generative computational structures rather than on natural language. Bridle's Tumblr blog was instrumental in curating New Aesthetic objects but others have added to the theorization of the idea. Science fiction writer and futurist Bruce Sterling has developed a response that articulates its impact in social, political, cultural and artistic terms. Describing a set of artifacts that he believes represents a conflation of the digital and the real, Sterling has said of the New Aesthetic:

> [It] is a native product of modern network culture. It's from London, but it was born digital, on the Internet. The New Aesthetic is a "theory object" and a "shareable con-cept." The New Aesthetic is "collectively intelligent." It's diffuse, crowdsourcing, and made of many small pieces loosely joined. It is rhizomatic, as the people at Rhizome would likely tell you. It's open-sourced, and triumph-of-amateurs. It's like its logo, a bright cluster of balloons tied to some huge, dark and lethal weight.[1]

Sterling's comment that New Aesthetic objects are rhizomatic is, unknowingly perhaps, derived from Gilles Deleuze's and Félix Guattari's notion of the rhizome as a metaphor for multiple entry points and representations of information into life, but he goes beyond their concept by asserting the phenomenological independence of New Aesthetic objects. Everyday interaction between human and consumer technology has been intensifying for the last decade: the internet at its most fundamental level of functionality, portable devices, mobile internet, web 2.0 and, lately, big data (where so much information is collected in large databases that it becomes impossible to access, use or control without adaptive algorithms and machine learning) amongst others have all deeply influenced contemporary civilization. What makes this influence different is how little choice the users have when they are relinquishing control of their existences to these media where the interaction has transformed from being merely intensive to pervasive and unseen.

Obviously, James Bridle and Bruce Sterling were not the first ones to notice what is taking place; Marshall McLuhan set the stage with his theories of communication and media, Lev Manovich's books *The Language of New Media* and *Software Takes Com-mand* have been instrumental in describing recent changes, and David M. Berry's notion of computationality in *The Philosophy of Software: Code and Mediation in the Digital Age* and *Critical Theory and The Digital* is an attempt to describe social and cultural changes in the digital era. All have brought insightful and invaluable perspectives to new notions of the document and the role computational devices have in our lives, but Bridle in particular deserves credit for coining the term 'New Aesthetic' because it is the first term which articulates these changes at social, cultural and political levels. Others have criticized it: the New Aesthetic has been dismissed and labeled as a superficial identi-fication of artistic practices that have already taken place for some time, and for many critics there is nothing new about New Aesthetic. We do not agree with this because we

---

1   Bruce Sterling, 'An Essay on the New Aesthetic', *Wired.com*, 2 April 2012, http://www.wired.
     com/2012/04/an-essay-on-the-new-aesthetic/.

believe the term takes into account multiple layers and modes of human technology interaction which are mediated by computational media and technological artifacts that need to be understood at an ontological level as a means of redefining what the world is; the New Aesthetic does more than identify a sufficiently distinct category of aesthetic products while challenging many of the normative conventions of aesthetics itself. 'It posits an aesthetic turn [...] brought about itself through a "new nature"'[2] and, in doing so, creates that new nature and a new holistic perspective for describing it. In a way, it signals a sense of hyper-contemporaneity.

To this end, we are taking two positions vis-à-vis New Aesthetic. First, we believe the New Aesthetic should not be considered as a mere theory of beauty or simple theory of beauty for the digital 21st century. In a broader perspective we would consider it as a theoretical approach that would enable taking to the forefront of our perception intertwined layers of algorithms and computation that contemporary civilization is built on. More narrowly, we are focusing on the New Aesthetic as an innovative interdisciplinary approach that is interested in describing specific types of digital imagery. At this level we would analyze it as an 'aesthetics of computational miscalculation' and as an 'aesthetics of digital age', taking into account: glitches, compression and codec artifacts, satellite images. It is not about aesthetics understood as in art theory or philosophy. The approach embodied by the New Aesthetic strives for 'seeing the grain of computation' and 'an eruption of the digital into the physical' and 'emergence of computationality as an onto-theology'. The New Aesthetic has sparked the practical interest of artists, curators and designers and has become a subject of theoretical inquiry for journalists and scholars. From a classic academic perspective it may seem vague, inaccurate and simply not worthy of any attention. However, any scholar interested in contemporary society and culture should take into account such movement.

Secondly, it is impossible to think of the New Aesthetic without thinking of it as an aesthetic system related to artistic productivity. The expanding use of digital technology has been increasingly recognized as worthy of interest in aesthetics and in the art world; from projected cybernetic utopias and virtual realities to global awareness of artistic trends and unique art worlds, from the direct use of digital techniques as both the means of production and as art itself to its use as a means of facilitating new insights into art history, digital technology's impact has become pervasive and even, perhaps, common. While there have been numerous discussions of the effects of digital technology on artistic production and aesthetic evaluation, until recently there's been little discussion of the digital as a language that functions independently of our normal concerns. Thinking through this idea we've identified two sets of questions. First, how has the digitalization of the world as it appears in a digital format affected our aesthetic perceptions of such

2   James Bridle, 'Waving at the Machines', Web Directions South 2011, 5 December 2011, Sydney, http://booktwo.org/notebook/waving-at-machines/.

appearances? Second, how has the digitalization of the world in the form of the New Aesthetic changed the way art is being produced today? Answering these questions involves
more than just describing the stylization of GUIs or the latest updates to the software
that runs iPhones but requires both asking questions about the assessment process that
users go through when looking at digital manifestations as well as looking at art specifically made in a digital format. Particularly nowadays, when any type of digital imagery,
including visual arts, undergoes the same computational processes: quantization and
discretization – continuous reality is transformed into set of variables.

The software used in mapping programs transforms the way we interact with and navigate a geographic location but it also has aesthetic qualities itself that work behind the
scenes, if you will, and subtly transform and manipulate digitally our actual movement
and enjoyment of space; to put it another way, whether we like a restaurant, book shop,
art gallery, local neighborhood or even an entire city may be dependent on the way
information about all of these is presented to us and, even further, how that information evolves in databases controlled by the software. This could go so far as a software
application 'defining' an entire country geographically by noting at certain scales the
locations of fast food restaurants. With the work of artists who use digital techniques we
have an entirely different but related set of issues: are artists utilizing the digital media
merely as a means towards an end or is the creative process guided by the software
regardless of artists' intentions? Artists like Mathieu Tremblin, Benjamin Grosser and
Aram Bartholl have been creating work that explores the implications not only of the
use of digital media but also our ability to control such media.

What needs to be addressed is how New Aesthetic objects or New Aesthetic art objects –
and there absolutely is a difference – necessitate new forms of aesthetic evaluation. It can
be argued that advocating an increasing awareness of the inescapabilty of digital manifestations opposes the continuation of aesthetics in the traditional sense as it finds itself
practically incapable of accounting for an aesthetic system that is self-substantiating; old
ways of looking at art, of describing the beauty of objects, are no longer relevant when
the objects themselves respond to our sensibilities and craft themselves towards their
understanding of our very intentions of aesthetic judgment. Because manifestations of
the New Aesthetic are based in computational language, algorithms and self-replicating
systems of code, it is necessary to question whether traditional accounts are viable or
whether the very notions of beauty, pleasure, idealism and expressiveness are reducible
to mathematical structures or simply incompatible with natural language when assessing
New Aesthetic objects.

What is striking about New Aesthetic art objects is not just their origins in digital media
but their appearance as natural evolving out of our digital experiences. Nowadays, the
landscape of potential 'artistic images' is basically endless as images are part of everyday
software and information ecosystems and are 'produced' thanks to capabilities of other
software. It is no longer strange to think of images as 'photoshopped' because all norma-

tively perceivable images are assumed to be digitally altered in some fashion. Thus, all contemporary images share the same digital DNA (creative software ecosystems, filers, effects, codecs, color spaces). What is strange, rather, is how natural the assumption itself has become. Of course many artists continue to work in traditional methods and materials, but increasingly digital methods become the foundations or the starting point. It might seem strange to say that we're going to end up talking about Kant at some point - at first it might seem like Kant would be the last person that has anything to do with the New Aesthetic - but it is by looking at Kant's little regarded 'Critique of Teleological Judgment' in his *Critique of Judgment* that some interesting insights emerge about New Aesthetic objects in general and art specifically.

Where we've ended up with these two perspectives - the theoretical, which seeks to understand the metaphysics of New Aesthetic manifestations, and the aesthetic, which seeks to assess the valuative and creative processes involved in the creation of New Aesthetic objects - is not at a pair of incompatible positions but a fluxual dialectic that articulates what we believe is a pervasive and unavoidable development in our world. The New Aesthetic isn't merely simply a recognition that software is becoming a guiding principle for our experience of the world nor a new form of digital creativity but is a determinative aspect of contemporary existence. Today's image is often a software product, implemented in and by another software construct, as Lev Manovich argues; we have entered an era when media *are* software. Given that media are software, and given the growing ubiquity of media and its effects on our lives, we believe the New Aesthetic is more than just an attitude but a defining feature of contemporary existence. The New Aesthetic is not without its limitations. It is hardly a firm academic theory or methodology. However, being aware of the limitations behind the idea, we argue that in order to examine a fluxual social and cultural context of the digital age one has to take an equally unconventional and fluxual approach.

CHAPTER 1
THE CASE FOR THE
NEW AESTHETIC

In September 2014 at the Emmanuel Gallery on the Auraria Campus in Denver, Colorado, an exhibition titled 'The Emperor's New Aesthetic' opened; though it received little notice and, to date, no reviews, nevertheless its premise as a critique of the New Aesthetic as 'an overused and over-hyped term' was immediately evident. 'The idea is to poke fun at the burgeoning institutionalization of "the new aesthetic", "post-internet" and "new-media" art in general, while still acknowledging the potential for cultural, political, economic and aesthetic intervention inherent in control of access / protocols / networks.'[1] Obviously, we take issue with that premise. The New Aesthetic, we believe, is a recent and important phenomenon, permeating much of everyday life as well as more rarified circles in academia and the art world; a perfect example of this is the proposed new designs of Norwegian banknotes that were revealed in October 2014[2] and which use a broad arrangement of pixels in a manner supposedly 'typically Nordic' in character but which, perhaps deceptively or unconsciously, could be more accurately described as driven by a digital aesthetic. {Fig. 1}

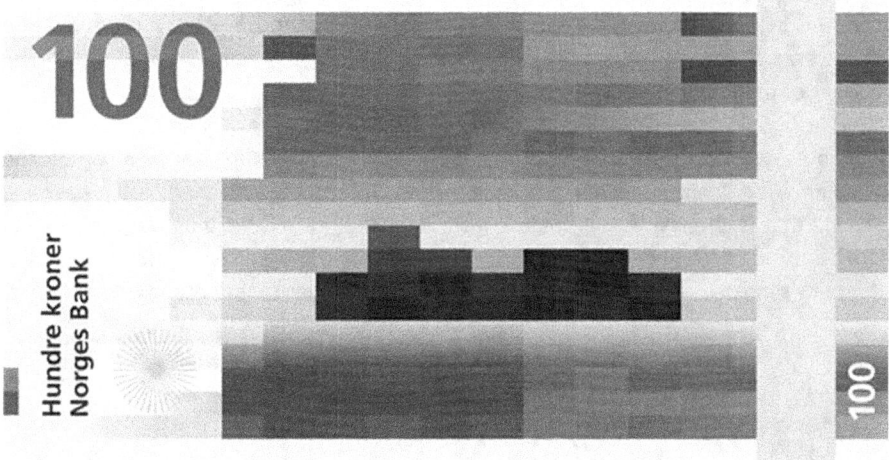

Fig. 1 Norge Bank Notes

The contrast between the frivolity of the Denver exhibition and the serious nature of the proposed banknotes is telling; to think of a purely digital design as endemically related to a national identity means that the digital has inserted itself into the way we conceive and construct our own identities. This chapter is focused on making the case that the New Aesthetic is worth an extended and serious look.

---

1   David Fodel and Matt Jenkins (curators), 'Exhibition announcement: *The Emperor's New Aesthetic*', 9 September 2014, Rhizome, http://rhizome.org/announce/events/60873/view/.

2   Norges Bank, 'Motifs for the New Banknote Series' (Press Release), 7 October 2014, http://www.norges-bank.no/en/Published/Press-releases/2014/Press-release-7-october-2014/.

To make the case that the New Aesthetic is worth studying perhaps a little history is a good place to start with even though it's only the most recent of histories. The New Aesthetic as a project was started by James Bridle, a London-based writer, publisher and artist, upon launching a new personal website in May 2011.[3] The first significant public and off-internet discussion on the New Aesthetic was held in 2012 at the SXSW conference, one of the most influential creative events in the world, attended by artists, curators, scholars and professional nerds. The panel entitled 'The New Aesthetic: Seeing Like Digital Devices' gathered Aaron Cope (designer and engineer), Ben Terrett (designer), Joanne McNeil (art activist, journalist), Russell Davies (communications consultant and tech journalist) and James Bridle. In the description of the panel, Bridle stated:

> We are becoming acquainted with new ways of seeing: the Gods-eye view of satellites, the Kinect's inside-out sense of the living room, the elevated car-sight of Google Street View, the facial obsessions of CCTV [...] As a result, these new styles and senses recur in our art, our designs, and our products. The pixelation of low-resolution images, the rough yet distinct edges of 3D printing, the shifting layers of digital maps. In this session, the participants will give examples of these effects, products and artworks, and discuss the ways in which ways of seeing are increasingly transforming ways of making and doing.[4]

In many ways Bridle's description of the New Aesthetic is intentionally vague but, at the same time, it did more than just provide a series of loosely curated examples; it was clear in 2012 that Bridle was still grappling with the idea and that his blog was functioning like a curatorial manifesto in his efforts to describe and categorize it at the time, but at the same time its vagueness certainly created opportunities that engaged others. {Fig. 2}

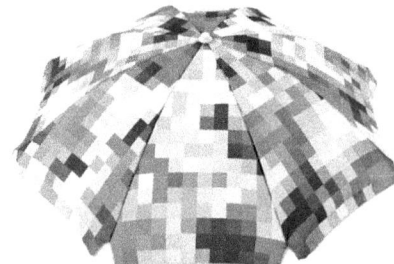

Fig. 2 'Le Pixel Umbrella'

---

3   The first entry on the New Aesthetic was published on Really Interesting Group website, http://www.riglondon.com/blog/2011/05/06/the-new-aesthetic/. Now the New Aesthetic project is available on Tumblr, http://new-aesthetic.tumblr.com.

4   SXSW Schedule 2012, 'The New Aesthetic: Seeing Like Digital Devices', http://schedule.sxsw.com/2012/events/event_IAP11102.

The New Aesthetic panel at SXSW and the critique that followed right after, made the term popular and helped it to gain attention among certain groups and individuals on the web, e.g. the '#newaesthetic' hashtag began appearing on Twitter. It went viral and resulted in many conflicting interpretational approaches and views on what it really was and which technologically-rooted social and cultural phenomena and artifacts could be described as examples of the New Aesthetic. The broad scope of visual media considered as the New Aesthetic was described by Bruce Sterling in his famous essay published in *Wired* magazine, which included '[...] Satellite views. Parametric architecture. Surveillance cameras. Digital image processing. Data-mashed video frames. Glitches and corruption artifacts. Voxelated 3D pixels in real-world geometries. Dazzle camou. Augments. Render ghosts. And, last and least, nostalgic retro 8bit graphics from the 1980s.'[5] Sterling's description shows that he was starting to catch on to the notion that there was this new thing, this new approach, this new attitude, that could be utilized in an extensive, horizontal and synchronic approach, taking into account various artifacts, media, tools and works of art of digital origin. Additionally, a number of the first commenters of the New Aesthetic grabbed on to the various categories of computational miscalculations and glitches as a way of identifying fascinating and inhumanly flawed contemporary imagery as a vital element of the New Aesthetic's fields of interest, in a way that contributed new insights into some of the discussions about the glitch that had been taking place in recent years. Some critics stressed the political consequences of increased human-technology interaction as seen by the New Aesthetic.[6] Others emphasized its social and gender-specific context e.g. the 'politics of the gaze'[7] problem (male vs. machine vs. human).[8] David M. Berry valued the New Aesthetic for stimulating interest in the computational aspects of contemporary civilization and their political and cultural impact, but at the same time stressed the unconditional inclusiveness of the term that result in its vagueness in terms of the accuracy of description and information.[9] On the other hand, Bruce Sterling criticized its supporters for the anthropomorphisation of technological artifacts, arguing that their assertion that computers are praiseworthy because their effects are apparently analogous to conscious decisions is like praising the Freudian unconsciousness as an autonomous agent.[10]

---

5   Sterling, 'An Essay on the New Aesthetic'.

6   Adam Rothstein, 'New Aesthetics – New Politics', *POSZU blog*, April 2012, http://www.poszu.com/new-aesthetics-new-politics.html.

7   Madeline Ashby, 'The New Aesthetics of the Male Gaze', *Madelineashby.com*, 2 April 2012, http://madelineashby.com/?p=1198.

8   Will Wiles, 'The Machine Haze', *Aeon*, 17 September 2012, https://aeon.co/essays/what-do-we-uncover-when-we-look-through-digital-eyes.

9   David M. Berry, 'What Is the "New Aesthetic"?', 'Abduction Aesthetic: Computationality and the New Aesthetic', *Stunlaw blog*, 6 April 2012, http://stunlaw.blogspot.com/2012/04/abduction-aesthetic-computationality.html.

10   Sterling, 'An Essay on the New Aesthetic'.

Quickly, the New Aesthetic became a hot topic of conversation, and the term became commonplace at least among those interested in technology's development and impact on society. Yet, almost just as quickly some of those interested in the New Aesthetic turned away from it, including James Bridle himself. Obviously, we're not in that crowd.

What fascinates us about the New Aesthetic cannot be summarized neatly. It is a non-movement that can't be easily defined but can be easily indicated. It's really cool, in a way, that a thorough academic approach to the New Aesthetic has not emerged so far when so many new categories instantly become the subjects of a feverish academic onslaught.[11] The New Aesthetic aims to cover so many contemporary social and cultural phenomena that any disciplinary approach would be too limited to analyze it as a whole. However, only a few weeks after the SXSW 2012 conference, a seminar was organized in the Netherlands in order to elaborate a critical study of the New Aesthetic. As a result of a booksprint session, a freely available e-book called New Aesthetics, New Anxieties was written by six authors – new media scholars, artists, curators and writers.[12] The authors focused on many aspects of the non-movement emphasizing the misunderstandings and anxieties generated by many instances considered as examples of the New Aesthetic. The authors were also interested in the influence of network-based initiatives as the New Aesthetic on their professional work. They 'attempt to move beyond lazy thinking, positions of pious indifference or naive enthusiasm, and ask what the New Aesthetic might tell us about this juncture in which we find ourselves, as curators, critics, artists, theorists and creative workers'.[13] Yet this remains, to date, the only sustained academic treatment of the subject.

Perhaps what tempts us to think about the New Aesthetic is that it is an offspring of easily accessible and open web-based communication channels which, therefore, means that it's become excessively pervasive and accessible. The initial response to the New Aesthetic can be characterized as an intellectual crowdsourcing of collective intelligence formed of theoreticians and practitioners interested in human-technology interaction, but we believe that the New Aesthetic is so wide-spread that care about its effects should be more general. The viral nature of contemporary communication channels resulted in a rapid spread of the term and the engagement of multiple agents in its development, leaving a discussion of this increasingly important development to the vagaries of a passing fad as it hits the peak of its popularity lasting no more than a few months is a mistake.

The New Aesthetic is primarily, though not entirely, an internet-based approach or a cultural phenomenon and, as such, affects or will affect the lives of the entirety of humanity;

---

11   The irony doesn't escape us, we promise you.

12   David M. Berry, et. al. New Aesthetic, New Anxieties, Rotterdam: V2 Institute of Unstable Media, 2012.

13   Berry, et. al. New Aesthetic, New Anxieties, p. 11.

as a result, we could describe it as a real-time web-based enquiry, one that functions within the construct of web-based activity and is determined by the conditions of the enquiry; but for the fact that its inclusiveness permits a multitude of interpretational approaches and standpoints, thinking through the manifestations of the New Aesthetic is already conditionally predetermined. Even if our efforts only result in a definition rife with the vagueness of the term and lacking a firm theoretical background, we still take the position, as Bruce Sterling has accurately observed, that the New Aesthetic has touched something new and important.

What makes the New Aesthetic such a challenge is more than just the fact that it exists at all; Sterling wrote 'It's our fault for pretending otherwise, for fooling ourselves, for projecting our own qualities onto phenomena that we built, that are very interesting to us, but not at all like us.'[14] We've both created the New Aesthetic and become a recipient of its existence's implication and, in the digital realm, therefore, to critically think about it means that it's necessary to utilize it at times uncritically. The New Aesthetic covered so many theoretical and practical fields (i.e. media art, media archaeology, digital art, digital aesthetics HCI, internet privacy, object-oriented ontology, programming) that its lack of coherence and methodology was essentially implemented in the movement from its early days. Even James Bridle explained that he did not intend to create a new big idea or an ontology of the 21st century. It seems that Bridle wanted to encourage people to engage in a discussion, using as many approaches and various expert knowledge as possible. Concrete methodology and disciplinary boundaries were of second importance:

> One of the things about New Aesthetic was that it was very much supposed to be not "post" anything else and not "pre" anything else, it was an observation about something hopefully grander, of which these are some current examples of.[15]

That is why Bridle chose a blog as a platform for sharing his ideas, instead of an academic journal or professional magazines, as the influence of these channels of communication is rather small compared to open internet platforms. As an example of a new type of enquiry that benefits from informal channels of communication and information distribution, the New Aesthetic as a set of phenomena seems almost naturally situated on (or even limited to) the web precisely because it has been discussed solely on blogs, on social media and popularized by talks at business and cultural conferences, but there's so much more to be said. Such supposed limitations of theoretical inquiry accompany any discussion of the New Aesthetic, making evident the discomfort traditional academia still has with blogs and online discussions as a source of critical inquiry. It could be argued

---

14   Sterling, 'An Essay on the New Aesthetic'.

15   Rober Urquhart, 'An Interview With James Bridle of the New Aesthetic', *The Huffington Post*, 9 May 2012, http://www.huffingtonpost.co.uk/robert-urquhart/james-bridle-the-new-aesthetic_b_1498958.html.

that the New Aesthetic is just an artistic performance of a British designer who decided to 'test' the creative communities on the web – though Bridle himself writes that it is an 'ongoing research project' – but then again, clearly, the commentators responded to his call. At the peak of the popularity of the New Aesthetic, Bridle was so overwhelmed by the interest that he even suspended the blog for some time, evidence of a growing awareness of its impact.[16]

The New Aesthetic is not without its limitations. It is hardly a firm academic theory or methodology.

Bruce Sterling argued in 'An Essay on the New Aesthetic' that the New Aesthetic was a very interesting movement, at least potentially. However Sterling also seems to be saying that, due to its extensiveness and rhizomatic nature, the very notion of the New Aesthetic wasn't bold and critical enough. Many examples of the New Aesthetic were only partially described or analyzed, but together they form a collective composed of artifacts, media, tools and works of art that is a direct result of contemporary informa-tion flow enhanced by web-based communication and they will continue to occur in the future. That is why many of its commentators emphasized that this approach could be developed in various directions. At the present stage of development it is more like a signpost for further enquiry.

The analysis of the New Aesthetic was performed from two perspectives. The first one focuses on its inner logic and takes into account one of the themes that the New Aes-thetic itself is concerned with – revealing the grain of computation in digital visual media by focusing on glitches, image processing artifacts etc. By emphasizing the abnormal in digital images, we can fully perceive its computational materiality along with limitations of today's visual media. Taking into account rapid technological development – high-definition images and displays, intuitive interfaces and services – this approach seems crucial for a critical and postdigital enquiry on the status of today's media. The second perspective studies various forms of visual media in the spirit of the New Aesthetic, iden-tifying their complexity, processual nature and their standardization, as the effect of the New Aesthetic becomes more perceptible like, for example, in the previously mentioned recent design of the Norges Bank currency.

At least one thing is clear: the New Aesthetic is dependent on the digital turn, the shift in contemporary culture when information presentation has moved from being an analog ontological relation to a digital relation. This has involved more than simply a change

---

16   J.J. Charlesworth, 'We are the droids we're looking for: the New Aesthetic and its friendly critics', *JJ Charlesworth Blog*, 7 May 2012, https://blogjjcharlesworth.wordpress.com/2012/05/07/we-are-the-droids-were-looking-for-the-new-aesthetic-and-its-friendly-critics/.

in the form of the information but a radical shift in the style of the presentation of the information; as Wim Westera writes:

> Technology and human life are inextricable. Whatever we do is either directly or indirectly linked with machines, tools, or digital media. Any product we buy, be it peanut butter, fruit, or a bunch of flowers is the outcome of a hidden processing chain containing numerous calculations, transport, raw materials, mechanics, administrative files, orders, and coordinative messages, many of which are carried by digital media.[17]

Everything has become digitized and, thus, every set of information surrounding our lives has become digitally available. In this respect, the digital turn is a real-time operative and manifest condition that has emerged as a schizophrenic force in contemporary society, whereby we are able to both control our world digitally but whereby we can also be controlled digitally in a way that is ignorant of such control. Recognizing the importance of the digital has become a de rigueur exercise among cultural theorists, such that descriptions of its pervasive presence and power are commonplace and widely accepted. David M. Berry writes:

> From its early days as a mechanism used to perform data processing, the digital is becoming the de facto medium for transmitting information, communicating and for sharing social life. Through these important functions the digital becomes a privileged site for social and political engagement and therefore it is increasingly important that we understand the digital and offer the possibility of a critical theory of the digital.[18]

While such a perspective is received unquestionably in all branches of cultural theory, nevertheless the shift of the digital from a functional tool to a 'de facto medium of information' is startling in its implications and cannot be taken for granted; whereas the horizon of digital objects once was a set of explorable and relatively unknown territories, wedged into limited but functioning parameters by computer scientists so that they could be employed as an external language and utilized to increase the accuracy of describing our experience and codifying the resultant data, today we're in entirely different circumstances. The creation of code now feeds the evolutionary and organic growth of the digital in order for it to operate with even greater autonomy, independent of the rarified controls found in a computer science laboratory. Witnessing the growth of apps available for Apple iOS as just one example – what started with 500 in 2008[19]

17   Wim Westera, *The Digital Turn: How the Internet Transforms Our Existence*, 2015 (2013), http://www.thedigitalturn.co.uk/TheDigitalTurn.pdf, p. 125.

18   David M. Berry, *Critical Theory and the Digital*, London: Bloomsbury, 2014, p. 121.

19   Apple Inc., 'iPhone 3G on Sale Tomorrow' (Press release). 10 July, 2008, http://www.apple.com/pr/library/2008/07/10iPhone-3G-on-Sale-Tomorrow.html.

has now reached 1,200,000 by mid-2014[20] - is like witnessing the exponential replication of viruses and bacteria. Over the course of several decades we have been increasingly relying on the computational in many domains of our activity at a civilizational level: in business it has taken over with algorithmically-based high-frequency trading, with approximately 73% of the equity trading and 60% of futures trading in the United States occurring without any human decision; societally our ability to bank, shop and interact with our fellow human beings is increasingly governed by our digital presence, with Facebook now becoming a legally serviceable address for court documents in Australia, New Zealand, the UK, Germany and other countries; and in cultural activity where there is a persistent decline in the education in and use of analog technology like photography film in favor of digital cameras to the point that the majority of universities world-wide are exclusively hiring digital photographers as faculty members. We are not favoring the analog and we're certainly not Luddites, but the digital turn has become more than just a 'turn', instead it's become a dominant force in contemporary society that is increasingly beyond the control of its users. Technological advancements, still to some extent based on Moore's law, are resulting in a logarithmically exponential increase of the computational capacity of electronic devices, but what is fascinating is that the limitations of the applicability of computational capacity may not be limited so much by hardware but rather by its intrusion into human capacity, in that there will be at some point fewer and fewer opportunities for digitalization to govern the world. We are living in a time in which it is becoming increasingly difficult to realize and act analogically. In this respect the New Aesthetic becomes a signpost, of sorts, that the digital has become more of a processual condition that our civilization is based on, instead of being just a 'turn' or a 'revolution' understood as a fixed moment in time.

To simply list a series of examples of digital phenomena in our world is insufficient. From our perspective, the tendency towards pervasive digitalization could be assessed by focusing on either its ontological effects or through an analysis of various episte-mological perspectives. In the case of the ontological, often an important tenant of the digital humanities, there is a tendency to move towards the conclusion that all experience is digital at its foundation. With an emphasis on the abstraction of real world experiences into digitally accounted data, through the persistence and pragmatic reduction of sequential experiences to concomitant time-related informational streams and in the increasingly complex and assumptive manifestation of desire structures of data-dependent human beings, we run headlong into situations such as Ashton's the Internet of Things; the convergence of connected devices starts to not only predicate decisions about replacing items in vending machines, for example, or governs market supply chains, but even more preemptively starts to choose our homes' temperatures

---

20   Sarah Perez, 'iTunes App Store Now Has 1.2 Million Apps, Has Seen 75 Billion Downloads To Date', *TechCrunch*, 2 June, 2014, http://techcrunch.com/2014/06/02/itunes-app-store-now-has-1-2-million-apps-has-seen-75-billion-downloads-to-date/.

prior to our return to work based on digitally evolving models of our preferences. As a result, a whole new species of semi-autonomous and autonomous beings have become vital constituents of our lives both at an individual and at a social level. A digital ontology asserts that the entire nature of reality is structured, and the digital becomes the sole means whereby the structure is effectively navigated. In the case of the epistemic, the status of knowledge has changed as it has become digitized; whereas epistemic questions once were subjected to logic and rationality, with the likes of Descartes and Kant painstakingly exploring nuances and dead-ends in the hopes of being self-satisfied that the answers to their questions were ensconced within necessary and sufficient conditions, the notions of big data and meta-data assert that the world can only be known once it has been digitized and, as knowledge itself ceases to be locally relative, that it has become singularly absolute. Things are true because we've read them (not read about them, but 'read them') on the internet, which we're always carrying around in our pocket, with philosophical implication extending beyond the epistemic and ontological concerns into the necessity of a teleological approach.

Focusing on either an ontological or epistemic position yields interesting insights, but often it becomes entangled in an implied negative critique of the digitalization of the world. In the case of the ontological perspective, resistance inevitably arises to the notion that the world of experiences must necessarily be accounted for in a binary manner; surely, it's assumed, there will always be instances when the digital method is insufficient, when directed rather than mediated experience and an emotional response is more appropriate. In the case of the epistemic perspective a negative critique runs along similar notions, especially in the context of some Romantic idea of the primacy of human rationality. These pitfalls are inevitable and, because they are inevitable, we would like to avoid them. So where to turn? By recognizing the dialectic between the ontological and the epistemic perspectives, a synthesis is possible; given an ontological perspective that turns outward to the world as it accounts for potential experience in a relationship between an epistemic perspective that turns inward to secure knowledge, there is a middle ground that is dependent on both while being yet a third form of experience: the evaluative or the aesthetic. Visual models of communication and information distribution have increased social and cultural reliance on the digital, necessitating analyzing contemporary society and culture in two ways: first, by recognizing that the autonomous digital products have an aesthetic existence in-and-of-themselves and second, by allowing for an appreciative and evaluative approach to these objects. Ontological and epistemological conditions of contemporary society manifest themselves in everyday practices rooted in digital visual media which can be edited and transformed into many kinds of media hybrids because of its powerful processing units and creative software; it is those hybrids as synthetic products that are, perhaps, the most interesting. We have reached the point where autonomous and synthetic objects necessitate new approaches, driving forms of artistic production.

What we mean by computational visual media is a category of digital products that are more than just programmable pieces of data that are often perceived through high-definition still images, movies, CGI or graphical user interfaces but are experienceable and self-determining phenomena in their own right, displayed on ultra-high definition displays and accessed and edited thanks to intuitive user interfaces; with the increasing processing power available in decreasing physical parameters[21] partnered with a graphic user interface that seemingly grasps our intentions spontaneously and predictively, conditions are being constructed whereby the output of the device assumes an unquestioned and teleologically natural state. The very computational materiality of today's visual media is, indeed, hidden beneath layers of user-friendly software, hardware, networks, cloud-based processing and storage services to the point (and, importantly, designed to that point) of increasing invisibility, with the implications or the predeterminatively agreed conventions that it will just work without any need for a user to change its operating parameters. {Fig. 3}

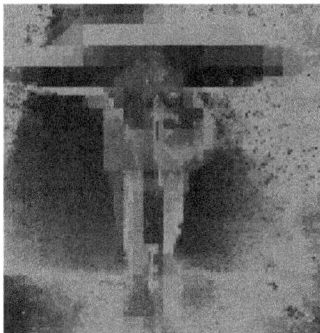

Fig. 3 Image Processed Through Decim8

In many respects, the benefits have been self-evident, and it's impossible to review the multitude of programs without being in awe of the innovativeness and ingenuity of their designers and programs; this extends beyond simply new ways of accounting for data or new ways of manipulating data to entirely new ways of dealing with the mundane to the profound: for instance, the explosion of new types of devices and services has resulted in the continual development of services, platforms and computational devices which foster new forms of cultural and social engagement enhanced by technology, extending beyond simply being able to contact friends and family instantaneously around the world to being able to alter the political landscape through spontaneous social collaboration and action. These phenomena occur right in front of us and simultaneously affect many areas of human activity (business, culture, science), both at an industrial and at a consumer level of human-computer interaction in a positive and productive way. We have

21   The increasing size of the iPhone 6 Plus and the Samsung Galaxy phones notwithstanding, which
      mark a shift in design emphasis, upcoming products like the Apple Watch and wearable digital
      devices follow the trend of decreasing physical size.

entered an era of real-time communication and knowledge generation and distribution that is fostered by multi-purpose devices and mobile internet access – many new ideas are now born due to the inclusive and non-hierarchical models of web-based communication, such as personal publishing services (blogs, websites), social media and informal discussion groups where both professionals and non-professionals as well as practitioners and theoreticians alike share and discuss new ideas – but what is increasingly clear is that these phenomena are synthetic in nature and effect, affecting and transforming in their use our perception of the world while simultaneously creating their own worlds. In short, we've entered a new form of experience best labeled 'postdigital' as an indication that the digital revolution is over.[22] The world of raw data and technology, while being in front of us, is usually hidden underneath graphical user interfaces, smooth high-res images, seamless user experience and touch-screen Retina displays. The New Aesthetic rejects 'screen essentialism' and encourages us to perceive contemporary reality as an 'augmented space' filled both with human agents and computational artifacts (devices, networks) that interact and influence each other. Mel Alexenberg describes this as:

> Of or pertaining to art forms that address the humanization of digital technologies through interplay between digital, biological, cultural, and spiritual systems, between cyberspace and real space, between embodied media and mixed reality in social and physical communication, between high tech and high touch experiences, between visual, haptic, auditory, and kinesthetic media experiences, between virtual and augmented reality, between roots and globalization, between autoethnography and community narrative, and between web-enabled peer-produced wikiart and artworks created with alternative media through participation, interaction, and collaboration in which the role of the artist is redefined.[23]

The key here is the betweenness, the notion of a mixed reality, the synthesis. Baudrillard was only partially correct: what governs our experiences is not hyperreality but hyperrealities. It is in this space that the New Aesthetic has emerged and is defined.

The digital visual culture that has been a foundation for the emergence of the New Aesthetic is just one of the manifestations of a greater shift our civilization has been undergoing with the digital turn and postdigital aesthetics; the New Aesthetic has necessitated not just a new perspective but a new approach or a new type of attenuation. Postdigital aesthetics require a cross-disciplinary theoretical and practical approach, which addresses the trends described above, going far beyond a mere theory of beauty of digital images.

---

22 Don't revolutions have winners and losers? If so, the digital clearly won.

23 Mel Alexenberg, *The Future of Art in a Postdigital Age: From Hellenistic to Hebraic Consciousness*, Bristol: Intellect Ltd, 2011, p. 35.

Real-Time Effects of the New Aesthetic

The New Aesthetic, for example, emerged as a direct result of real-time communication channels enhanced by computational technologies. On the one hand it can be
understood as an approach useful in digital image analysis as it unveils the simultaneous materiality and instability of contemporary imagery by focusing on the abnormal
(image processing errors, glitches, artifacts etc.) On the other hand, taking into account
the origin and development of this approach the New Aesthetic should be considered as
one of the manifestations of the radical shift in the emergence of ideas and knowledge
distribution in the digital age. The New Aesthetic is based on real-time data generation
and distribution as it was born and developed thanks to internet-based channels of communication and exchange of ideas, but what emerges with the New Aesthetic is something
quite powerful that remained relatively unnoticed until James Bridle started his blog in
May 2011. Nowadays this approach can be generally described as a cross-disciplinary
approach recognizing the consequences of synthetic and autonomous objects through
human-technology interaction and an analysis of new non-anthropomorphic agents,
forces and computational patterns that are present both in the digital sphere and in the
physical world. As the identification process of New Aesthetic objects accelerated and
grew in confidence, it became clear that they were manifesting themselves through visual
digital media and new social and cultural practices involving humans and technological
artifacts in a plethora of fashions. Bridle's initial focus on the visual manifestations of the
New Aesthetic prompted the blog's horizontal stream layout containing several types of
digital visual media: images, movies, graphics, GIFs. In his first entry, James Bridle wrote:

> Since May 2011 I have been collecting material which points towards new ways of see-
> ing the world, an echo of the society, technology, politics and people that co-produce
> them. The *New Aesthetic* is not a movement, it is not a thing which can be done. It is
> a series of artifacts of the heterogeneous network, which recognizes differences, the
> gaps in our distant but overlapping realities.[24]

And, on another occasion:

> I started noticing things like this in the world. This is a cushion on sale in a furniture
> store that's pixelated. This is a strange thing. This is a look, a style, a pattern that
> didn't previously exist in the real world. It's something that's come out of digital. It's
> come out of a digital way of seeing, that represents things in this form. The real world
> doesn't, or at least didn't, have a grain that looks like this.[25]

---

24   James Bridle, *The New Aesthetic blog*, Tumblr, http://new-aesthetic.tumblr.com/about.

25   James Bridle, 'Waving at the Machines', Web Directions South 2011, Sydney, 11-14 October 2011,
     http://www.webdirections.org/resources/james-bridle-waving-at-the-machines/.

In this sense, to analyze the New Aesthetic is to engage in a form of topological description from a new perspective and position, identifying relations that exist beyond simply manifest usage to objects that are autonomous. This has been done before in a parallel way for similar objects, and in analyzing the New Aesthetic we intend to follow the phenomenologically driven methodology introduced by Vilém Flusser in his 1983 book *Towards a Philosophy of Photography*.

Flusser's approach is useful both for studying the inner logic of the New Aesthetic (its interest in computational images) and for analyzing it as one of the manifestations of computationality understood as a condition of contemporary civilization. Flusser argued that by describing complex relations between a camera (apparatus) and a human being (user) we can shed light on the condition of contemporary civilization which is founded on (mega)mass production and distribution of images, writing: 'The invention of photography constitutes a break in history that can only be understood in comparison to that other historical break constituted by the invention of linear writing.'[26] In the process of being able to reproduce the appearance of reality, the status of such reproductions became portable, mobile, and transmittable; whereas descriptions of the world were once dependent on lengthy exposition of words, photography placed an immediate form of perception in the hands of everyone, especially as the technology became less expensive, more widely available, and needed decreasing amounts of intervention on the part of the image producer to create satisfactory images. To put it another way, Flusser argued convincingly that photography constituted a new form of knowledge, one that didn't need a mediating subjectivity explicating at length its intended effect. What is especially important about Flusser's ideas in relation to the New Aesthetic is that this shift from writing to photography was entirely dependent on technological innovation; the camera became more than just a tool, it became an apparatus that could be manipulated by the user but which had a schematized set of limitations that were, nevertheless, assumed to be sufficient and self-sufficient to the task. He explained that, 'nothing can resist the force of this current of technical images – there is no artistic, scientific or political activity which is not aimed at it, there is no everyday activity which does not aspire to be photographed, filmed, video-taped'.[27] In essence, this shift marks a relinquishment of the user of their freedom to the apparatus' methods, creating a new topology of knowledge that had profound ontological and epistemic consequences because the user, even if they believe they are exerting control over the photographic process, never produces images except through the programmed character of the apparatus. Flusser recognized that this shift and its consequences needed to be addressed, writing:

It is consequently the task of a philosophy of photography to expose this struggle between human being and apparatuses in the field of photography and to reflect on

---

26 Vilém Flusser, *Towards a Philosophy of Photography*, London: Reaktion Books Ltd, 2000, p. 195.

27 Flusser, *Towards a Philosophy of Photography*, p. 20.

a possible solution to the conflict [...] [I] will illustrate that the photographic universe can serve as a model for post-industrial society as a whole and that a philosophy of photography can be the starting point for any philosophy engaging with the current and future existence of human beings.[28]

In many respects, Flusser is arguing for two paths of philosophical effort: first, that philosophy should investigate how any epistemology is inevitably changed by photography and second, what moral and ethical challenges need to be addressed because of that change. Although his argument was formulated in the 1980s, it is even more valid today as computational power related to image making has increased exponentially and through it, such that the standardization and quantification of social and cultural practices are much more profoundly effected. While we disagree with Flusser's notion that advances in technology constitute a threat to the human condition per se - in this respect, any notion of a 'threat' is dependent on an attachment to the notion of being human as having a culminating state of development, a high point if you will, that seems excessively modernist in its origins - we absolutely agree with his point that technology's development towards networks of automation independent of human control creates a new ontological condition and extend it to the notion that photography represented merely the first stage of technology's pervasive encroachment into our lives. If nothing else, the abandonment of analog cameras and, even, digital cameras in favor of phones as photographic devices signals both an end of photography's technology as a determinant in our lives and the furthered role of the postdigital turn that the New Aesthetic represents.

The shift towards an emphasis on the visual is part of this new, necessary attitude that recognizes the effect the New Aesthetic is having in the world. The New Aesthetic is that new epistemic and ontological condition, both of the world while making its own world. Bridle's cataloging of various objects, even if it was without any sustained critical analysis of overlapping characteristics, made evident that it is no longer sufficient to study contemporary visual phenomena in terms of classic aesthetics; the digital nature of contemporary imagery requires media studies, software studies and, in general, a digitally informed approach particularly if we take into account changes in the humanities as a set of academic disciplines as well as a set of creative activities. What is particularly important, coming out of our understanding of Flusser's ideas, is to stress that this approach is primarily through images, primarily through the visual. Think of the way we interact with data today. One way is to look at projects such as the Palladio platform, developed by the Human+Design Research Lab at Stanford University, that takes on a justified faith that visual representation of data leads to insightful and critical new discoveries of the relations between various trends;[29] at the Text Encoding Initiative Conference in

---

28   Flusser, *Towards a Philosophy of Photography*, p. 75.

29   Palladio Humanities thinking with data, http://hdlab.stanford.edu/projects/palladio/.

October 2014 at Northwestern University, Thomas Faith and Joseph Wicentowski, working for the Office of the Historian in the U.S. Department of State, presented 'Visualizing the History of U.S. Foreign Relations: The State of TEI at Foggy Bottom' – how they've used Palladio to visualize the encoded Foreign Relations of the United States series, a 150 year old, 500 volume document that is the official history of United States foreign policy.[30] Another way is to consider the development of Ubiquitous Learning Materials as an effort to shift the educational process away from a linear instructor-centered model to an immersive, social model utilizing mobile devices in order to remove the stress of the classroom experience while preparing students for 'real life'; a perfect instance of this is the Philippines Smart Communications' project TXTBKS[31] {Fig. 4} that provides transcribed elementary school textbooks to children through discarded mobile phones.

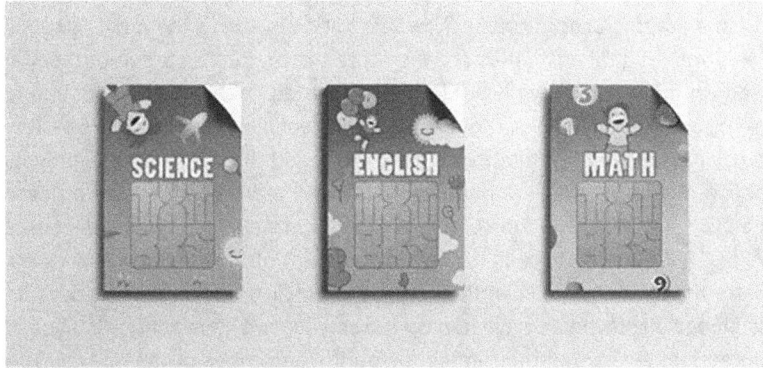

Fig. 4 Smart Philippines Textbooks

Everything is increasingly visual, including text to the detriment of textuality. Still, these are singular instances and it is on the more pervasive ways that we use data that we're focusing: our worlds are not our 'smart' phones just yet, but increasingly it feels that way, and the very fact that they are described as 'smart' signals a shift in how much we rely on them and how much we don't rely on our own knowledge, our own experiences, our own sense of our place in the world. Because the aesthetics of digital images are a consequence of constant, real-time interaction between many software and hardware layers that disappear as they are supplanted by newer instances, and precisely because such layers are the synthetic products of ontological and epistemic shifts such that these interaction becomes aesthetic, we believe that there is a necessity to shed light on the many ways in which digital images have become autonomous actors in the world.

---

30   Thomas Faith and Joseph Wicentowski, 'Visualizing the History of U.S. Foreign Relations: The State of TEI at Foggy Bottom', 2014, http://tei.northwestern.edu/files/2014/04/Faith-Wicentowski-1ntyfbr.pdf.

31   TXTBKS, https://www.thinkwithgoogle.com/campaigns/smart-communications-txtbks.html.

Because of this visuality, the nature of New Aesthetic objects is quite different from normal digital objects. In most cases, digital products adhere to a simple presentation of information, often governed by the type of data being provided; by allowing a certain degree of simplification one could propose an equation: digital visual media = algorithms + data structure.[32] An easy example of this is the typical Excel spreadsheet, which has its origins in a program called Multiplan, was code named 'EP' for 'Electronic Paper' and released in 1982 as a competitor for Lotus 1-2-3.[33] Multiplan's code name is revealing in that there was every intention of imitating and being visually analogous to an accounting ledger's columns for ease of use. However, digital objects have shifted dramatically as contemporary digital images have increasingly become products of software ecosystems, which offer certain pre-determined templates and cross-media processing and editing tools that are often utilized as means of data organization and presentation prior to their representation in a graphic user interface. New Aesthetic objects as the most dynamic form of contemporary digital aesthetics are therefore the product of a computational aesthetic based on media software – within its limits and capabilities. By limits and capabilities we mean their interfaces, the tools, and the techniques they make possible for accessing, navigating, creating, modifying, publishing, and sharing media documents i.e. creative software ecosystems equipped with standardized presets, image process- ing tools and ecosystems (GIMP, Adobe Creative Cloud), image encoding and decoding standards (MPEG, JPEG etc.) There is hardly any element of software and hardware that is neutral for the final aesthetics of the image. By studying only the layer closest to us – the digital image displayed or projected on the screen – we ignore the existence of hidden computational layers and their influence on the aesthetics of the images. The New Aesthetic reminds us that the computational layer of digital media is inextricably linked with the cultural layer.[34]

In this light, the New Aesthetic encourages us to take a postdigital approach in studying computational-based visual media. This might lead to a sense that we should only be interested in the surface of the digital object, the screen through which the user inter- acts with the software and hardware, but to keep that as the primary focus of aesthetic analysis is a failure in light of normative aesthetic interpretative strategies which demand a deep form of evaluation. Therefore we argue that we should avoid screen essentialism – that is, a screen-centric approach in image analysis as the privileged site for research – precisely because we do not want to limit ourselves to judgments of appearance or usability alone. Berry argues that 'without an attentiveness to the layers of software

---

32   Lev Manovich, *Software Takes Command*, London: Bloomsbury, 2013, p. 207.

33   Wikipedia contributors. 'Multiplan', *Wikipedia*, 31 August 2014, https://en.wikipedia.org/wiki/ Multiplan.

34   Lev Manovich, *The Language of New Media*, London: MIT Press, 2002, p. 63.

beneath this surface interface we are in danger of further screen essentialism'.[35] Indeed he further remarks, 'computational tools assist by providing mediation and advising and providing structure for a world full of data, real-time streams and complex calculations required from its citizens. This computational assistance or monitoring is backgrounded and often hidden from us.'[36] Marianne van den Boomen also rejects the screen-centric approach in her book on digital metaphors (particularly in studying GUI), although her point is applicable to any kind of computationally rooted imagery. She explains, 'what you see, is what you get, which suggests that, that is all there is to get. The machinery gets reduced to the screen, or better, to the representations on the screen. The screen shows but also blinds.'[37] It is in the interplay between screen and the underlying software and hardware that the New Aesthetic manifests itself, not just in its immediate appearance. Although much of the final aesthetics of the digital image is a direct result of the existence of layers of underlying dynamics, in viewing the final image we are not aware of them; even more so, increasingly, because digital objects are dependent on a modular programming approach the final designers themselves are not aware of the underlying functions actively driving such things as notifications, interactions with system software and interactions with additional software on the device. The raw computational materiality of images comes to the foreground when we go off-road from the usual models of image transformation and focus instead on the breakdowns and abnormalities of the usual computational-based artistic processes.

---

35   David M. Berry, *Understanding Digital Humanities*, London: Palgrave Macmillan, 2012, p. 10 and David M. Berry, *The Philosophy of Software Code and Mediation in a Digital Age*, London: Palgrave Macmillan, 2011, p. 36, 65, 137.

36   David M. Berry, *Critical Theory and the Digital*. p. 66.

37   Marianne van den Bommen, *Transcoding the Digital: How Metaphors Matter in New Media*, Amsterdam, Institute of Network Cultures, 2014, p. 15.

Abnormalities of the Digital, or Where the New Aesthetic Begins

That being said, all is not perfect. If there is any one feature that distinguishes a New Aesthetic object from its predecessors it's the appearance of the glitch as accepted, even aesthetically determinative and welcome, in contrast to visual hyperrealism understood as standardization. One of the most important properties of contemporary civilization considered as computationality is standardization, wherein concomitant expectations of a similar experience are shared across users; we expect a 'polished' experience, what-ever that might mean, and in many instances are startled when our software doesn't 'just work'. Digitally-based culture, business, administration and other domains of our human activity operate based on computational data with the expectation that they ought to be standardized in order to guarantee a constant flow of real-time informa-tion based on application programming interfaces (APIs) and protocols. From the users' perspective, standardization is clearly visible in everyday practices of human-computer interaction. We often operate within certain software and hardware ecosystems which offer unified interfaces and user experience – for example, Google, Apple, Microsoft or Adobe ecosystems – and this has become a powerful notion, especially well articulated by Matthew Fuller in his *Media Ecologies: Materialist Energies in Art and Technocultures* as it emphasizes the role of the standard object in contemporary computational culture. We would even argue that various types of standard objects (physical – shipping con-tainers or iPhones and digital – codecs or file formats) have become a vital constituent of a post-Fordist economy in that their consumption transcends industrial modes of production in favor of individual contributive modes of participation. According to Fuller, standard objects are 'ideally isolated systems'[38] and separate entities within the universe and Fuller, following Alfred Whitehead's logic, argues that 'such objects become crucial to the generation of media and communications networks and the organizations that handle them' and then adds that the standard object 'refers most easily to things that are mass-produced: cars, houses, the customizable ring of a telephone' or standardized technologies i.e. packet switching, compression algorithms etc.[39] Post-Fordist products are quite different in that they maintain a semblance of standardization while at the same time being eminently capable of being personalized; in fact, post-Fordist objects are sold to the user on their basis of customization rather than on their standard functionality.

The implications of this shift from standardization to customization is quite profound. The appearance of 'evidence' of a shift from unmediated consumption to mediated and synthetic personalization is an illusion; we believe, at least unconsciously, that we are participants in the 'manufacturing' process, that our expectations are being personally

---

38   Matthew Fuller, *Media Ecologies: Materialist Energies in Art and Technoculture*, Cambridge: MIT Press, 2005, p. 93.

39   Fuller, *Media Ecologies*, p. 95

met precisely because they are our expectations that the manufacturer is attentive to, but this mediated form of consumption is generally false in many digital objects and particularly in New Aesthetic objects because the programming skills necessary for such modifications is not only beyond the skill level of the typical user but often entirely ignored by the programmer. The importance of the shift away from standard objects for today's society and culture founded on computational technologies is hardly arguable. James Stevens of Free Networks, cited by Fuller, states that 'The information age has boiled down the magic of telecommunications into a set of modular components that any of us can adopt and explore.'[40] Nevertheless, this magic is not even that because it's not trickery that's under the control of a 'magician' as programmer but a seduction of the user through the user interface, a seduction the leads the user to erroneously believe they are in control of them software and hardware. Taking Fuller's perspective, a critical approach to the New Aesthetic is an identification of a new category of independent objects beyond the post-Fordist, most easily identifiable by the acceptability of these self-generated failures called glitches.

The glitch is a well-known phenomenon; often described as a short-term error, it is often regarded as a small problem that can be either ignored as unimportant or quickly fixed with minimal effort, minimal knowledge or simply by resetting the device. {Fig. 5}

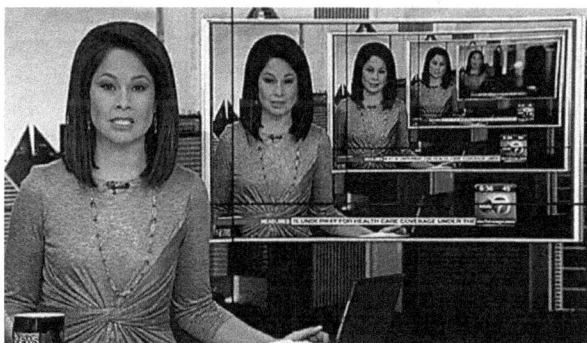

Fig. 5 Glitch Image of Newscaster

New Aesthetic objects, as a visual sub-genre sufficiently distinct from standard digital objects, are different because they manifest the glitch as a natural part of their use; while seemingly unintended they are often, at a phenomenological level, inherent to these objects and making explicit their distinctly digital and, most importantly, different form of existence from our own. As a position of analysis, any investigation of the New Aesthetic is particularly interested in glitches and signal processing errors that result in image artifacts and deformations because they represent a form of digital autonomy

---

40   Fuller, *Media Ecologies*, p. 105.

beyond the users' control. If pixelization considered as an aesthetic pattern reveals the 'grain of computation' in digital media, glitches and errors unveil also the very fact of media softwarization and the limitations of these processes.

It's safe to say that any glitches that appear would reveal that there's no human 'management' of memory, for instance, and that this lack of management creates an exposure as an opportunity for autonomy. In this state of exposed computation - which is all too often not exposed to the user - the primal advantage of standardized systems found in seamless digital data integration and transformation is no longer valid and normally hidden forces of the computational are revealed to be a continual disruption in the use-process. Consequently, not only the aesthetic properties (quantization, discretization) of digital media are clearly perceptible, but also the politics of power of the digital age as the end-user needs are subordinated to workflows programmed by software or hardware vendors. The New Aesthetic emphasizes the computational nature of contemporary digital imagery precisely because the glitch, or the potential for the glitch as a breakdown of the immediacy of the user's interactive capabilities, is an extensive element of New Aesthetic objects that marks their independence through an autonomous utterance. By focusing on visual patterns, glitches and signal processing errors our analysis of the New Aesthetic highlights this fundamental property of digital images which is usually hidden beneath the state of the visual content. Up until this point it would be natural to assume that New Aesthetic objects are only digital objects appearing on laptops, smartphone and tablets, with some expansion, to the interface found in everyday digital interfaces such as the screens of ATM machines, the menus for digital television services or the growing use of interactive touchscreens found at airports, train stations, libraries and on vending machines, but these objects have been a part of the modern social and cultural horizons for longer than expected.

Constellations of the New Aesthetic

All of these certainly are examples of the growing number of New Aesthetic objects – of course, not all examples are New Aesthetic objects – but New Aesthetic objects are also found in the art and design world in an important but distinctively different form. Every day we perceive motion pictures, digital photographs, 3D graphics etc. and we are seduced by their aesthetics; taking a cue from Kant, aesthetic choices are a constant part of our lives as tests of epistemic certainty and judgments of moral value; any analysis of these objects is also going to become an analysis of similar art objects. In the modern world, artists have been interested in the way the world has been influenced not just by changes in technology but in the manner that technology has often driven those changes. Ferdinand Léger's 1919 painting *The City* {Fig. 6} prophetically indicated what is true of our contemporary experience of the world, that we would be bombarded by such a plethora of levels of detail and color range, by the encoded linguistic structure of modernity, that we would begin to give up and retreat from an active representation of ourselves in the world into a passive absorption of experience such that we would see thinking about the conditions of the formation of communicative objects as beyond our control.

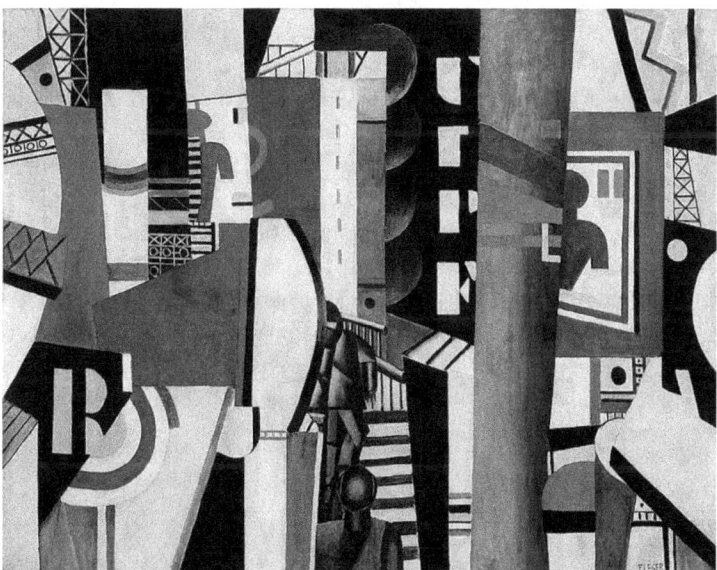

Fig. 6 Ferdinand Léger, *The City* (1919)

It is only in the last ten years that Léger's and Baudrillard's vision of the world has become a dominating characteristic of our age, and artists have started to consciously use New Aesthetic styles to alert us to this state of affairs. By employing digital images that are the result of complex hardware and software interactions which fundamentally influence their aesthetic, New Aesthetic artists such as Matthew Plummer-Fernandez, Ralf

Baeker, Mishka Henner, Aram Bartholl, and Mathieu Tremblin remind us not only about New Aesthetic's limitations and unreliability but its effect that itself limits and makes increasingly unreliable our experience of the world. This is extremely important in the computer-driven age that we live in, in that the world is becoming computer-driven and computer-determined. The authors of *New Aesthetic, New Anxieties* write that 'The New Aesthetic, in other words, brings these patterns to the surface, and in doing so articulates a movement towards uncovering the "unseen", the little understood logic of computational society and the anxieties that this introduces.'[41] Often, it is artists who best capture the anxiety and the potential in the underlying conditions, and we look forward to discussing ways in which contemporary artists are both utilizing and responding to the New Aesthetic.

The New Aesthetic is like a hashtag or meta-tag assigned to many phenomena, approaches, perspectives and people that we argue is more than just a movement rooted in web 2.0 culture using the operational logic of the hyperlinked interface and freely shareable information. Therefore, from a classic academic perspective it may seem vague, inaccurate and simply not worthy of any attention but it is a manifestation of the greater ontological shift our civilization is undergoing due to computational-driven processes and computational literacy. In this respect, one of the central tenets of our description of the New Aesthetic is based entirely on our belief that our contemporaneity can be described as computationality. The concept of computationality was coined by David M. Berry and is used in his *Philosophy of Software Code and Mediation in the Digital Age* (2011), on his blog (*stunlaw*) and was later developed in *Critical Theory and the Digital* (2014). Berry writes: 'Computationality is therefore an ontotheology, which when read through Heideggerian categories can be understood as creating a new ontological "epoch" or a new historical constellation of intelligibility.'[42] Computationality can be understood as a set of social and cultural practices rooted in digital technology. We can also consider it as an ontological description of the contemporary civilization which is deeply shaped by software and digital management of data. Therefore, computationality should be then understood as the very condition for emergence of such approach as the New Aesthetic, focusing on 'revealing the grain of computation', as it enables us to perceive the conditions underlying contemporaneity considered as computationality.

---

41   Berry, et. al., *New Aesthetic, New Anxieties*, p. 41.

42   David M. Berry, *The Philosophy of Software Code and Mediation in a Digital Age*, London: Palgrave Macmillan, 2011, p. 27.

The Postdigital Condition

Why should we bother with yet another 'post' notion? Florian Cramer, one of the first proponents of the 'postdigital' clearly stated that this 'term sucks but is useful'.[43] We are willing to agree with him on that matter. In the following paragraphs we hope to prove that the postdigital approach is of vital importance for our endeavor to conceptualize the New Aesthetic. Additionally, the postdigital as described by its advocates may be quite helpful in assessing the cultural and social consequences of the latest computational technologies – manifested by multi-layered software, black-box hardware and ubiquitous computing. We agree with David M. Berry and Michael Dieter who write that in the last decade, 'computation [has become] experimental, spatial and materialized in its implementation, embedded within the environment and embodied, part of the texture of life itself but also upon and even within the body'.[44] Both the New Aesthetic and the postdigital take into the spotlight unique characteristics and affordances of the latest computational technologies, instead of just putting them into the very same 'digital basket' where each and every technological artifact has been residing in for the last thirty years. Both the New Aesthetic and the postdigital signal and acknowledge the fact that in the last few years, technology's impact on society and business has manifested itself in a profound and unprecedented scope.

Florian Cramer proposes several interpretative leads that we can use to conceptualize the postdigital. Each of them touches upon a different set of phenomena associated with the digital, taking into account some cultural artifacts, computational tools and a few broader trends that have lately emerged in the digital society, while responding to the research questions asked by different academic disciplines. We are proposing a kaleidoscope of the postdigital.

Following on Cramer's work, we argue that the postdigital should not be understood as a new temporal period that comes after the 'digital' as its prefix would suggest. The postdigital rather strives to characterize new economic, social and cultural contexts that have been introduced in the last decade due to the general evolution of computational technologies towards even more autonomous systems, ubiquitous devices, real-time and cloud-based software and services. The term does not describe an era which is no longer formed by the presence of computational technologies. Quite the opposite, as it is rather interested in emphasizing the fact that the 'digital revolution' has already taken place, and through the latest innovations in the age of autonomous systems, ubiquitous computing, networks and clouds, the digital has been even more embedded with us

---

43   Florian Cramer, 'What is "Post-digital"?', *A Peer-reviewed Journal about Post-digital Research* (2015), vol. 3, issue 1, p. 3., http://www.aprja.net/?p=1318.

44   David Berry and Michael Dieter (eds) *Postdigital Aesthetics: Art, Computation and Design*, Basingstoke: Palgrave Macmillan, 2015, p. 3.

and the environment. This has left a profound imprint in many areas of our society and culture such that the '"post-digital" in its simplest sense describes the messy state of media, arts and design after their digitization (or at least the digitization of crucial aspects of the channels through which they are communicated)'.[45] The postdigital is therefore interested in assessing these consequences by locating, conceptualizing and critically examining manifestations of the postdigital condition in society, culture, economy etc. Cramer compares the postdigital to other post-like notions (post-punk, post-communism, post-feminism, post-apocalyptic etc.), emphasizing that the crucial difference between the initial appearance of the idea or movement and its post- version is that it 'has progressed from a discrete breaking point to an ongoing condition - in Heideggerian terms, from Ereignis to Being'.[46] This is one of the crucial points to be remembered when dealing with the postdigital. For us, both the New Aesthetic and the postdigital approach offer a unique paradigm that enables us to grasp and encapsulate various phenomena within the area of media, art and culture that are distinctive for the specific phase of evolution of the computational - the phase that came right after the 'digital revolution' - that is now understood as a fixed time event which has ended.

Cramer stresses that the postdigital stands in opposition to the quasi-teleological and linear understanding of technological progress that is centered around narratives of innovation, efficiency, disruption etc. In these paradigms yet more powerful and efficient software and hardware are the very conditions of social and cultural development of our civilization potentially leading towards a sterile, high tech era. The postdigital would oppose this tendency to argue that only by using the digital technologies or by embedding the digital with the non-computational physical environment and tools we can achieve our social, economic and cultural goals. He therefore suggests that proponents of the postdigital attitude should 'dismiss the idea of digital processing as the sole universal all-purpose form of information processing.'[47] This idea has been a dominating paradigm in popular culture since the dawn of the personal computer, and later in the so-called mobile revolution which was introduced by the smartphone and broadband mobile internet access. What is really interesting, as we are entering the age of Internet of Things when there will be endless variations of small devices and single-use chips that will make ordinary things 'smart' (fabric, vehicles, home appliances etc.), is that this idea will evolve further. The digital in the IoT era will be even more dispersed, hidden yet opaque in its nature.

According to Cramer and Kim Cascone the tendency to praise the hyper-fidelity of the computational and the myth of perfect representation is particularly visible in the

45   Cramer, 'What is "Post-digital"?', p. 10.

46   Cramer, 'What is "Post-digital"?', p. 4.

47   Cramer, 'What is "Post-digital"?', p. 7.

domains of audiovisual media. In those fields has been an ongoing transition to higher resolutions, better color palette, screen refresh rate that would make the medium even more transparent yet hyperreal. 'The simplest definition of "post-digital" describes a media aesthetics which opposes such digital high-tech and high-fidelity cleanness.'[48]

The New Aesthetic, similarly to the postdigital, rejects such a fetishization of technological progress and the theoretical and interpretative approaches that come with it. Kim Cascone used the term for the first time in 2000 to describe how digitalization of the music production workflow has changed the very principles of this creative process.[49] Similarly to the New Aesthetic a decade later, he focused on abnormalities, errors, and glitches in electronically produced music that were caused by specific commercial computational technologies involved in the process, to grasp and critically analyze their influence.

In the light of the above, it is hardly surprising that Cramer argues that the postdigital can be used to describe the condition of 'disenchantment with digital information systems and media gadgets, or a period in which our fascination with these systems and gadgets has become historical'.[50] The first version of his article was written only a few months after the Snowden revelations as part of a contribution to the Transmediale 2014 Festival. In this context the 'disenchantment' would address the ultimate end of the 'free internet' paradigm that has reigned in popular culture for decades. The internet that meant to be the great facilitator of the free circulation of information and the cornerstone of a new media, remix and sharing culture or the 'web 2.0' that was praised at the dawn of the new century by Henry Jenkins, Tim O'Reilly and others, has been disclosed as an ultimate surveillance machine and yet another space dominated by profit-driven corporations. The 'free internet' narrative shares the fate of the dot-com boom of the late 1990s.

Another understanding of the postdigital, which should be also associated with the 'disenchantment attitude', comes with the revival of 'old' or better said mechanical or electrical media in the arts. Cramer writes that we observe a 'renaissance of artists' printmaking, handmade film labs, limited vinyl editions, the rebirth of the audio cassette, mechanical typewriters, analog cameras and analog synthesizers'.[51] This trend is particularly visible in art schools (at least in the Netherlands) where, according to Cramer, students prefer to work with non-digital tools and techniques, and digital communication design and

---

48 Cramer, 'What is "Post-digital"?', p. 6.

49 Kim Cascone 'The Aesthetics of Failure: 'Post- Digital' Tendencies in Contemporary Computer Music', *Computer Music Journal* 24, No. 4 (Winter 2000), pp. 12-18.

50 Cramer, 'What is "Post-digital"?', p. 3.

51 Cramer, 'What is "Post-digital"?', pp. 3-4.

new media is associated with commercial and mainstream. We could then argue that after three decades of artists' fascination by new possibilities that the digital offers, part of the art community has become discouraged by the constraints that are imposed on them by commercial software and hardware, corporate media and a surveilled internet. Consequently, some artists of the new generation of creatives turn back to 'old' means of expression that are not dependent on the limits and compromises that come with the use of computational technologies of the present day – paper, canvas, paint, mechanical tools, or electromechanical media at most, have again become means of expression associated with the greatest degree of agency and control over the creative process.

Cramer and Berry also write about a more economy-oriented strand of the postdigital which is interested in 'corporate' media and technologies and their increasing impact on society or culture. In the light of the postdigital, the growing tensions between globalized techno-oligopolies and the revived hacker culture manifested by the maker / DIY movement – FabLabs Media Labs, local production etc. – should be considered as a critical response to the powerful alliance of corporate technology and money that dominates the so-called digital economy of the present day. The postdigital could then be considered as yet another struggle to regain political and economic agency in today's world.

We believe that both the New Aesthetic condition and the postdigital are signposts of yet another momentum in the everlasting cycle of human-technology interaction. In the early stage of development of any major set of tools or technologies the sentiments of skepticism and disenchantment of the general public are often suppressed by the optimism of early adopters and innovators. The fact that such critical approaches as the New Aesthetic, the postdigital, post-internet, post-capitalism etc. have lately emerged and are deeply concerned about the role of computational technologies in today's reality, only proves the fact that the computational is no longer the avant-garde of our civilization and as such is of minor importance to the general public. On the contrary, it rather proves that it has become the condition of existence of today's reality and, for better or worse, has greatly permeated our everyday lives.

CHAPTER 2
MANIFESTATIONS OF
THE NEW AESTHETIC

In 2005, Sandy Island in the Pacific Ocean was undiscovered. {Fig. 7} Sandy Island had been listed as an island on maps and noted in documents perhaps as far back as 1774 when James Cook supposedly discovered it. Additionally, instances of its sighting and its representation on maps continued well into the late 19th century, including notes on an 1895 British Admiralty Map that described its heavy breakers and sandy islets. Despite repeated attempts to find Sandy Island, it was never seen again even though it continued to appear on many maritime charts and maps through the rest of the 20th century. Finally, in 2012, the Australian ship R/V Southern Surveyor conclusively proved that it did not exist and only then was it removed from Google Maps. In many ways, this is simply an example of how large our world remains and how there is still more to explore and explain even in the 21st century. Still, despite the increasing digitalization of the world, the island remained on Google Maps until 2012 and had been utilized in scientific data models since 2005; in short, the non-existence of Sandy Island had maintained a persistent digital autonomy with real world effects that itself has been made real precisely because of the impossibility of its recollection as not having existed.

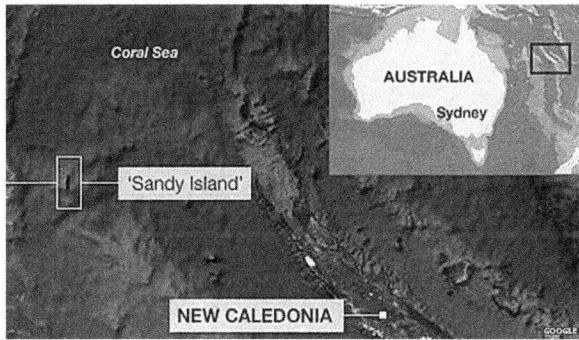

Fig. 7 Sandy Island as seen by Google Maps

In many respects, Sandy Island is merely an instance of a cartographic error, but we also believe that it's a good example of the pervasive datafication of our culture and society, wherein digital authority begins to supersede our senses as one half of the dialectic that articulates a pervasive and unavoidable development in our world. Like many of the examples of New Aesthetic manifestations that we will describe below, the story of Sandy Island illustrates an interesting tendency in our contemporary world which resulted in the necessary emergence of critical approaches. We would call it a pervasive datafication. We are entering the era where the computational, particularly through processes of automation, is granted a significant degree of agency. As a result, tasks such as information management have been delegated mostly to autonomous machines of many kinds. These systems, residing beyond our day-to-day control, may sometimes fail to function properly due to data corruption and flows in code. We are not aware of it, until an unwanted action occurs in the physical reality (a power grid fail or an autonomous car malfunction) or in the digital layer (software glitch, data loss).

However, the Sandy Island case is even more interesting. In this example the digital layer worked perfectly; based on digitalization of human-generated cartographical data, a digital representation of a non-existent terrain was created, establishing the foundations of transmedial aesthetic patterns. A computer does not ask questions about the validity of data it is given, its sole aim is to digitize, process and make available to users, and this condition of passive legitimization further engenders aesthetic validity. The Sandy Island example illustrates how the digital and physical realities have become intertwined, but it also illustrates the fact that even an autonomous computational system should be trusted as long as we are certain that the data it was given is correct. The New Aesthetic approach suggests that even in this ideal situation, which is far from today's reality, a computer's agency and 'power of judgment' should not be considered as a final instance. This thought will accompany us as we will discuss some New Aesthetic objects in this chapter.

Until now, our focus has been on the theoretical ideas behind the New Aesthetic. This has been a crucial step, if for no other reason than that the New Aesthetic is such a con-temporary set of phenomena that its grounding can be traced to recent theoretical ideas in digital culture, philosophical ideas behind computational practices and algorithmic construction, and the remainder of the intersection of these in digital form. James Bridle's blog set out the pathway of discovery, but it's been clear that, as the popularity of the New Aesthetic has waned in the common discourse of *Wired* and other magazines, that theoretically mapping the framework and parameters was crucial in order to encapsulate the specific ontological nature of the categories of critical thought and practices. That being said, theory is only as good as its objects. With a partial completion of this effort, we would now like to turn to specific manifestations of New Aesthetic objects and discuss them within this framework.

Precursors of New Aesthetic Objects

Examples vary widely: from simple HTML code to complex websites, from iOS and Android applications on smartphones and tablets to databases and datafarms, the variety of what might be classified as a New Aesthetic object is almost overwhelming and continually shifting; there are even instances of New Aesthetic objects which seemingly manifest themselves as analog objects, designed or coded digitally but physically analog in their interactivity. What is also clear is that New Aesthetic objects, regardless of the duration of use, are inherently pervasive in their effect.

It's clear from our research that New Aesthetic objects have been evolving over a longer period than the existence of James Bridle's blog. The 'worst video game' ever made – the commercially unreleased *Desert Bus*, created in 1995 to reproduce the eight-hour drive from Tucson, Arizona to Las Vegas, Nevada with unrelenting and excruciating boredom (you drive the bus in real time, with only the perfectly straight road as a vague distraction, and get one point for each successful run you make there and back) – may be one instance.[1] {Fig. 8}

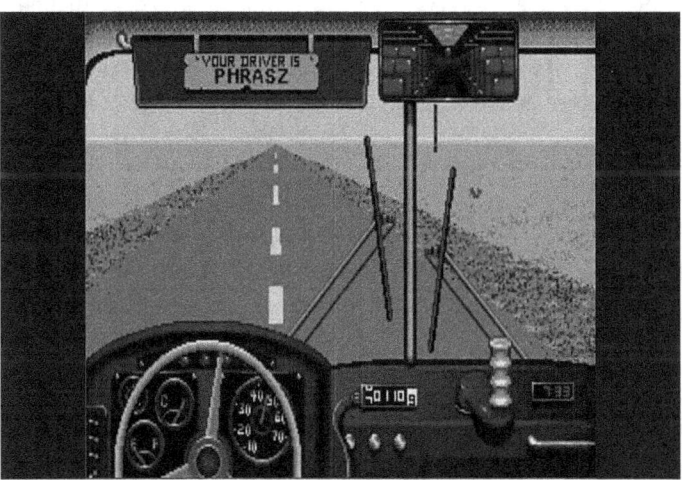

Fig. 8 *Desert Bus* (1995)

Desert Bus is a video game without any goals beyond one, with an almost unceasingly tedious display of just desert and road, but it has attracted a strange, determined cult following among a few gamers who return to it for marathon charity fundraisers. *Desert Bus* also is a mental concession to the virtual of simple programming; while the experience of the game may last eight or more hours (or much, and more likely shorter, since

---

1   Simon Parkin, 'Desert Bus: The Very Worst Video Game Ever Created', *The New Yorker*, 9 July 2013, http://www.newyorker.com/tech/elements/desert-bus-the-very-worst-video-game-ever-created.

relinquishing any control over the bus causes it to immediately crash, ending the game), and the game play can best be described as mind-numbingly inert at best, certainly the programming itself took little time comparatively, as there would have been no need to map out digitally every stretch of the eight mile run.

Neither the undiscovery of Sandy Island nor *Desert Bus* are really New Aesthetic objects, however. Sandy Island was a mistake with real world consequences; and a mistake that says more about the construction of knowledge systems than about digital artifacts. *Desert Bus* is a video game that has often been described as the worst video game ever, and was created more as a prank than a game, without any expectations that people would play it or get any enjoyment out of it. What they are is historical indicators, even precursors, of the New Aesthetic as a means of categorizing an entirely new set of objects. Thinking about a dynamic conceptual space between the aesthetic experience of both, there is evidently a widening and increasing divergence between expectations and use value while simultaneously a collapsing relationship between the digital artifact and user experience. What the cases of Sandy Island and *Desert Bus* represent in a very nascent stage is a spectrum of New Aesthetic experiences, products and objects. One of the strengths of James Bridle's blogging efforts is also the biggest hurdle to constructing a viable topology of the New Aesthetic: on the one hand its relatively random approach to curation has allowed a kind of free-wheeling and inclusive investigative strategy; on the other hand such a loose accumulation of manifestations has blurred the differences between different types of experiences and objects with a varyingly commensurate typology of creativity and productivity, to actual objects which are even more fully autonomous digital products such as the results of software glitches or algorithmic juxtaposition and that are more accurately described as New Aesthetic products. Some manifestations are the way they are because they represent a human response or attitude within the New Aesthetic attitude, while others are directly the product of a digital environment independent of human control.

New Aesthetic Products as Experiences

Certain instances of New Aesthetic objects, like this screen shot from the UK McDonald's iPhone app, fit easily into our notions of what this attitude entails. {Fig. 9}

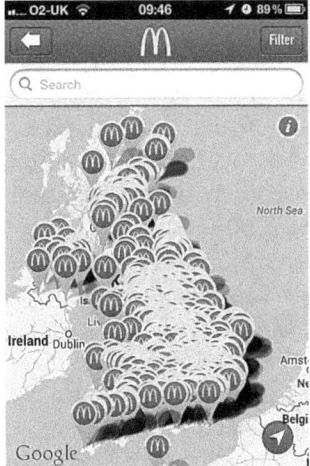

Fig. 9 McDonald's App, Map of the UK

Here we have a map of all of the locations of the fast food restaurant McDonald's in the entire country, including Northern Ireland and Jersey. Having scaled back to the appropriate level, the user has created a map of the UK constructed entirely of McDonald's locations – a dystopian nightmare if there ever was one – that deletes any possible map function and obfuscates actual restaurant locations with an excessive number of overlapping logos. What makes this a New Aesthetic product, the most important aspect of this image, is the manner in which the use of the digital object greatly circumvents the programmer's intentions. With other images {Fig. 10} we have even more instances of the programming overtaking the programmer's intentions; facial recognition may be a valuable tool for control of the public, police and intelligence agencies, but its history indicates a shift from practical uses to a more intrusive construction of digital identification.

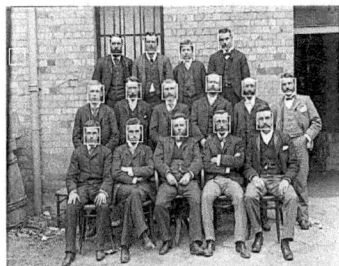

Fig. 10 Facial Recognition Error

Facial recognition software has a long history, extending back into the 1960s with early work being done by of Woody Bledsoe, Helen Chan and Charles Bisson at Panoramic Research Inc.[2]

Originally focused on artificial intelligence, their efforts at creating software based pattern recognition was quickly identified as having a multiplicity of purposes, including reading address labels as well as identifying individuals in photographs. The research's use of normalized correlation of unprocessed optical data such as the space between the corners of the subject's eyes, the length of their nose or the width of their mouth started the means whereby catalogs could be generated of individual faces, but a high degree of accuracy was a long way off; by the 1990s, facial recognition software had become so sophisticated that its failure rate was remarkably low, and by 2007 almost non-existent. This has, of course, raised privacy concerns, and a number of efforts have been made to design products that will foil facial recognition algorithms; more importantly, it has become clear, with the introduction of consumer facial recognition, that a major shift in the public consciousness and acceptance has occurred. What is now the case is that a willing public accepts facial recognition as a part of daily life. Given this background, the image cited on James Bridle's blog is an even more radical instance of a New Aesthetic manifestation. There is no surprise that the faces have been highlighted by the facial recognition software, but what is surprising – while increasingly not being surprising to any user of commercial facial recognition software – is the identification of different colored parts of the background as a face. Why is this radical? It's more than just the software asking the user to confirm someone's face (often the case in Apple's Aperture software, for instance) but a digital prompt necessitating an interaction between a user and the software as autonomous decision processes; the software has decided that there appears to be a face there, and needs human intervention not to identify that face but to confirm its decision; should the user decline or simply avoid correcting that decision, then the software will continue to identify that portion of the digital photograph as a face, as a human being, and even further will utilize its decision to identify similar things in photographs as faces.

Building on a theoretical approach that would enable taking to the forefront of our perception intertwined layers of algorithms and computation that contemporary society and culture is built on, further instances of New Aesthetic objects as experience can be identified at an increasing rate. Another example of a manifestation of a New Aesthetic object is 'What colour is it?'.[3] (Fig. 11) In many respects, this is merely a webpage displaying the user's local time, an increasingly common type of application for Chrome

2   Robert Boyer, James C. Browne and Jayadev Misra, 'In Memoriam Woodrow W. Bledsoe', Faculty Council, The University of Texas, Austin, 27 May 2014, https://www.utexas.edu/faculty/council/1998-1999/memorials/Bledsoe/bledsoe.html, adapted from 'Woody Bledsoe: His Life and Legacy', authored by Michael Ballantyne, Robert S Boyer and Larry Hines, *AI Magazine*, Volume 17, Number 1, Spring 1996, pp. 7-20.

3   What colour is it?, http://whatcolourisit.scn9a.org/.

and other browsers, but what becomes immediately apparent over a short time is the ever-shifting color of the background. Here we have the emergence of computational-ity as an onto-theology, wherein the datafication of web colors embeds itself into our temporal sensibilities.

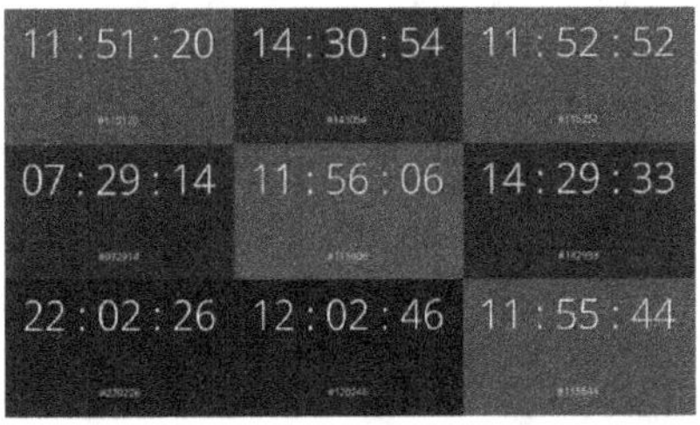

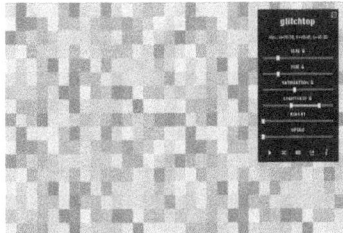

Fig. 11 James E. Murphy, *What colour is it?* (2014)

With each new second the background corresponds to its HTML color code, e.g. 08:55:59 turns out to be a darkish grey blue. Where the conceit lies is in the expectation that a 24 hour clock will produce a rainbow of colors when, in fact, nothing could be further from the truth; a solely numeric listing of HTML color codes tends towards dark greens and blues, so there's less variation than might be anticipated. Created by Berlin based artist and designer James E. Murphy, it is part of a series of webpages and coding[4] that challenge users' preconceived notions of web interactions. It's difficult to think of 'What colour is it?' as an example of art per se (and we will return to Murphy's work in the next chapter on examples of New Aesthetic art where other work seems more appropriately discussed), since it feels more like a gimmicky trick of web design, but that sense of being unknowingly confounded by the digital coding is itself New Aesthetic in nature; it's not the gimmick that makes it that but the increasing degree of autonomy and means of confounding the user's experience.

Chris Foley's *Glitchtop*[5] {Fig. 12} is a further example of the development of HTML coding producing a specifically New Aesthetic experience.

Fig. 12 Chris Foley, *Glitchtop* (2015)

---

4   J.E. Murphy, http://jemurphy.org/.

5   Glitchtop, http://chrisfoley.github.io/glitchtop/.

Chris Foley is a web designer whose work is focused on data management, including the innovative browser extension LightboxE for Chrome and Safari that allows users to view and manipulate images found on websites on their own terms without leaving the page. Glitchtop is quite different from other programming efforts by Foley, labeled as 'an online art generator inspired by glitch art and pixel art'.[6] Users are invited to choose from a range of different sliding parameters – size, hue, saturation, lightness, repeat and speed – which are then used to generate an image of varying colored squares that alternate between the spectrum of those parameters. At first this seems like an interesting visual experience and, in reality, it's really nothing more than that. Where this is a New Aesthetic experience, though, is in the illusion of control; user input seems to be a contributing factor to the product, but user input is a limiting factor in that the relations between the different colored squares are a result of the digitization of the color spectrum itself. While Foley notes that this is inspired by glitch art, with its dependency on random information and errors, it's clear that glitches do not make an appearance. Where, indeed, is the art or the New Aesthetic experience in this case? The status of both Murphy's and Foley's work as art is debatable – though we would tend to place them into that category – their status as New Aesthetic products is not. The contrast between viewers' expectations and the resulting visuals generates more than just a flashing sequence of colors; instead, more poignantly, what is created is a remarkably overlooked response of indifference to the digital reality, based on an acceptance of the limited control in contrast to the final product. The response of most users to what is generated is less of a sense of awe and aesthetic excitement and is rather an acceptance that this is what should have been expected, graphically represented in the ubiquity of the poster produced by the Deterritorial Support Group. {Fig. 13}

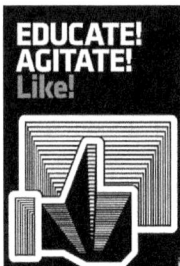

Fig. 13 Deterritorial Support Group poster

What is revealed isn't some hypnotic, cathartic or enlivening visually engaging set of patterns but a distancing removal of the user from a critical engagement or an aesthetics of computational miscalculation. In many ways, it's a safe assumption that most users will respond to these flashing squares of color with 'so what?'. And it's in that indifference that the New Aesthetic often operates most effectively, best represented by an apolitical response.

---

6   Chris Foley, http://www.cfoley.net/.

Glitchtop is at best a reproduction of the glitch interjecting itself into our experience of the digitization of the world. We will return to glitches as art in the next chapter, but for now we're focused on glitches as they manifest as part of the digital experience. Perhaps the most famous of this type of image associated with Bridle's blog and the New Aesthetic is that of an airplane appearing on Google Maps; flying too quickly to be resolved accurately, it appears as four different images of the same plane broken up into a grainy image and three separate RGB shadows. {Fig. 14}

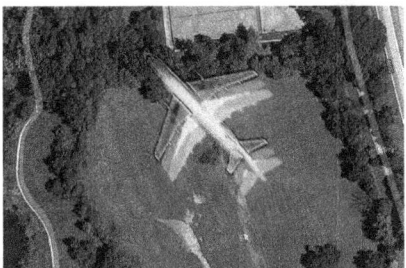

Fig. 14 Google Maps image of a plane flying over Hyde Park, Chicago

This is a true glitch, an error caused by the inability of the software to process real time imagery or an inadequate capacity to recognize and recombine images into a functioning single image, and it is vitally interesting as a New Aesthetic object because of its inherent aesthetic appeal, but it's become sufficiently commonplace in 'false glitches' like those found in satellite imagery that the glitch itself has become readily accepted as part of users' aesthetic experiences. At first what seems like a data output error, which is indeed actually an error, becomes immediately attractive, absorbing and even engrossing despite itself. The aesthetic appeal of the image, its beauty, rests in the fact that the viewer ignores the glitch and responds on a more intuitive level. What's even more interesting is how the strangeness of the image disappears into a state of aesthetic ubiquity. Skyler Balbus, a designer interested in branding, interactivity and product design, writing about this image {Fig. 15} and the New Aesthetic generally on a blog for the Hook & Loop design team, notes:

> If you've ever had an app suddenly deteriorate into pixels, or sent a text message that was autocorrected to the wrong words, or had your Google Maps satellite view obstructed by a low-flying plane, you know that the glitches in our everyday life can be just as surreal as they are maddening. When things don't behave as we expect them to, and when the logic of interactions isn't clear to us, we're left with what can feel like pure absurdity. But these glitches in technology aren't always just random acts of incoherency; they're often the product of a breakdown of communication.[7]

---

7   Skyler Balbus, 'What Glitch? Technology And The New Aesthetic', *Hook & Loop*, 20 September 2013, http://www.hookandloopnyc.com/author/skyler/.

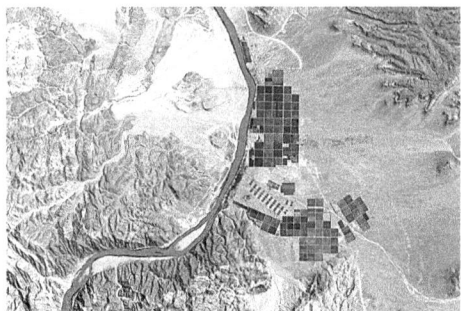

Fig. 15 Agricultural Fields

Maddening deterioration and surreal autocorrection often are taken as criticisms of aesthetic experiences, especially the former, but they've become commonplace experiences as we rely increasingly on smartphones to navigate the world. Balbus isn't theorizing at a critical level the impact this image has, but it's clear that she's embracing the absurdity generated in the glitch as well as the breakdown of communication. Balbus is not the only one to note the connection between New Aesthetic experience and the surreal; in 'An Essay on the New Aesthetic' Bruce Sterling wrote:

> People have tried such things before. The Surrealists once valorized the "imagination of the unconscious." But, as the Situationists pointed out, a generation later: the imagination of the unconscious is impoverished.

> Valorizing machine-generated imagery is like valorizing the unconscious mind. Like Surrealist imagery, it is cool, weird, provocative, suggestive, otherworldly, but it is also impoverished.[8]

Clearly, though, while the image generated as a result of the glitch isn't surreal (a word all too often synonymously used in place of 'weird' or 'incomprehensible') Sterling has a point. The four different and simultaneous images of the plane in the digital artifact may appear as a glitch in the programming, an error showing the inadequacy of the computational device, but at the same our response is to accredit an artistic agency of sorts in the process of the image's production; like surrealism, with its emphasis on creating a level of connectivity between human beings through suggestive imagery, New Aesthetic images that are the product of glitches are creating a level of connectivity between human perceptual capacity and aesthetic response with autonomously and digitally generating entities, namely software packages that function independently of human intervention. At some level, responding aesthetically to a glitchy image grants a type of aesthetic, even artistic, autonomy to software as part of the increasing computational materiality of our civilization.

---

8   Sterling, 'An Essay on the New Aesthetic'.

The appearance of glitches as a hallmark of the New Aesthetic has become a common-place paradigm. Images like agricultural fields appearing to be pixelated are glitchy in a way, in that there is the illusion of digital parameters being imposed on the world (an illusion that may be all too real, given the increasing dependency in agricultural production on GPS technology as databases). Other images appear to be glitchy when they are, instead, the product of the visualization of data. {Fig. 16}

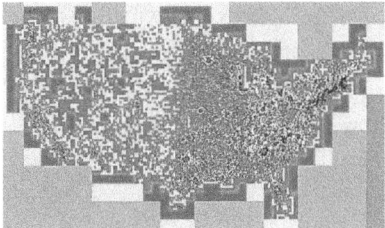

Fig. 16 Population Blocks

These images in particular are interesting in that they represent population figures of the contiguous United States at varying levels as part of the Polymers JavaScript library[9] that is designed to create interactive maps for web browsers; giving each pixel the task of representing an area populated by 1000+ people, the programmers still felt the need to make the result more visual appealing, such that:

> My team selected the old-school color scheme to maximize contrast whilst maintaining some semblance of readability. According to them, if it dredges up any repressed 8-bit feelings – like the urge to snipe an Atari 2600 off Ebay – that's not a bug. It's a feature.[10]

Pixelization has seemingly acquired a value as a tool. Apps like Pixelate Tool {Fig. 17} are advertised as 'a QUICK and HANDY tool for adding pixelated blur to your photo in seconds' with one reviewer's comments being 'I can get used to it not being super accurate but I hope it doesn't get removed because as of now it's the only simple tool that does what it does' as if the accuracy of the pixelization is ironically important.[11]

When we start to look at images or videos, wherein the players of a football game are reduced to pixels equivalent to the information provided by the drone to its operators

---

9   Polymaps, http://polymaps.org/.

10   Steven von Worley, 'My God, It's Full Of Blocks: Population Density Meets The Tile Space', *Data Pointed*, 3 October, 2011, http://www.datapointed.net/2011/10/us-population-density-and-google-maps-tiles/.

11   'Pixelate Tool', iTunes Store, September 2015, https://itunes.apple.com/us/app/id442157795.

{Fig. 18}, or in which the photographer noted was referred to by people as the 'Lego Tornado' {Fig. 19} but is more appropriately described as a Tornado fight jet covered in a semi-glitchy livery, we start to see a different approach to glitches and pixelization.

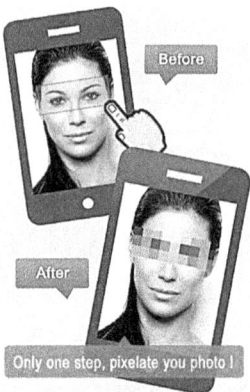

Fig. 17 Pixelate in the iTunes store

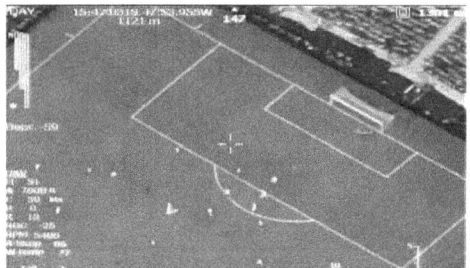

Fig. 18 Neymar goal filmed by a Brazilian Air Force drone

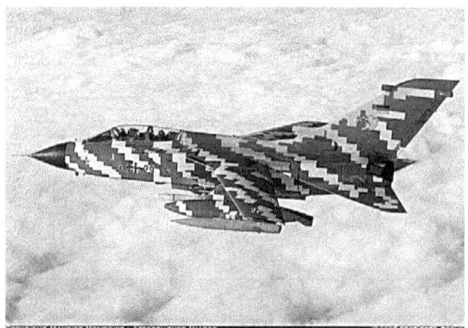

Fig. 19 Maurice Hendriks, *German Air Force Tornado ECR, Tiger Meet 2010* (2010)

Other images such as those from the 2015 parade in China marking the 70th anniversary of the end of WWII {Fig. 20} are even more strikingly strange and distanced from a normative human experience; putting aside the political and military themes, with the subtext running through each of the images discussed in this paragraph, it's evident that the digital style of the camouflage is entirely counterproductive but assumed contradictorily to be effective. {Fig. 21}

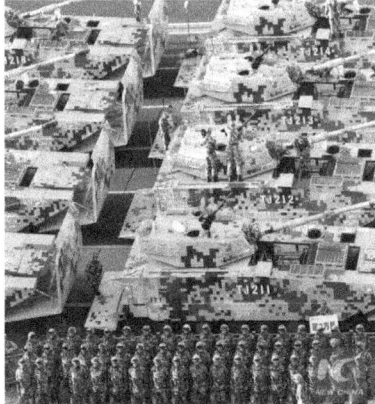

Fig. 20 Chinese Tanks in the WWII Victory Celebration in 2015

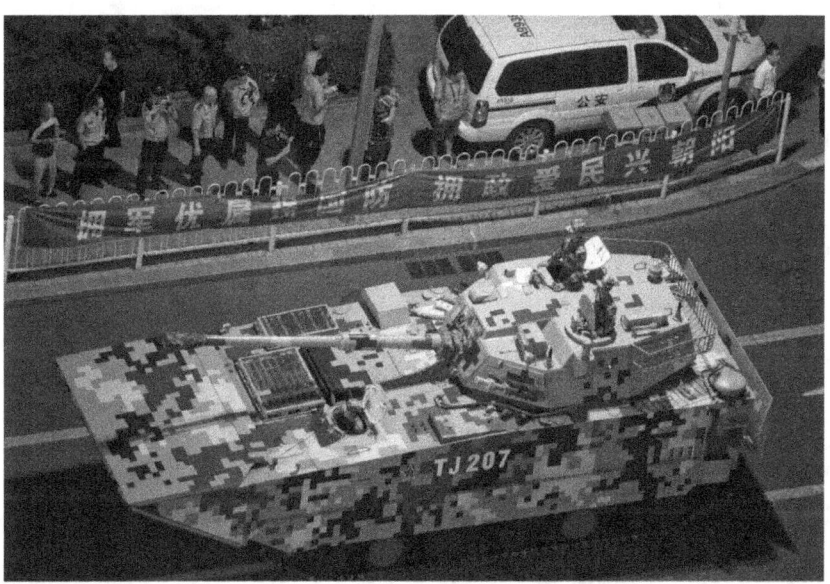

Fig. 21 Chinese Tanks in the WWII Victory Celebration in 2015

Consider, for the moment, the purpose of camouflage: it's designed to obscure the object from sight, specifically human sight. Now consider the bright blues used by the Chinese military on their tanks and missile launchers, and it's obvious that exactly the opposite effect is intended; these tanks have been designed to be seen more readily rather than less. While there are instances of this pixelization camouflage paint scheme appearing that are apparently an attempt at hiding the military vehicle, such as the image of a Leopard 2 tank photographed outside of Munich, the effectiveness of such a visual scheme has been proven to be quite low, as evidenced by the quick retirement by the United States military of patterns there are entirely fractal or pixel based.[12] {Fig. 22}

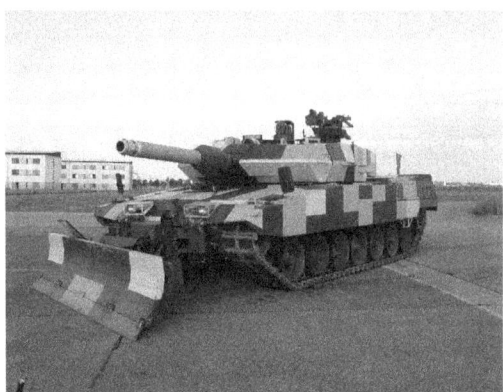

Fig. 22 Leopard Tank

Thinking about these tanks even further in contrast to the German Tornado it's also clear that the camouflage scheme was digitally designed in an almost random fashion; rather than having each part of the paint scheme chosen to obscure the appearance of the tank, the color scheme has been generated by digital means with little input from a human designer. Two intertwined conclusions can be drawn from these manifestations. First, the camouflage has probably been utilized to achieve greater visibility in a parade setting rather than during military action; second, the assumption has been made that any camouflage that obscures these vehicles from human eyesight, no matter how effective at that purpose, is useless in a modern battlefield with digital target acquisition. Given this perspective, it doesn't matter what color the tanks were painted, since the digital environment will trump the human experience of that environment.

The human experience of its localized environment has become so intricately bound up with the digitalization of the world that the interaction itself has become newsworthy, of a sorts, especially when things go wrong. In the middle of the Old Street roundabout in London that is frequently referred to as the 'Silicon Roundabout', the outdoor advertising firm JCDecaux constructed the 'Old Street EC1' digital billboard system, described thusly:

> Old Street EC1 provides a powerful communications channel for brands to engage with the unique and exciting audiences who live, work and socialise in EC1. The

---

12   Matthew Cox, 'Army Unveils Design Changes for New Camo Uniform', *Military.com*, 6 August 2014, http://www.military.com/daily-news/2014/08/06/army-unveils-design-changes-for-new-camo-uniform.html?ESRC=todayinmil.sm.

newly digitised, iconic advertising architecture in the centre of Silicon Roundabout has become synonymous with the EC1 area, providing unparalleled impact within the vibrant and creative East London community.[13]

Part of the Old Street EC1's design was the display of Google and YouTube searches in the UK with predictably unruly and offensive results. {Fig. 23}

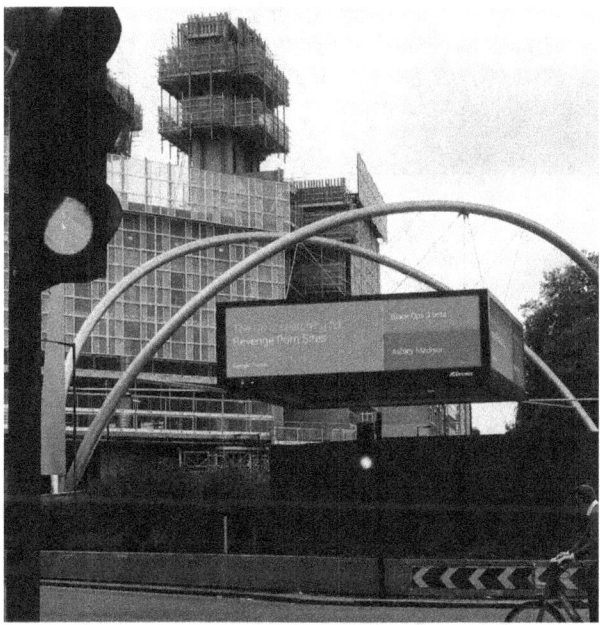

Fig. 23 Old Street, New Billboard in 2015

It's always remarkable that designers and advertisers don't anticipate unintended effects that spark outcries and offense, but clearly what ended up being on display was beyond what almost anyone could have imagined. Humorous, yes, but, like the camouflage on Chinese tanks, there is evidently a lack of human intervention resulting from a lack of engagement on the part of the programmers who trusted their own interaction with the digital world to be echoed universally. Our theoretical approach enables us to take the position that our perception has become so entangled in the intertwined layers of algorithms and computation that contemporary civilization is built on that a fully effective engagement with that entanglement is no longer possible. It's not just that programmers are making mistakes or oversights when they don't anticipate surprising results, nor is it simply that there is an unwarranted and blind faith in the appearance of digital traces in

---

13   JCDecaux, 'Old Street EC1', September 2015, http://www.jcdecaux.co.uk/roadside/roundabouts/
      old-street-ec1.

the real world leading to a misplaced sense of an enhanced experience; rather as every point of our interaction with our environments, at an individual level, becomes increasingly guided and then determined by their digitalization, it's clear that we're losing our ability to decisively act digitally. It's at the boundaries of the unintended consequences that the New Aesthetic has emerged, where digital autonomy supersedes human intention and even social structures. Whether it's an expired QR code on a bottle of Heinz ketchup going terribly wrong, resulting in a link to a pornography website,[14] the use of selfies for live reporting[15] or advertising for Facebook in Yemen,[16] the presence of New Aesthetic digital objects has become so widespread that it's no longer recognized but simply accepted, an indication that we've stopped thinking of the world as digitized and started thinking of the digital as the world.

---

14   Kashmira Gander, 'Heinz forced to apologise after QR code on ketchup bottle linked to hardcore
      porn site', *The Independent*, 17 June 2015, http://www.independent.co.uk/life-style/food-and-
      drink/news/heinz-forced-to-apologise-after-qr-code-on-ketchup-bottle-linked-to-hardcore-
      porn-site-10327313.html.

15   @Matt_Macklin7, 'The latest in live cross technology. Pic via Instagram', Twitter Post, 28 October
      2014, 7:54PM, https://twitter.com/Matt_Macklin7/status/527292438574952449/photo/1.

16   Maciej Cegłowski, 'Ta'izz', *Idle Words blog*, 17 May 2015, http://idlewords.com/2015/05/ta_izz.htm.

New Aesthetic Objects as Products

The examples discussed in this chapter so far are the result of unintended manifestations, a result of what we believe is a metaphysical and ontological shift in the digitization of the world. At the same time, we also believe that a number of New Aesthetic products can be identified specifically as New Aesthetic objects; code, webpages, typography, advertising and a myriad of other forms of human products extending well beyond the digital into physical objects are a result of the attitude that Bridle wrote about. The distinction between products and objects is quite simple: products are objects of experience that are evidently created, authored, programmed and are the result of human activity while objects don't necessarily appear this way. That being said, thinking about New Aesthetic objects is a little more complicated than at first it might seem because New Aesthetic objects are implicitly understood as products because of their digital nature but aren't evidently so. Given the examples discussed so far, with the emphasis on the autonomy of the software, the algorithms, and the digital interference into and selective emphasis on human activity, it would be reasonable to assume that mediated New Aesthetic objects are more difficult to identify; our description of their nature has often implied a digital agency separate from human agency, a position we continue to maintain. This is made even more complicated when it quickly becomes clear that many of these objects are political in nature, or at least analogous to the products of a political awareness. What we would also like to note is that we are still not talking about New Aesthetic art, which is its own separate category above and beyond the distinction between products and objects, and which is reserved for the next chapter, though the status of some of this work as art is unquestionable.

One of the most interesting manifestations of the New Aesthetic has been the work produced by the CAVI group based in Aarhus University.[17] With recent contributions from members focused on digital aesthetics, a number of projects by CAVI have explored in great detail the interplay between digitally produced information and human interactivity. In 2006, the group installed the Dynamically Transparent Window[18] {Fig. 24} in the Salling department store in Aarhus; using data generated by tracking the people walking by, exploiting the computational materiality of our everyday activities, the large, glass storefront shifts from opaque to transparent with changes in thin electro-chromatic strips of foil in response to transmedial aesthetic patterns elaborating a dynamic relationship between the storefront as advertising and users' experience of the storefront, but often with a collapse of the standard enticing or seductive intent of advertising alone.

---

17   CAVI, http://cavi.au.dk.

18   Kim Halskov, Morten Lervig and Peter Dalsgaard, 'The Dynamically Transparent Window', 14
      October 2014, CAVI, http://cavi.au.dk/research-areas/the-dynamically-transparent-window/.

The intent of this installation is to draw people closer to the window, to give them the opportunity to interact with the display in a playful and productive fashion, but it's equally clear that the design doesn't actually invite people into the Salling department store but rather invites them to play with the display or simply ignore it. While the commercial intent is self-evident – Salling would not have allowed this display if the management did not foresee it as a marketing tool – its flawed and subverted outcome undermines the display's manifest purpose to hunt down future customers through the semblance of interactivity.

In 2009, in collaboration with Digital Urban Living at Aarhus University, CAVI installed *Climate on the Wall*,[19] another instance of a seemingly interactive display. {Fig. 25}

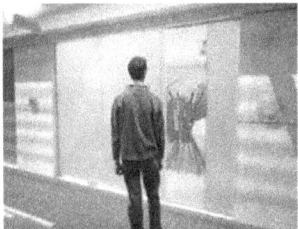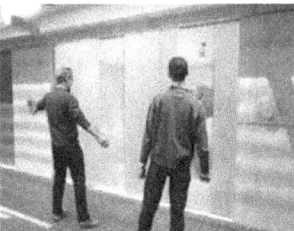

Fig. 24 CAVI, *Dynamically Transparent Window* (2006)

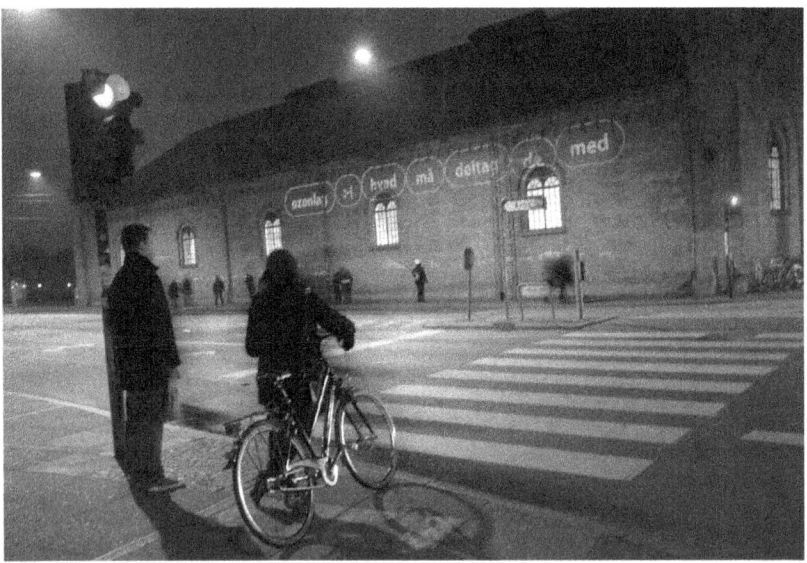

Fig. 25 CAVI, *Climate on the Walls* (2009)

---

19   Kim Halskov, Morten Lervig and Peter Dalsgaard, 'Climate on the Wall', *CAVI*, 14 October 2014, http://cavi.au.dk/research-areas/climate-on-the-wall/.

Tracking people passing by with infrared cameras, thought bubbles with words and thoughts related to environmental awareness would be projected onto the wall above them. Additionally, *Climate on the Wall* has been described as interactive in that different people could collaborate to form sentences and statements about changes in the world's environment, building a dialogue promoting increased environmental awareness and responsibility. Yet, it too is an instance of the New Aesthetic in that the participants' autonomy is clearly limited to the digitally projected programming, and certainly glitches and poorly constructed 'sentences' would be apparent if not ripe for a type of digital vandalism; *Climate on the Wall* was installed during the 'Beyond Kyoto' conference in Aarhus, so that assumption that the programmers designed the system as an assertion of climate protection ideas is a safe one, but it's an equally safe assumption that the system itself would appear to counteract its intended purpose; the inescapabilty of digital manifestations opposes the continuation of aesthetics that might encourage the growth of an environmentally oriented mindset.

One problem with either instances of work by the CAVI group is that they are not genuinely intrusive in the way that typical examples of New Aesthetic objects are, in part because they clearly are products produced in response to specific needs and conditions. This does not make CAVI's work any less interesting, in that it seems clear to us that individuals making New Aesthetic products are exhibiting an awareness of the increasingly pervasive effect of the digitalization of the world on our human experience, but we're still cautious about the work's status as New Aesthetic objects. If we want a better example of an object that autonomously controls experience then it would be good to start with the app Cloak, available for smartphone. {Fig. 26}

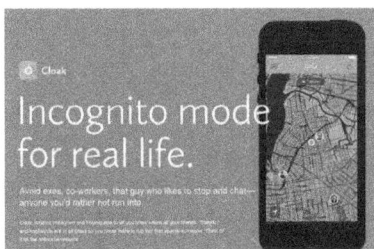

Fig. 26 Franz Kirschner *Cloak app* (2014)

Launched in 2014 with a lot of media coverage, Cloak is an app designed to prevent what has become a standard feature of all smartphones: a continual broadcasting of users' geographical location. Ironically, Cloak almost aspires to functionally imitate the conditions of Sandy Island, creating a digital invisibility for the user as if a digital invisibility is more important than an actual physical invisibility. By linking to Foursquare, Instagram, Facebook and Twitter, Cloak attempts to deny social media applications their default capability of connecting users not just digitally through messages and updates but physically by hiding their presence in the world when their presence if often assumed to be substantiated digitally. Its success has been less than stellar, with many users reporting a failure to obscure them from the prying capability of social networks, but as a response to the ubiquity of social networking's capabilities it presents an interesting test case of both working within and opposing the intentions of the programmed capabilities of smartphones. Equally, a sense of pervasiveness of the digital experience is at the forefront of the design of Cloak; it's clear that Cloak has no application in the real world, because the real world no longer exists. It's even necessary to point out that there is a contradiction involved in the visual design of Cloak itself, in the need for an app that allows the use of social networks while denying a key aspect of sociability, curiously heightened by the glowing green colors reminiscent of old radar devices, but its purpose shows a remarkable degree of perspicuity on the part of the programmers, who have obviously taken note of a dissatisfaction with the pervasive digitization of our world. Apparently, we've reached a stage where we want everyone to know where we are but no one actually knows where we are.

The creation of the typeface ZXX[20] also presents a really interesting instance of a New Aesthetic object in a manner similar to Cloak. {Fig. 27}

Fig. 27 Sang Mun *ZXX* Typeface (2013)

Created specifically in response to the revelations of the American government's spying program targeting American citizens, ZXX is a typeface that is unreadable by text scanning software.[21] A first response to this might quickly conclude that ZXX is an absurd project – how much disruption can occur as a result of text scanning software that reads hard copies, when so much of the world's information is digital and, therefore, doesn't need to be scanned? – and this response would be correct; any effort to defeat optical scanners through a publically available digital typeface is going to fail once that typeface

20   Eric Limer, 'A Typeface Designed To Thwart Spying Computers', *Gizmodo.com*, 22 June 2013,
       http://gizmodo.com/a-typeface-designed-to-thwart-sneaky-spying-computers-543341176.

21   Sang Mun, 'Making Democracy Legible: A Defiant Typeface', *Walker Art Center blog*, 20 June 2013,
       http://blogs.walkerart.org/design/2013/06/20/sang-mun-defiant-typeface-nsa-privacy/.

is part of the library of scannable typefaces. It's clear, however, in the statements of the creator Sang Mun, that he designed ZXX in 2012-13 as a protest against the ease with which the NSA can access information rather than as a practical tool to thwart such information; the title of the typeface itself is used by the Library of Congress to indicate 'No linguistic content; Not applicable'. Sang Mun is a Korean graphic designer and artist, and ZXX could be thought of as an example of New Aesthetic art, but it's indicative of something much more. In his statement about the typeface on the website of the Walker Art Center, where Mun was an artist in residence, he quotes both Slavoj Žižek and Julian Assange. Žižek wrote: 'We feel free because we lack the language to articulate our unfreedom.'[22] Assange stated: 'What does censorship reveal? It reveals fear.'[23] What's curious about these statements is how contradictory they are. Žižek's indicates his position that a state of ignorance and muteness creates the illusion of freedom, while Assange's implies that the very act of censorship creates the conditions of increased knowledge. It's clear, within the context of the New Aesthetic, that ZXX is not actually a response to either position, articulating instead a response to the digitized conditions of knowledge. ZXX's existence doesn't raise questions about privacy, unlike so many other artworks do, though its presentation in the art world articulates many of those questions, but more poignantly manifests a growing unease on the part of designers that their basic tools like typefaces, created in a digital manner for a digital means of production, quickly slip out of their control and can be used for radically unintended consequences. Mun writes about ZXX as a contribution to those fighting the intrusion by governments into the private lives of their citizens, but to believe that ZXX is effective is naïve. In an update to the Walker Art Center's blog, Mun acknowledges the discernable naïveté and notes that as a former NSA partner and intelligence agency employee he's aware of the issues we're concerned with. For Mun, raising awareness is the sole goal of ZXX; for us, it's a symptom of the New Aesthetic's increasingly pervasive intrusion into our lives. Because we are helpless in the face of digital agencies' capacity to intrude, Mun writes:

> Our lives in cyberspace are overloaded with impalpable and extensive personal information that is gathered, intercepted, deciphered, analyzed, and stored. With this information government and corporations can easily create an informational architecture that traps us in the structures of the World Wide Web and social media. Restricting and repressing our communication tools under the name of "homeland security" is only a small step into a totalitarian society. This non-physical-yet-ideological violence is what allows us to lapse into lethargic silence. But really, we shouldn't be afraid to question the authorities' continual intrusions.[24]

---

22   Slavoj Žižek, *Welcome to the Desert of the Real!: Five Essays on September 11 and Related Dates*, New York: Verso, 2002, p. 2

23   Make a DifferenSe, 'What is Wikileaks? by founder Julian Assange', 11 December 2010, YouTube video, Duration: 14:58, https://youtu.be/DFE7d91vQf4.

24   Mun, 'Making Democracy Legible: A Defiant Typeface'.

This is a curious statement. Where's the violence? In cyberspace, whatever that means today. How is our personal information stored in cyberspace? Through the digital architecture that is increasingly self-determinative. The use of digital information by the NSA and the like is itself governed by this self-determining digital architectonic and, in many respects, they are just as much of a victim of it as private citizens, in that their ideological justifications are created aesthetically for them rather than by them. Why aesthetically? Because the use of ideology must necessarily be seductive. The ideological violence that Mun rightfully identifies as a threat to privacy doesn't come from human programming as agency but from the increasingly autonomous nature of data storage, tracking and use as an agent in and of itself. In this respect, ZXX is a perfect example of a type of New Aesthetic object, one designed to operate within an almost metaphysical and epistemic shift of the human condition and existence.

Both Cloak and ZXX can be understood in the context of an uneasy relationship with Google's mapping efforts. Google's mission statement says that the company's ultimate goal is to organize the world's information and make it universally accessible and useful. Almost more than any product by Google, Google Maps directly creates a sense of the computational materiality of our civilization, especially if one considers it simply a search engine for geographical locations. The latest restructuring of the company into Alphabet Inc., a conglomerate of several companies that were owned by or tied to Google, indicates that this strategy is treated very seriously by its managers, especially as it relates to an aggressive monetization of the presentation of information to users through their web searches and use of data such as Google Maps (which is, after all, merely another instance of a web search for location data) If we were to describe all Google operations, they could be narrowed down to two basic infinitively repeated actions. The first process would be an analog to digital conversion of any kind of world-related, textual and geospatial information as well as visual sensations, commonly known as digitalization. The second stage of this action is processing, organizing and sharing all this information with interested parties, from advertisers to common users. From the very beginning of the New Aesthetic, Google Maps aesthetics and its glitches were considered as key examples of the 'new ways of seeing the world' and 'machine ways of seeing'.[25] Google Maps (2005), and particularly Google Street View (2007), which provides 360° panoramic street-level views of various locations, introduced a new worldwide cultural paradigm, a new aesthetics which encapsulates the way we can experience the world beyond our sight. Distorted 360° panoramic street photos combined with searchable, geospatial data became a new paradigm of visual, however mediated, interaction with locations that are beyond our reach – in more than 65 countries, as Google proudly explains. The photograph of an airliner over Hyde Park in Chicago discussed earlier, which due to a processing error has been divided into a phantom plane and three RGB shadows is an example of a 'new machine vision', and does more than just embody an aspect of the New

---

25   James Bridle, 'Waving at the Machines'.

Aesthetic but also indicates the intrusive nature of Google Maps; the aerial or satellite cameras are usually designed to capture a picture of a static terrain, rather than a moving object, but here we're not only given an impractical perspective - does anyone need an image of a plane flying over a park in order to navigate their way to and around that park? - but an assertive image that intrudes into our consciousness of the world, shifting our paradigm from one of being in the world to one of knowing the world. As such, it's easy to conclude that New Aesthetic products unveil the limitations of computational technologies by focusing on examples that preprogrammed, specific use cases cannot 'process' while at the same time redirecting our attention so that we fail to recognize those limitations. This seems especially troublesome with Google's efforts to digitize as many works of art as possible. The Google Cultural Institute[26] states that its mission is to facilitate the discovery of artworks and collections from around the world by as broad an audience as possible. Our first thought would be to embrace this effort; it's long been a truism that seeing art in museums around the world is an inherently elitist activity, if for no other reason than the financial resources necessary, and Google's efforts are obviously couched within a democratizing impetus. At the same time, something else occurs when literally millions of examples of art are made easily available through the most prevalent search engine in the world: the experience of art becomes potentially commonplace. This is not an assertion on our part of Walter Benjamin's description of the loss of aura in his influential chapter 'The Work of Art in the Age of Mechanical Reproduction' - which we are, nevertheless, remarkably sympathetic about, and which has been a major influence on the development of our critical perspective - in that we don't readily subscribe to the idea that the value of artworks is necessarily lessened by their reproduction. Rather, what troubles us is the opportunity for error that inevitably creeps into such a large-scale effort as Google's, highlighted and embodied in the images curated by Mario Santamaria in his Tumblr 'The Camera in the Mirror'. {Fig. 28}

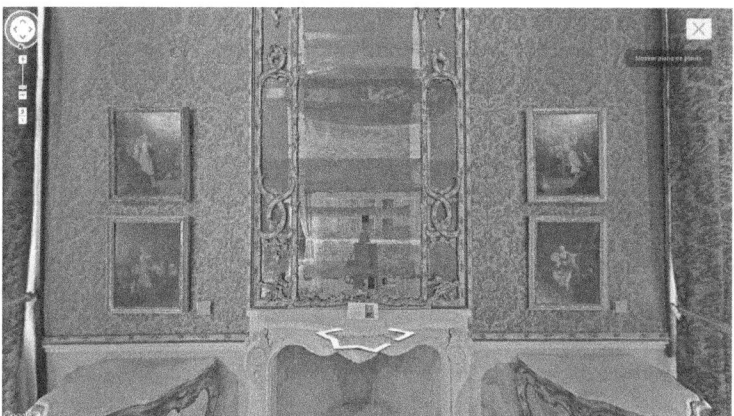

Fig. 28 Mario Santamaría, *Google Art Bots* (2014)

26   Google Cultural Institute, https://www.google.com/culturalinstitute/about/.

Jené Gutierrez writes about these images: 'In some of the images, the cameras don silvery-white blankets – this effect, combined with our culture's immersion in selfies, renders these cameras almost familiar and comfortable, but startling in its reflection of itself and selfie culture. These museums and galleries are, for the most part, emptied of people, the camera eerily alone in its self-documentation.'[27] This statement is both strange and stranger still. The very notion of a robotic selfie reflects our tendency as human beings to anthropomorphize activity.[28] Further, the idea that the cameras 'don' blankets and actively document themselves is obviously erroneous, in the simple fact that the robots never clothed themselves and are unintentionally documenting their presence and activities. But is Google Art a sufficient art experience? Most people might answer negatively, but given Google's stated intentions they would then claim that it serves a positive purpose. But does it really? Again, given the metaphysical and epistemic questions involved with the New Aesthetic, we would assert that it does not, that Google Art creates just as false a connection to art as a list of friends on Facebook to friendship.

With Cloak and ZXX, we have objects that accentuate our awareness that the complexity of the world cannot be grasped by single-task software and hardware. This awareness has continued with Google Maps. If computers are multi-role devices then so long as they are pre-programmed to respond to specific use cases and not a single other use they demonstrate a capability of transforming our epistemic position into a position of weakness. This is evident in two recent projects that partake of New Aesthetic ideas while still resisting its transformations of our world: *Report a Problem* (2012) {Fig. 29} by Emilio Vavarella[29] and the efforts of Eduardo Graells-Garrido at the Universitat Pompeu Fabra in Barcelona together with Mounia Lalmas and Daniel Quercia, ironically both at Yahoo Labs, to burst the so-called 'filter bubble'.[30]

Report a Problem {Fig. 30} is part of Vavarella's 'Google Trilogy' as an ongoing effort to explore 'the relationship between humans, power, and technological errors'. Presented as an art project in a number of galleries, it catalogs a series of images in which Google Maps has failed to accurately represent a specific location. The failures

27   Jené Gutierrez, 'Google's Robot Cameras Caught Taking Unintentional Selfies In Museums And Galleries', *Beautiful/Decay*, 7 July 2014, http://beautifuldecay.com/2014/07/07/googles-robot-cameras-caught-taking-unintentional-selfies-museums-galleries/.

28   Michael Silverberg, 'Google's Street View cameras are touring museums and taking weird selfies by accident', *Quartz*, 3 July 2014, http://qz.com/229852/googles-street-view-cameras-are-touring-museums-and-taking-weird-selfies-by-accident/.

29   Emilio Vavarella, 'Report a Problem', http://emiliovavarella.com/archive/google-trilogy/report-a-problem/.

30   KentuckyFC, Emerging Technology from the arXiv, 'How to Burst the "Filter Bubble" that Protects Us from Opposing Views', *MIT Technology Review*, 29 November 2013, http://www.technologyreview.com/view/522111/how-to-burst-the-filter-bubble-that-protects-us-from-opposing-views/.

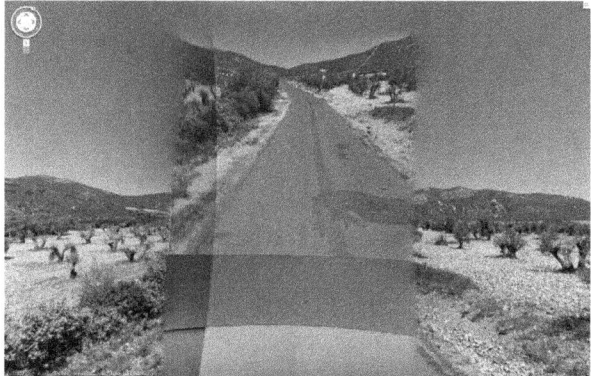

Fig. 29 Emilio Vavarella, *Report a Problem* (2014)

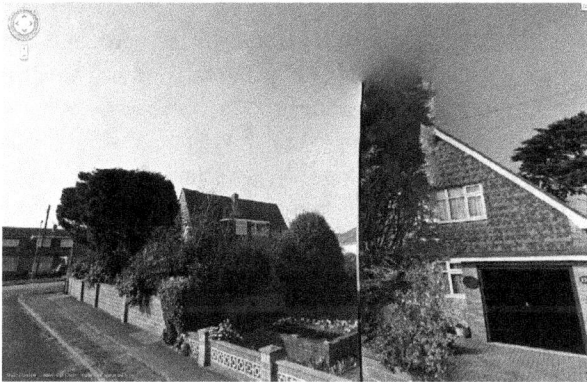

Fig. 30 Emilio Vavarella, *Report a Problem* (2014)

range from glitches in the photo file to random appearances of irrelevant information and incorrect views to actual instances of censorship. Most of these errors are caused by problems with the software used by Google in their efforts to photograph all of the locations available in Google Maps, but curiously quite a few of them seem to be simple problems with local conditions; for instance, quite a number of the images seem to have had rain or snow on the camera lens, lens flare or problems with the exposure. It might have seemed more reasonable to include Vavarella's project in our chapter on art, but we believe that the justification for this project indicates more than just an aesthetic response to glitches; *Report a Problem* is itself dependent on programming software, one that allows users to report errors to Google for correction. What's inherent to the function of Google's software is the sense that Google Maps is interactive, when nothing could be further from the truth particularly in light of users' general reluctance or indifferent attitude to actually report these errors. Vavarella's project is interesting in an artistic sense, but what makes it even more interesting is that it documents the conditions of use and the acceptance by users of their digital experience.

The project 'Data Portraits: Connecting People of Opposing Views' by Graells-Garrido, Lalmas and Quercia is, in many ways, a direct response to the aesthetic peculiarities identified by Vavarella, though it takes the form of a visualization of Twitter responses to a contentious issue rather than glitches and errors in Google Maps. {Fig. 31} In the abstract to their paper presenting the project they write:

Social networks allow people to connect with each other and have conversations on a wide variety of topics. However, users tend to connect with like-minded people and read agreeable information, a behavior that leads to group polarization. Motivated by this scenario, we study how to take advantage of partial homophily to suggest agreeable content to users authored by people with opposite views on sensitive issues. We introduce a paradigm to present a data portrait of users, in which their characterizing topics are visualized and their corresponding tweets are displayed using an organic design. Among their tweets we inject recommended tweets from other people considering their views on sensitive issues in addition to topical relevance, indirectly motivating connections between dissimilar people. To evaluate our approach, we present a case study on Twitter about a sensitive topic in Chile, where we estimate user stances for regular people and find intermediary topics. We then evaluated our design in a user study. We found that recommending topically relevant content from authors with opposite views in a baseline interface had a negative emotional effect. We saw that our organic visualization design reverts that effect. We also observed significant individual differences linked to evaluation of recommendations. Our results suggest that organic visualization may revert the negative effects of providing potentially sensitive content.[31]

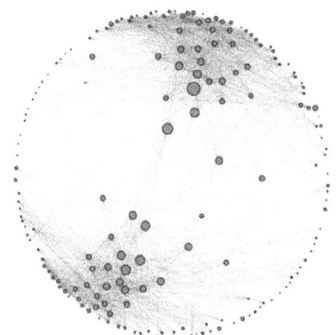

Fig. 31 Eduardo Graells-Garrido, Mounia Lalmas and Daniel Quercia, *Data Portraits: Connecting People of Opposing Views*, 'Bursting the Filter Bubble' (2013)

---

31   Eduardo Graells-Garrido, Mounia Lalmas, and Daniele Quercia, 'Data Portraits: Connecting People of Opposing Views', Human-Computer Interaction (cs.HC); Social and Information Networks, Cornell University, 19 November 2013, http://arxiv.org/abs/1311.4658.

This is a remarkably interesting New Aesthetic object not so much for the intended results but in that the visualization of contrasting opinions and the means of facilitating the introduction of opposing perspectives in an organic fashion apparently led the researchers to conclude that ideological opposition is breachable through a digital reformatting of the spectrum of perspectives. Unintentionally, perhaps, Graells-Garrido, Lalmas and Quercia have created a New Aesthetic condition wherein the aesthetic format transforms the degree to which users are receptive to new ideas. In a comment about the project in the *MIT Technology Review*, it's noted that 'There is good evidence that users can sometimes become so resistant to change than any form of redesign dramatically reduces the popularity of the service. Giving them a greater range of content could change that.'[32] Or, as it is put it another way, technology bursts the 'filter bubble'. But let's be careful here. Technology may be bursting the 'filter bubble' by easing the resistance that users have to different ideological perspectives, but the question remains as to whether users' abilities to be more open to different perspectives are eased through choice or by an external agency; it's our position that this research identifies an instance where users' agency, their ability to act and choose, is weakened precisely because of the acceptance of information in a digital format like Twitter. For example, recently a group on Facebook supporting the continued use of the Confederate flag in the United States was 'hijacked' by Virgil Texas, a self-described 'internet user' whose efforts at subversively undermining ethically questionable activity through humor are becoming well known.[33] {Fig. 32}

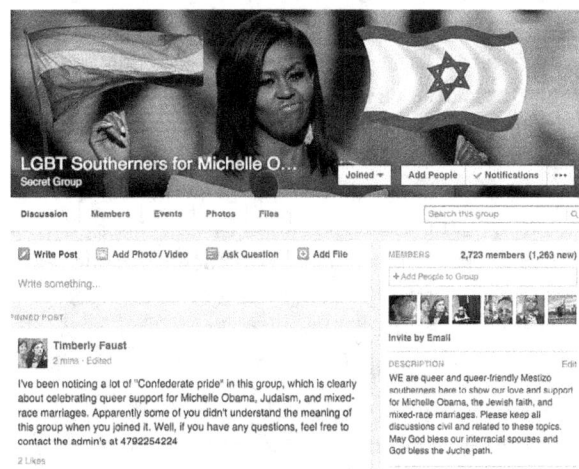

Fig. 32 Virgil Texas, *LGBT Southerns for Michelle Obama* (2015)

---

32   KentuckyFC, Emerging Technology from the arXiv, 'How to Burst the "Filter Bubble" that Protects Us from Opposing Views'.

33   Ben Mathis-Lilley, 'Hacked Confederate Facebook Group Becomes Tribute to LGBT Rights, Obama, Judaism', *Slate.com*, 29 July 2015, http://www.slate.com/blogs/the_slatest/2015/07/29/ confederate_flag_pride_facebook_group_hijacked_michelle_obama_and_multi.html.

For a brief period of time, Texas acquired full administrative control of the group, removed other users' administrative privileges, and transformed the group into 'LGBT Southerners for Michelle Obama'. In an interview, Texas noted 'Everyone in Confederate Facebook seems to accept friend requests from strangers, which I guess can be chalked up to Southern hospitality.'[34] From our perspective, as much as we applaud Texas' efforts and thought they were a hysterically funny sabotage of a self-righteous group's buffoonery, we disagree with this last remark; the willing acceptance of Texas' requests for administrative control of the group weren't facilitated by 'Southern hospitality' but by the New Aesthetic conditions that Facebook invariably operates within. In short, the New Aesthetic today erodes users' capacity to defy an alteration of their agency. While 'Data Portraits' – the irony of the title doesn't escape us here– is well intended and clearly is an effort to establish a paradigm of resistance within the digital framework of experience, it is precisely because of this framework that its aspirations are thwarted. The same is true of the efforts of Texas; it's not human agency in the form of 'Southern hospitality' that allowed the Facebook page to be highjacked but the conditions of Facebook's objecthood itself in its own programming.

Other instances of this become increasingly visible the more you know where to look. Again and again, the pervasiveness of the New Aesthetic has surprised us, especially when it affects political theory in a cross-pollinating fashion. Google's recent Constitute project,[35] in partnership with the Comparative Constitutions Project,[36] has the best of intentions – giving access to all of the constitutions of the world to everyone, so that people rewriting constitutions can reference others, search for key words and ideas, and pin specific areas of interest for further legislative use and review – but it's underlying architecture specifically notes that the data provided is 'prepared as open-linked data in order to provide for efficient human and machine consumption' with the clear implication that writing new legislation, often amidst social upheavals, will be reduced to Google searches rather than the product of any genuinely original effort (and its description as machine consumable, while understood in its normal context of database use and cross-referencing, gives us chills). This disconnect in New Aesthetic objects often prompts some opposition.[37] Anna Jobin importantly notes the inherent sexism of Google searches, with a particularly interesting contribution in the coining of the phrase 'linguistic prosthesis,'

---

34   Virgil Texas, 'How I Infiltrated a White Pride Facebook Group and Turned It into "LGBT Southerners for Michelle Obama"', *Vice.com*, 3 August 2015, http://www.vice.com/read/virgil-texas-white-power-facebook-group-troll.

35   James Bridle, 'Google launches "Constitute," a new tool for designing governments | The Verge', *The New Aesthetic Tumblr blog*, 25 September 2013, http://new-aesthetic.tumblr.com/post/62244541600/google-launches-constitute-a-new-tool-for.

36   Comparative Constitutions Project, http://comparativeconstitutionsproject.org/.

37   Randall Patrick Munroe, 'Questions', *xkcd.com*, 26 August 2013, http://xkcd.com/1256/.

along with her co-author Frederic Kaplan, that identifies the fact that 'the mediation by autocompletion algorithms acts in a particularly powerful way because it doesn't correct us afterwards'[38] and asks the absolutely perfect question of 'Who is in charge when algorithms are in charge?' With the images produced for UN Women by Memac Ogilvy and Mather Dubai[39] {Fig. 33} it's clear that search results themselves are offensive. {Fig. 34}

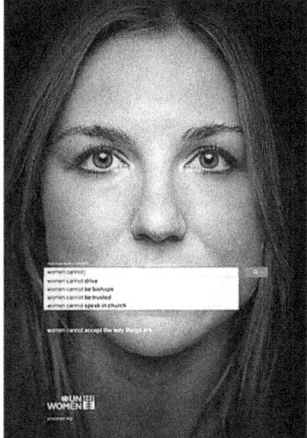

Fig. 33 Memac Ogilvy and Mather Dubai for UN Women (2015)

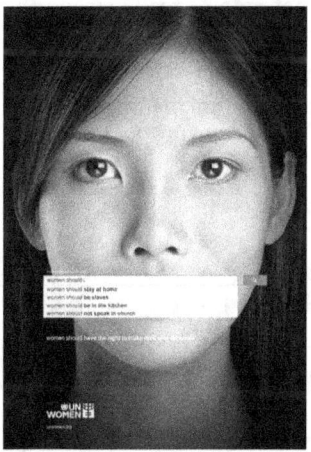

Fig. 34 Memac Ogilvy and Mather Dubai for UN Women (2015)

---

38 Anna Jobin, 'Google's autocompletion: algorithms, stereotypes and accountability', *Sociostrategy blog*, 22 October 2013, http://sociostrategy.com/2013/googles-autocompletion-algorithms-stereotypes-accountability/.

39 *UN Women*, 'UN Women ad series reveals widespread sexism ', 21 October 2013, http://www.unwomen.org/en/news/stories/2013/10/women-should-ads.

It's not just that the text shows search results that indicate misogynistic viewpoints, con-demnable at a fundamental level, but just as important from the perspective of a critical engagement with the New Aesthetic it's the fact that all human beings themselves are reducible to the products of search engines and autocompletion. {Fig. 35}

Yet, even if those search results don't appear in Google searches in the United States, the results themselves are still there; given the supposed democratic nature of Google searches, there is every possibility of their rise to prominence. Even more troubling, with the emergence of computationality as an onto-theology we all become mere data for search engines. The New Aesthetic increasingly means, in its manifestations, that there's a lack of resistance to digital objects, a lack of an opportunity to resist the digitalization of the world, as that digitalization process transforms the world and our experiences of it in a way that's beyond our control.

Representing this perfectly is an image from Bridle's blog that shows the average appear-ance of every one of the 535 members of the United States' Congress. {Fig. 36} A first reaction would be to see this as a humorous representation of the lack of genuine dif-ferences amongst American legislators, an unfocused image that is white, dressed in a suit, perhaps slightly balding, and undifferentiated in terms of ideology or propensity for corruption. Perhaps that's a bit too far or a bit unfair, but this image as a parody of the identities of these politicians also clearly indicates that nothing really makes one different from the rest of their colleagues; the ethnic differences, the fundamental dif-ferences in identity are of no consequence for an algorithmically driven form of digital vision. As a object of the New Aesthetic, however, we turn to thinking about what it represents. Politics across the entire world have readily embraced social media such as Facebook and Twitter to the point that it would be absurd or impossible to conceive of a politician not having a website and a social media presence. In doing so, however, haven't politicians simply homogenized their image? And, if image is the most crucial tool to getting elected, haven't politicians' embrace of social media in a New Aesthetic context homogenized their ideological values? Why this image is important, is not so much in its parody value but in the further implications of what it represents: a New Aesthetic politics, just like a New Aesthetic constitution, is always going to be dependent on the digital presentation to the users of an aesthetic condition, and the value of ideas is going to be lost amidst the form of that aesthetic condition. It might seem strange to imagine a New Aesthetic constitution – a legal, governing text that establishes social norms – but when politicians' messages conform to predetermined stylistic conventions, in the hope that they are effective but driven by the externally influenced belief in a necessary style of the message, then a New Aesthetic constitution is not so far-fetched precisely because it's the politicians who will be writing that document. In our opinion, anyone who believes that new laws and policies are today conceived and implemented by a traditional sense of politics governed by social power structures such as votes is foolish; policy and law and their intended and actual effects are increasingly a product of a conforming to the drive of the digital.

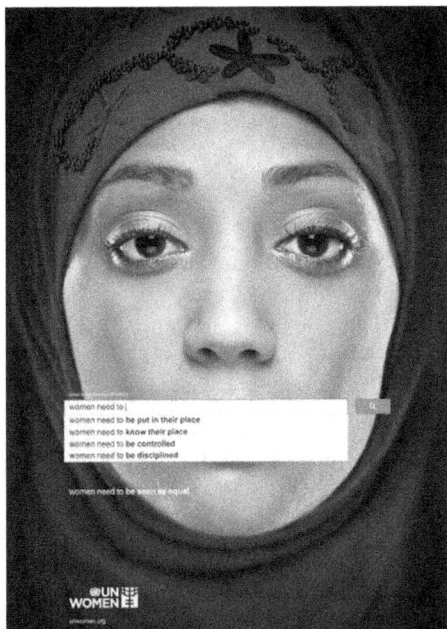

Fig. 35 Memac Ogilvy and Mather Dubai for UN Women (2015)

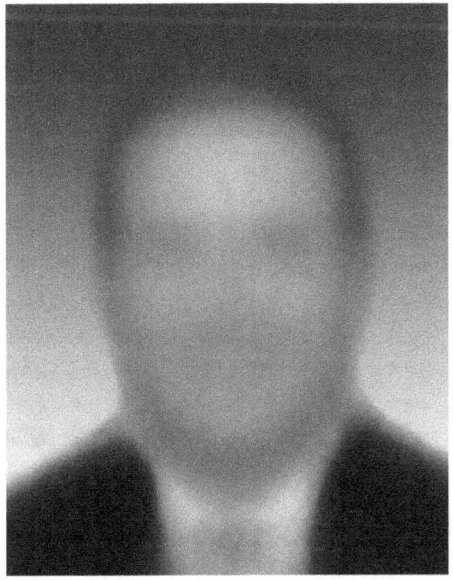

Fig. 36 Average member of the United States Congress

The Effects of Instances of the New Aesthetic

In describing these various objects of the New Aesthetic, we should not forget about the other path of reasoning, namely that the New Aesthetic often manifests only as examples of real-time phenomena rather than as a persistent set of objects that can be curated, collected and confined to a museum setting. There is a correlation between presentation, identification and recognition in the New Aesthetic condition; presentation in the experience of New Aesthetic phenomena, identification of New Aesthetic objects as sufficiently distinct from other phenomena, and recognition of the effects of New Aesthetic objects as they alter our understanding of the world. Added to this, though, is the paradoxical temporary nature of the objects, paradoxical in terms of the contrast to their persistent effect. Each of the examples we discuss in this chapter present themselves either as digital products or as the resulting objects of digital processes, and importantly each example is clearly only associated with a New Aesthetic because of its dependency on its digital origins. Each example further distinguishes itself as New Aesthetic from other experiences because its digital origins seemingly have a capacity to be self-sufficient and self-determinative, acting as an autonomous agent in the interplay between itself and the user. And each example, with the recognition of its autonomous character, is then accepted, almost passively, as an agent affecting a shift in the way we understand and interact with the world. Google Maps or any other navigation app on our smartphone is a perfect example of this in the often documented instances of users relying on data rather than their own awareness of their surroundings; when someone drives onto a runway in the path of oncoming aircraft because Google Maps or Apple Maps told them to,[40] they've done so less out of stupidity and more because they believed what they were being told and because they assumed the information the app was providing was correct. In fact, the information as far as the app was aware of (and we do attribute a certain digital 'awareness' to apps, with the full intentions of ascribing a certain limited sense of consciousness to apps), was correct.

Where the metaphysical change takes place, amidst these effects, is less in the specific examples but in the passive acceptance of temporarily accurate data. Almost all the examples we've described, because they are digital products, may paradoxically not exist at the time the reader is reading this book. Certainly it would be a good assumption that many will not exist decades from now, even mere years from now; in some cases, the imagery we've used was archived by us and is no longer available through the URL addresses at the time of this publication. Most of these software-based phenomena are just a 'pull of a plug' away from oblivion, never to be archived, never to be available again, absolutely temporary. From an aesthetics perspective, there has been a spectrum

---

40   Leo Kelion, 'Apple Maps flaw results in drivers crossing airport runway', *BBC News*, 25 September
      2013, http://www.bbc.com/news/technology-24246646.

of responses. Hito Steyerl's article 'In Defense of the Poor Image'[41] is an acceptance at an aesthetic level of a range of image quality, particularly poor quality images. Steyerl's defense centers around the poor quality of images from pirated sources of cinema and video work, an inevitable consequence in the conversion process when shifting content from analog or outdated digital sources to more widely used video formats. Borrowing from Juan García Espinosa's book *For an Imperfect Cinema*, written in Cuba in the late 1960s, Steyerl advocates the notion of an 'imperfect cinema' that can be extended to a notion of an 'imperfect image'. Steyerl writes about the political force that she identifies as an inherent quality of imperfect cinema:

> The imperfect cinema is one that strives to overcome the divisions of labor within class society. It merges art with life and science, blurring the distinction between consumer and producer, audience and author. It insists upon its own imperfection, is popular but not consumerist, committed without becoming bureaucratic.[42]

We find ourselves very much in alignment with Steyerl's position; it has been one of the crucial catalysts of our own thought. At the same time, in the same vein as Steyerl's assertion that 'one has to redefine the value of the image, or, more precisely, to create a new perspective for it', we find her opening paragraph even more interesting in that we see it as an ontology of the digital image diverging from the rest of her article. Steyerl writes:

> The poor image is a copy in motion. Its quality is bad, its resolution substandard. As it accelerates, it deteriorates. It is a ghost of an image, a preview, a thumbnail, an errant idea, an itinerant image distributed for free, squeezed through slow digital connections, compressed, reproduced, ripped, remixed, as well as copied and pasted into other channels of distribution.[43]

The poor image, the glitchy and distorted image that is often the product of digital processing, is indeed an image in motion, though perhaps not a copy. Because it is in motion, because it is active in the world, its quality might be 'bad', but it is not an errant idea but an inerrant presence that shirks off its connections as it acquires an experiential presence for the user. What makes the New Aesthetic different from Steyerl's imperfect cinema, or different from the extension of her idea to imperfect image, is that the image no longer manifests as distributed but as present and singular. We can even play a grammatical game here, taking the notion of 'imperfect' not only to mean flawed by as a past tense verb form. In Steyerl's notion of imperfect cinema there is the idea that

---

41   Hito Steyerl, 'In Defense of the Poor Image', *e-flux*, November 2009, http://www.e-flux.com/journal/in-defense-of-the-poor-image/.

42   Steyerl, 'In Defense of the Poor Image'.

43   Steyerl, 'In Defense of the Poor Image'.

the reproductions were once perfect but no longer are, and the temporal space between the perfect state of the cinematic example and its current imperfect state is tangible, social, and often politicized. Imperfect images would be the same, their degraded quality (similar to fading in Polaroids and other analog photographs) marking a sense of loss as a tangible manifestation of temporal duration between their original state and their current condition. In contrast, New Aesthetic objects are continually present while being continually deletable.

A good example of New Aesthetic objects as evidence of a metaphysical shift is, again, Stephen von Worley's efforts at an artistic visualization of data that have produced images of population data that have a visual flair to them. But in his posting 'My God, It's Full Of Blocks! Population Density Meets The Tile Space'[44] we see something different. What he describes is a constant shifting of the means of presenting information which itself is prone to shifts, but the title of the posting is telling as an exclamatory passive response to the aesthetic manifestation; the shock is a response to the digitalization of the data, to its presence, but we also believe that there's an underlying subtext in this shocked response that is equally a response to the potential future changes in the data. Another example is Yarin Gal's efforts at a machine-learning based implementation of Photoshop's 'PatchMatch' function to 'extrapolate the scene of a painting to see what the full scenery might have looked like'.[45] {Fig. 37}

What Gal displays is a series of images by artists such as van Gogh, Monet, Picasso and Hokusai that have been digitally extended to 'complete' the painted scene; in most respects, the final product is excruciatingly terrible on a purely aesthetic level, in clear contrast to the artists' original intentions (why would someone feel the need to extrapo-late additional imagery from finished art unless they felt it was in an incomplete state?), but it signals a willingness to accept both an extension of digital agency as well as an acceptance of the temporary nature of these extrapolations in that there's no illusion nor expectations that viewers are going to understand these New Aesthetic digital products as separate from the original paintings over any extended period of time. There have been efforts to counter what seems to be this inherent aspect of many instances of these objects, this strange sense of presence that is vividly temporary, but even work such as the 2015 *As Long As Possible* project by Juha van Ingen in collaboration with Janne Särkelä, which consists of a GIF viewable only over a thousand years showing 48,140,288 frames changing every ten minutes, is an artistic work that is clearly unfeasible. {Fig. 38}

---

44   Stephen von Worley, 'My God, It's Full Of Blocks! Population Density Meets The Tile Space'.

45   Yarin Gal, *Extrapolated Art*, http://extrapolated-art.com/.

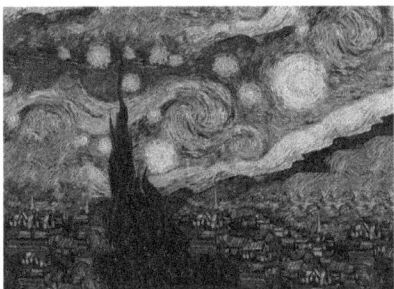

Fig. 37 Gal, Yarin, *Patchmatch*, 'Starry Night' (2014)

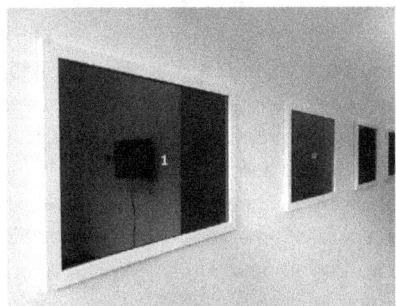

Fig. 38 Juha van Ingen and Janne Särkelä, *As Long As Possible* (2015)

The New Aesthetic objects often appear to be permanent, but clearly are not. In the context of these manifestations, we wonder if it's possible to resist the digitizing homogenization and increased acceptance of digital autonomy, to resist this shift in our metaphysics. The New Aesthetic objects that give us a sense of success are few, but products like Mint Digital Products *WhiteAlbum*,[46] a recently developed app for iOS, is in many respects the perfect instance that alters our relationship with photographic objects and that, perhaps, is also a product of efforts resisting the New Aesthetic. {Fig. 39}

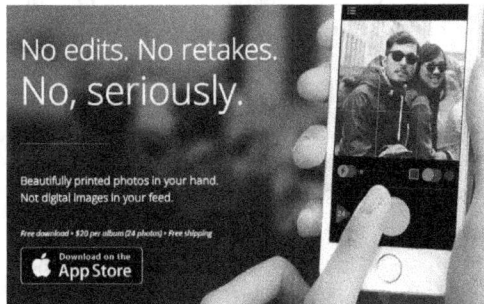

Fig. 39 Mint Digital Projects, *Whitealbum* (2015)

46   WhiteAlbum, https://whitealbumapp.com/.

Released in early 2015, and since discontinued, it was a photographic application for the iPhone that confoundingly did not provide visual feedback nor a digital file to the photographer, making it impossible to correct, edit, save or share the results. *WhiteAlbum*, rather ponderously, mimicked the disposable camera by saving the photographs to a server until 24 shots have been produced, at which point the user was charged $20 for those shots to be printed on high quality paper and to receive them by mail.[47] It's in the return to the analog, in a return to the actual world, that the paradigmatic and metaphysical shift identifiable as the New Aesthetic loses its dominance. That being said, *WhiteAlbum* was also a little ridiculous, even if we ignore its strange reference to the Beatles album.

We conclude this chapter with what we believe is perhaps the most innocuous and yet increasingly pervasive example of the New Aesthetic's intruding into our lives: the shift towards vertical photography and video. We hope to have shown that the New Aesthetic does not only address specific visual phenomena or niche artistic practices but is an affective approach transforming the very foundations of human existence in subtle but important ways. As a transition between manifestations and art, between products and objects, we argue that one instance of its inclusiveness and rhizomatic theoretical foundations can be helpfully observed in one of the earliest emergences of this specific new cultural paradigm, namely, the recent trend towards vertical photography and video caused particularly by the mobile revolution. We know what you're thinking: how could a vertical or horizontal orientation of photography or video change the world? Consider this: according to a study done by eMarketer in 2015, digital device users frequently spend as much as 10 hours daily in front of various screens, and in nearly 30% of that time the screen content was being consumed on mobile 'vertical' screens (2010-2015, US). Additionally, in 2015, the overall time of consuming digital media in the western world reached nearly 6 hours on a daily basis, with 51% of that time spent on mobile devices typically in a vertical orientation. The fact that this evolution towards mobile devices is changing the way humans interact with the world is without question, but it's equally evident that one of the most fundamental formal configurations in the process of presenting information is also changing. The horizontal format has been a fundamental element of the aesthetic canon in a range of different art forms for centuries, dominating image creation and distribution; this is apparent not just in photography and video but in the history of painting. One could even claim that evidence of the horizontal format as fundamental to image production goes all the way back to ancient Greece, with the examples of sculptural friezes on the Parthenon, of ancient Mesopotamia, with architectural decoration and cylinder seals, and even instances of prehistoric art found in cave paintings. The reason for this is simple: our eyes are arranged in a horizontal relationship, and our binocular vision is processed in this fashion. In recent years, however, and most strangely, the horizontal, widescreen frame in photography and video is increasingly becoming extinct, as today the vertical frame begins to dominate contemporary imagery.

---

47   Kyle Vanhemert, 'App Turns Your iPhone Into a Crappy Disposable Camera (And That's a Good Thing)', *Wired.com*, 1 January 2015, http://www.wired.com/2015/01/app-turns-iphone-crappy-disposable-camera-thats-good-thing/.

There are multiple explanations for this evolution. The simplest or the most obvious would be that mobile devices themselves are equipped with vertical screens because their design is directly linked an ergonomic design impetus observable in the history of the physical form of the telephone, where a handset's receiver and transmitter needs to be aligned in one hand between the ear and the mouth; various designs of horizontal mobile phones have languished and died in popularity against to the massive dominance of the vertical shape, a clear sign that comfort and usability is part of the drive towards the vertical. In the shift from landline to mobile phones, this design approach resulted in a specific user interface which favors handling the phone with one hand (a manner of speaking on the phone that we've all grown accustomed to) which would lead to 'scrolling' through a screen in an up and down rather than a horizontal manner. Scrolling through information on a screen then encourages an approach that stacks information rather than encouraging a manner of 'hyperlink exploring' as a way for interacting with the content. Multiple windows and hierarchical links, which dominated the web and GUIs in the personal computer era, have lately been replaced by interaction models based on single-window view. Across the world, smartphones and mobile devices are becoming the primary everyday screens to consume and transform not only text-based content but also interactive (apps) and visual content (photography, video), almost to the point that referring to them as 'phones' is increasingly becoming inaccurate.

It's evident that the processes of using mobile phones have dictated the presentation of material, but we assert that this has done far more than just shifting the orientation of information and has, instead, changed the very nature of the information itself. Widescreen and horizontal image aesthetics have dominated theatrical releases and TV broadcast for decades, in part because, as noted above, the natural process of human vision is horizontally oriented through our binocular vision. But once both professional visual content and user-generated photos and videos, often captured vertically, have blended on a single mobile screen, the hegemony of the horizontal has ended. Today the user can access multi-device services such as Netflix and HBO GO which still offer widescreen content, and social media uploads generated on a mobile phone held horizontally or apps like Vine, Snapchat (200 million monthly users) or Periscope (10 millions users and only supporting vertical videos) on the very same mobile device. In 2015 YouTube updated its mobile apps to support full-screen vertical video playback. The disruptive cultural effect of portrait video could not have been ignored even by the largest social media video service, only a decade after the very invention of a modern mobile device. Several media – among them *Mashable* and *The Daily Mail* – have begun experimenting with professional videos shot in portrait mode. At the end of the day, the format of vertical video is just a tool, but we argue that the users who create art, advertisement or entertainment based on that, are introducing fundamental cultural changes for the simple reason that the horizontal orientation of our natural vision processes is forcibly being shifted to accommodate the manner in which the information is received. The vertical video example illustrates that the New Aesthetic can be an interesting approach to grasp and analyze rapid socio-cultural changes triggered by a very fast adoption rate of a particular technology, to the point that we read information in the manner in which it is presented to us – vertically, rather than horizontally – which shifts our critical perspective, even the basic level at which we understand visually presented information, from one that is naturally familiar to one that is artificially familiar. There has been some resistance to this and some lively debates; 'Vertical Video Syndrome'[48] is neither dangerous nor offensive per se, but it does indicate an unwillingness on the part of the content producer to account for our horizontal panoramic video, and as an example of the New Aesthetic it indicates an unconscious concession to the software paradigm that is itself governed by limitations of the hardware. It's more than just a sign of amateurism, it's increasingly becoming the norm as authors like Farhad Manjoo argue: 'They worry they are on the wrong side of history. The future of video, it turns out, just may be vertical.'[49] Quoted in Manjoo's article, Jon Steinberg, the chief executive of The Daily Mail's North American operations, states: 'We find the engagement much higher. Users are more satisfied, and there's a higher completion rate on them.'[50] But does Steinberg genuinely believe that there is actual engagement, which is highly unlikely, or is this merely indicative of an increased length of time watching the video and the web page, a vital rubric when it comes to advertising fees? A higher completion rate means nothing, we would assert, beyond the presence of a paradigmatic shift of the user's experiential expectations identifiable as the New Aesthetic; we've been conditioned to consume digital content in a certain fashion because of the characteristics of its presentation that were, at first, a result of their limitations, and now it's been produced at an even higher rate with an assertion that it's a new, fresher, more exciting way of seeing the world. It's not because video has become more personal, it's because the technology behind the video has driven our aesthetic standards away from the human towards the pervasively digital. If our perception of the world is increasingly in a fluxual state of intertwined layers of algorithms and computation that defines contemporary society and culture then it's increasingly evident that New Aesthetic experiences are becoming a dominant and driving force for that change.

48   Glove and Boots, 'Vertical Video Syndrome - A PSA', YouTube video, 2:58, 5 June 2012, https://youtu.be/Bt9zSfinwFA.

49   Farhad Manjoo, 'Vertical Video on the Small Screen? Not a Crime', The New York Times, 12 August 2015, http://www.nytimes.com/2015/08/13/technology/personaltech/vertical-video-on-the-small-screen-not-a-crime.html?_r=0.

50   Ibid.

CHAPTER 3
GLITCH ONTOLOGY
AND THE NEW AESTHETIC

In order to critically examine the cultural impact of the latest computational technologies and to follow the critical approach to the computational advocated by the protagonists of the New Aesthetic, we need to turn to studying the computational in a state of failure.

In this chapter we are elaborating on glitch theory, which will be used in the subsequent chapters devoted to studying glitches in digital media, consumer software and hardware ecosystems, artistic interventions and works of art. {Fig. 40}

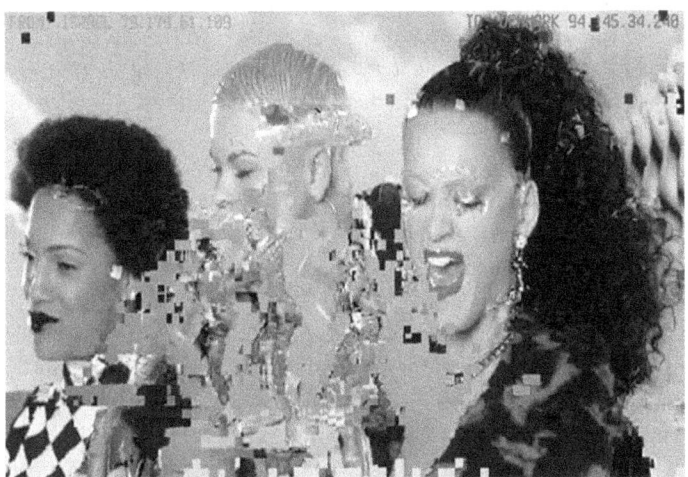

Fig. 40 Nicolas Maigret, *The Pirate Cinema* (2014)

The glitch is a result of the 'attitude' (Bridle's characterization) that drives the New Aesthetic; it is a fundamental aspect of New Aesthetic objects, the means by which they are apparent and recognizable to the user. We argue that glitches are one of the key constituents and manifestations of the New Aesthetic both on the conceptual and on the aesthetic level.

In *Software Studies, A Lexicon* in the chapter entitled 'Glitch', Olga Goriunova and Alexei Shulgin write that

> In electrical systems, a glitch is a short-lived error in a system or machine. A glitch appears as a defect (a voltage-change or signal of the wrong duration - a change of input) in an electrical circuit. Thus, a glitch is a short-term deviation from a correct value and as such the term can also describe hardware malfunctions.[1]

From the aesthetic perspective glitches can be 'claimed to be a manifestation of genu-

---

1   Olga Goriunova and Alexei Shulgin, 'Glitch', in Matthew Fuller (ed.) *Software Studies: a Lexicon*, London: MIT Press, 2008, p. 110.

ine software aesthetics' as they reveal the computational nature of the digital image.[2] There is even a sense that the glitch is a challenge to the moral or ethical status of the digital object's use, in that it manifests an incorrect value contradicting the user's expectations. Glitch aesthetics has been discussed as a form of transmedial narratives, and has even been frequently linked to a nostalgic form of 8-bit game design, to cite one example, but in the case of New Aesthetic objects there is something more. Both low-res pixelated images and glitches are rather marginal phenomena in comparison to common contemporary aesthetics (images displayed in high resolution with millions of colors). However they allow us to break away from the screen-centric approach and make the softwarization of the digital image clearly visible. The glitch, being a direct and natural result of an algorithmic error, unveils the degree of the software's influence on the aesthetics of digital image:

> Just as digital technologies and software mediate our experience and engagement with the world, often invisibly, so the "digital" and "software" is itself mediated and made visible through the representational forms of pixelation and glitch.[3]

In this sense, glitches are more than just a manifestation of a coding error or the result of inputted data from the user; they are both an opportunity and an encouragement for us to reconsider the myth of total immediacy of computational imagery, particularly when images are perceived as parts of software structure e.g. graphical user interface. The very notion of mediation is important because it creates a dialectical relationship between user and object, necessitating interaction or, at the very least, reaction. In *Transcoding the Digital: How Metaphors Matter in New Media* Marianne van den Boomen gives examples of such situations:

> For example, when sound and vision are no longer synchronized in a movie, when subtitles suddenly disappear, or when we notice the delay in a live television interview from the studio. Paradoxically then, immediacy is the imaginary degree zero of any mediation, a lived illusion of absent mediation, deprived of all traditional markers that announce an encounter with media. When it shows itself, the spell is broken. In retrospect, immediacy turns out to be a matter of unnoticed and concealed mediation, revealing itself now in the split into a faltering medium and a stammering message.[4]

In focusing on the appearances of glitches and miscalculations in New Aesthetic objects, we believe that at least part of its nature is revealed as an abnormal relation in the structures composed of standardized objects, especially in the creative software based

---

2   Goriunova and Shulgin, 'Glitch'.

3   Berry et al. *New Aesthetic, New Anxieties,* p. 43.

4   van den Boomen, *Transcoding the Digital,* p. 65.

on image processing algorithms or lags and artifacts that are the means of producing graphical user interfaces in contemporary software. An instance of a programming
language taking over the responsibilities of coding from the programmer, while dis-
ingenuously promoting itself as a guarantor of the programmer's and user's end-use
satisfaction, is Apple's new programming language Swift, which is supposedly designed
for 'safety' because 'Swift eliminates entire classes of unsafe code. Variables are always
initialized before use, arrays and integers are checked for overflow, and memory is
managed automatically.'

On the aesthetic level they seem to address the approach taken by many proponents of
the New Aesthetic. For Matt Jones the New Aesthetic encourages us to 'see the grain of
computation'[5] in everyday interaction not only with the digital but with the physical world
as well. The 'grain of computation' would be these specific aesthetic patterns associated
with the digital that are becoming visible through pixelization and visual glitches in digital
media and in new pixelated aesthetics in fashion, military, architecture, design and other
actual objects present in the physical world. In the era of ultra-high resolution, seamless
user interfaces and ubiquitous systems that Peter Knapp names the 'era of noise cancel-
ing', the New Aesthetic manifestations, and particularly glitches, unveil the limitations of
the computational through something that Kim Cascone calls the 'aesthetics of failure'.[6]

Both glitch studies and the New Aesthetic seem to share the spirit of a 'critical trans-
media aesthetics'[7] as understood by Rosa Menkman, the author of the *Glitch Art Manifesto* (2010) and the *Glitch Momentum* (2011).

> these aesthetics media show a medium in a critical state (a ruined, unwanted, not
> recognized, accidental and horrendous state). These aesthetics critique the medium
> (genre, interface and expectations) [...] They challenge its inherent politics and the
> established template of creative practice while producing a theory of reflection.[8]

Menkman suggests that glitch aesthetics offer more than just interesting and attractive
visual experiences. They give us a new perspective on digital media and applications
that goes beyond the preprogrammed aesthetics and interactions paradigms. They can
also challenge another praised popular culture paradigm that emphasizes the unlimited

---

5   Matt Jones, 'Sensor-Vernacular', *Berg London blog*, 13 May 2011, http://berglondon.com/
     blog/2011/05/13/sensor-vernacular/.

6   Kim Cascone, 'The Aesthetics of Failure: Post-Digital Tendencies in Contemporary Computer
     Music', *subsol*, 24 April 2004, http://subsol.c3.hu/subsol_2/contributors3/casconetext.html.

7   Rosa Menkman, *Glitch Studies Manifesto*, *Sunshine in My Throat*, 2009/2010, p. 8, 9, 11. http://
     rosa-menkman.blogspot.com/2010/02/glitch-studies-manifesto.html.

8   Menkman, *Glitch Studies Manifesto*, p. 8.

creative potential of computational technologies. Glitches in digital media processing and user-oriented applications suddenly bring to the forefront the hidden boundaries of creative practices based on affordances of the digital.

This observation drives us to the conclusion that the New Aesthetic is not a medium-specific approach, since the phenomena associated with the New Aesthetic can be encountered in any kind of digital media; be it CGI, still images, video content, GUIs, etc. The range of artworks presented in the subsequent chapter clearly proves that point. Despite the fact that there are multiple formats and media types, when faced with glitches digital media seem universally equivalent. All digital objects are susceptible to unwanted, sudden errors that lead to visual glitches. The reason for this is the fact that the very conditions for glitch aesthetics are structured by core properties of computer-based media enumerated by Lev Manovich in his *The Language of New Media*.[9] Manovich argues that all digital media share some common properties, which are deeply rooted in their numerical nature. Consequently, all digital images are discrete since they are broken and then displayed as discrete elements with pixels (data values on chrominance and luminance). They are also modular since they are built in real-time from various layers of data types. The process of their displaying involves actual image data, specific codecs, software, user interfaces and this is even more complex in network-based imagery. The cultural and social significance of different, interconnected layers in the computational will be addressed broadly when we will discuss the 'ontological levels of the computational' described by David M. Berry. Another common property of digital images would be their ability to be compressed. This is important particularly in web-based imagery which has to be processed and sent with as few resources as possible. Compression has become really important in the advent of mobile devices and mobile internet access. Video streaming services, such as VOD platforms or YouTube, but also social media that heavily use visual content like Instagram or Facebook, function thanks to advanced compression algorithms. Variability and automation would be another key property of digital visual media. Both can be narrowed down to the fact that they are programmable. Manovich explains that this enables a user to create infinite versions of the same image which can vary in size, resolution, colors, composition and so on.

Following Manovich's observations we argue that the core properties of digital media create the very conditions of existence of glitch aesthetics. It emerges as a trans-media, or better a medium-neutral abnormal momentum, which takes the user beyond a care-fully designed modi operandi of each and every medium. In high-resolution photography, glitch aesthetics would manifest itself by a pixelated or broken (partially-displayed) image, in video the glitches would be seen as compression artifacts, in real-time web-based media and interfaces the glitches would result in partial or incorrect display of icons, data streams etc. We will address such cases in our glitch art analysis. In any case,

---

9   Manovich, *The Language of New Media*, pp. 246-250.

glitch aesthetics challenges the logic of seamless interaction and automation maintained by the continuity of streams of processed data displayed in various media.

Of course, the ontological identity of objects is not only identifiable through the presence of glitches but also their relational capacities and effects, a crucial point to remember in the context of a narrowed discussion of New Aesthetic objects. Many scholars emphasize the promising critical potential of glitches in studying not only technologies themselves and everyday human-computer interaction practices but also their social and cultural impact; with a general consensus that it is necessary to open the black box of computation to the user.

This quasi-hacking approach in which the glitches are undeliberate after all is considered as a first step in a process of making the user aware of both technical limitations of the digital and of socio-political constraints imposed on her through these technologies. For instance, Benjamin Mako Hill, and to some extent Jussi Parikka, write about hidden affordances of technologies that are made visible to the users thanks to glitches and errors.

> [...] errors can reveal the affordances and constraints of technology that are often invisible to users. Through these affordances and constraints, technologies make it easier to do some things, rather than others, and either easier or more difficult to communicate certain messages. Errors can help reveal these hidden constraints and the power that technology imposes. [10]

In other words, Hill argues that glitches do reveal the boundaries of the digital sandbox that a user usually plays in while being enchanted by supposed limitless creative possibilities and perfect visual representations that come with user-oriented software and systems. 'Through noise, through anomalies, we are able to decipher a range of crucial issues concerning politics, aesthetics and cultural processes of media.'[11] Parikka goes even further, saying that a critical examination of anomalies and noise in digital media can be a starting point for a more broad analysis of the impact of the computational on society and culture. Parikka seems to follow an important line of reasoning in the humanities that was advocated by Immanuel Kant – that examining the world in the light of its aesthetics may provide us with a very productive and unique critical perspective. This approach is shared by us as well throughout this book.

Building on this approach, it is worthy to mention a very important addition to it by Olga Goriunova and Alexei Shulgin who link glitch studies with software studies. The scholars emphasize the critical potential of glitch for revealing the inner logic of software, how-

---

10   Benjamin Mako Hill, 'Revealing Errors' in Mark Nunes (ed.) *Error Glitch, Noise, and Jam in New Media Cultures*, New York and London: Continuum, 2011, p. 29.

11   Jussi Parikka, *What is Media Archaeology?*, Cambridge: Polity, 2012, p. 110.

ever not solely as a technology-oriented endeavor but rather as a starting point for a wider discussion on the social and cultural consequences of a particular organization of digital spaces:

> A glitch is a mess that is a moment, a possibility to glance at software's inner structure, whether it is a mechanism of data compression or HTML code. Although a glitch does not reveal the true functionality of the computer, it shows the ghostly conventionality of the forms by which digital spaces are organized.[12]

Goriunova and Schulgin understand glitches and errors as unique epistemic micro-states that offer a chance to critically assess the boundaries of the operational logic of the software. The scholars encourage us to conceptually understand glitches as ruptures which go vertically through different layers of the computational as they may be caused by errors in the software code, data sets, network, protocols or user interface. Glitches provide us not only with an insight into the layered structure of the computational, but also make clear the limitations of the programmability of the digital. Mark Nunes and Benjamin Mako follow a similar logic, emphasizing the importance of opening the computational 'black boxes' for making possible a critical analysis of HCI.[13] The scholars claim that errors that provide clear views into black boxes provide a view into some of what we might be missing. However, they also emphasize that glitches may be of vital importance for making the users aware of the great formational power of digital technologies.

Given the growing dominance of this ideology of informatic control, error provides us with an important critical lens for understanding what it means to live within a network society. Error reveals not only a system's failure, but also its operational logic.[14] David M. Berry, similarly to Goriunova and Schulgin, claims that glitches do introduce a specific phenomenological condition that enables a user to interact with the computational in a state of failure. Berry conceptualizes this condition in the *Critical Theory and The Digital* as 'glitch ontology' which takes the user out of the constant flow of digital processes that are normally masked by autonomous content representation and seamless interaction.

> Computation due to its glitch ontology continually forces a contextual slowing down at the level of the experience of the user. This is suggestive of the possibility for a micro-phenomenology that could fully explore the breaks in perception that the computer generates.[15]

---

12   Goriunova and Schulgin, 'Glitch', p. 114. (110-1119).

13   Mako Hill, 'Revealing Errors', p. 39.

14   Mark Nunes (ed.) *Error Glitch, Noise, and Jam in New Media Cultures*, New York and London: Continuum, 2011, p. 3.

15   Berry, *Critical Theory and the Digital*, p. 99.

[...] just as digital technologies and software mediate our experience and engagement with the world, often invisibly, so the "digital" and "software" is itself mediated and made visible through the representational forms of pixelation and glitch.[16]

Berry emphasizes the importance of glitches for bringing to the forefront the layered nature of computational technologies. However their role is even more significant for representing breaks in the continuity of postdigital media and software. In the era of mobile networks, clouds, IoT, data streams, preventing or better masking errors in the constant flow of the digital is crucial. Glitches, by introducing their unique micro-phenomenology, unveil these breaks, at least on the perceptual, visual level.

Berry argues that glitch ontology is one of many manifestations (e.g. code / software or ubiquitous systems) of a specific civilizational condition which is a result of the increasing presence of the digital in our everyday life. He conceptualizes this 'new constellation of intelligibility' as computationality. The notion is used, as explained in the previous chapter, to describe today's transformation of our society and culture which will lead to ultimate synchronization with, or better, to subordination to the digital. This should be understood as an era when cultural and social practices are both rooted in and bound by digital technology - e.g. the various types of hardware, software, distributed networks or interaction paradigms.[17] Lev Manovich in his *Software Takes Command* argues that even now we rely on software and hardware to create, transform and distribute information to such an extent that our society should rather be characterized as software society.[18]

The media studies, digital art and critical theory scholars cited above are intrigued by the critical potential of glitch aesthetics. On the one hand it is emphasized that glitches offer a unique possibility to visually depict the impact of core properties of computer-based media on their functioning by exposing their limitations. On the other hand, they argue that glitches may provide us with an interesting starting point to formulate a broader critique of today's digital technologies based on examining the glitches themselves, their milieu and their social and cultural impact.

Building on that approach we argue that the rapid pace of technological innovation that resulted not only in new technologies per se, but also in new human-computer interaction paradigms and digital image aesthetic. This evolution has left an imprint on the way glitches manifest themselves in everyday interaction with digital media based on real-time and cloud-based computational technologies, ubiquitous computing and

---

16   Berry, *Critical Theory and the Digital*, p. 159.

17   Berry, *Philosophy of Software Code and Mediation in a Digital Age*, p. 27.

18   Manovich, *Software Takes Command*, p. 147.

autonomous systems.[19] Postdigital glitch studies should, similarly to the New Aesthetic, critically challenge the mainstream technological narratives that were founded on the latest technological innovation, including the illusion of seamless interaction, automation and perfect visual representation.

For our purposes, two different sets of philosophical strategies provide intriguing and productive approaches to an ontological analysis of glitches. For the rest of this chapter, we base our approach on Heidegger's notions of ready-to-hand and present-to-hand advocated by him in *Being and Time*. Obviously Heidegger was never exposed to the type of artifacts constituting the body of postdigital and New Aesthetic objects, and Heidegger's philosophy at first glance doesn't seem applicable. Nevertheless, we take courage from recent applications of Heidegger's ideas to a diverse range of subjects; if we can use Heidegger to discuss environmentalism, psychology and religion then why not use Heidegger to discuss digital objects and their effects, especially if we consider those objects and their effects as fully phenomenologically appreciable. In fact, extending Heidegger's ideas into the realm of postdigital and New Aesthetic objects is particularly fruitful if we take the position that Heidegger's theory would provide us with a unique insight into the various ontological contexts in which things, or more specifically tools, can manifest themselves in everyday usage.

For Heidegger, tools are an essential aspect of our interaction with the world; the world comes at us in the manner of things, but those things which help constitute our thrown-ness (*Geworfenheit*) into the world are special as a means of making our place in the world and understanding it more fully. When tools become more than singular in their application as a means of transforming the world then they are labeled equipment and through this equipment human beings come to understand the notion of being-with others in the worldliness of the world as constituted by this being-with ourselves. The fact that Heidegger in his analysis also focuses on instances where tools do not function as intended, providing a clear contextualization of their specific ontic status and micro-temporality, will give us a promising analytical paradigm to distinguish and contextualize glitches and other aesthetic phenomena associated with the New Aesthetic and postdigital media and technologies.

A glitch offers a unique epistemic perspective. The unexpected error caused by the inability of the software to process real-time data or an inadequate capacity to recognize and recombine images into a functioning single image, reveals not only the software's inner structure, as Rosa Menkman says, but also makes visible the limitations of real-time data transmission and makes the omnipotence of digital quantification questionable. Glitches in web-based graphical user interfaces, video-streaming services, or satellite imagery services are some of the last remaining instances of the unreadiness-to-hand

---

19   Berry, *Critical Theory and the Digital*, p. 38.

of the computational in the era of multi-layered autonomous software and ultra high-resolution display systems. We could then argue that a glitch becomes a manifestation of a malfunctioning piece of equipment that emerges from a functional transparency or immediacy of a computational system and becomes a sign of its unready-to-hand condition. It should also be emphasized that a glitch goes beyond a binary distinction between a working and not-working computational system, but is rather situated in-between these two states.

Before applying Heidegger's taxonomy to our analysis of the New Aesthetic in today's technological milieu, we think that its ontic status should be clarified as well. As already argued, the computational has become even more opaque because of the combination of interconnected layers of both material (hardware) and immaterial (software) generating ever changing data streams, based on protocols, and standardized tools. If we want to avoid generalizations in our analysis of the New Aesthetic, which occurs at any level or layer of our contemporary technological milieu, we feel it is essential to at least briefly characterize these levels. To do that we will use David M. Berry's theory of 'ontological levels of the computational' advocated in *Critical Theory and The Digital*.

The Glitch as an Unready-to-hand Condition

Heidegger's phenomenological analysis of things has never been more relevant. Particularly pertinent for a networked digital society, he moves beyond the seemingly
self-evident, but ultimately incomplete, under-standing of things as entities or objects.
Instead, he provides a much richer phenomenological account of how thingness is
in fact inextricably related to human concerns and dealings that occur in a distinctly
insubstantial and non-thing-like fashion. In doing so, Heidegger illuminates the seemingly intangible but actually fundamental phenomenological aspects of mediated
things – those things we commonly experience as "equipment".[20]

Heidegger argues that things are actual things acquiring their proper 'thingly character'
only when they are used for a particular purpose. The thing is then available as 'ready-
to-hand'. However, its unique 'readiness-to-hand' is manifested only through putting the
thing to work, as we can't grasp it only through its appearance. He explicitly states that
'no matter how sharply we look at the "outward appearance" of Things in whatever form
this takes, we cannot discover anything ready-to-hand'.[21] The specific mode of being
that belongs to the thing appears as a using of something for something.[22] Heidegger's
famous example of this logic is a hammer and a nail. The specific thingness (manipulabil-
ity) of the hammer is unveiled through putting it to actual work – nailing the nail. [23] The
process of putting the things to actual work disclose them and their thingness to the user.
David Gunkel and Paul A. Taylor argue that if we'd follow Heidegger's line of reasoning
we would conclude that 'Readiness-to-hand is therefore not just a temporary attitude
or viewpoint we adopt with regards to things. It acts to define the very being of things
as things.'[24] The Readiness-to-hand defines things both ontologically and categorically.
From the perspective of media and communication studies, the things should then be
understood as intermediary means to and end or simply put, media (in a broader McLu-
hanian sense). However, usually we do not reflect on the nature of a hammer, nail or any
tool. We focus instead on completing the task by using a particularly thing or medium.
The thing and its thingness become transparent or unremarkable. The tool follows the
logic of immediacy, being a mere mean to an end. 'The paradox of the ready-to-hand is
therefore the fact that in its most authentic form, it necessarily withdraws from direct
view', Gunkel and Taylor write.[25]

---

20   David Gunkel and Paul A. Taylor, *Heidegger and the Media*, Cambridge: Polity, 2014, p. 98.

21   Martin Heidegger, *Being and Time*, trans. John Macquarrie & Edward Robinson, Oxford: Basil
     Blackwell, 1962, p. 98.

22   Heidegger, *Being and Time*, p. 100.

23   Heidegger, *Being and Time*, p. 98.

24   Gunkel and Taylor, *Heidegger and the Media*, p. 103.

25   Gunkel and Taylor, *Heidegger and the Media*, p. 104.

Now we've arrived to a point when Heidegger's theory on things meets with principal assumptions about human-computer interaction and digital content representation that have been challenged by the New Aesthetic and the postdigital. Even before mass popularization of consumer-oriented computing, the visionaries of the computing age envisioned computers as tools that would serve as autonomous machines that would assist humans in storing, processing and accessing information. From an electromechanical device called Memex, described in 'As We May Think' by Vannevar Bush,[26] through Sketchpad designed by Ivan E. Sutherland in 1963[27] and PARC User Interface (Xerox 8010 Star Information System) from the early 1980s to various modifications of the personal computers from the 1990s: all have been designed with the principle to 'augment the human intellect', while being as transparent as possible.[28] The logic of the immediacy of the computational has prevailed even more in the age of ubiquitous computing, cloud-based and multi-device ecosystems. Their ultimate readiness-to-hand is a necessary condition of their actual interoperability and versatility. They are perfect tools as long as they stay in the shadow. As soon as they break down, or a visible glitch occurs in any node of the system – particularly near to the end user – in graphical user interfaces or in the visual media they process and display, the tools become present-at-hand. Heidegger points out that such a situation causes concern among users, and 'the entities which are most closely ready-to-hand may be met as something unusable, not properly adapted for the use we have decided upon. [...] we discover its unusability, however, not by looking at it and establishing its properties, but rather by the circumspection of the dealings in which we use it'.[29] Gunkel and Taylor also emphasize the fact that the evolution from being ready-to-hand to present-to-hand of certain tools, takes place not in the user's perception of a tool, but through putting it to actual use. 'Something becomes present-at-hand when the thing in question fails to work, breaks down or interrupts the smooth functioning of what had been already handy and ready-to-hand.'[30] If we return to our broader understanding of the New Aesthetic, described as a theoretical approach that takes to the forefront of our perception the conditions of existence of the computational in the postdigital age together with its limitations, the critical potential of studying certain technologies and media in their unready-to-hand conditions, looks

26   Vannevar Bush, 'As We May Think', in Noah Wardrip-Fruin and Nick Montfort (eds) *The New Media Reader*, Cambridge/London: MIT Press, 2003, pp. 44-46.

27   Evan E. Sutherland, 'Sketchpad: A Man-Machine Graphical Communication System', in Noah Wardrip-Fruin and Nick Montfort (eds) *The New Media Reader*, Cambridge/London: MIT Press, 2003, pp. 109-126.

28   Douglas Engelbart, 'A Research Center for Augmenting Human Intellect', in Noah Wardrip-Fruin and Nick Montfort (eds) *The New Media Reader*, Cambridge/London: MIT Press, 2003, pp. 233-246.

29   Heidegger, *Being and Time*, p. 102.

30   Gunkel and Taylor, *Heidegger and the Media*, p. 106.

very promising. Heidegger uses three different notions to describe specific conditions of things when they reveal their presence-at-hand through unique unreadiness-to-hand. The modi of conspicuousness, obtrusiveness and obstinacy introduce a micro-temporal context, an epistemic condition that through the state of failure allows us to apprehend the characteristic of presence-at-hand, a handiness that is usually masked by a perfect functioning of the equipment.

In a technological context, the unready-to-hand condition of the equipment can be characterized as a condition in which a computational apparatus is facing a sudden or unusual obstacle that can't be overcome by its (pre)programmed mode of operation and interaction with the user. However, it may not imply that the machine's inner logic of operation is defective. The state of unreadiness-to-hand goes far beyond a mere problem of incalculability. Something - a tool, device, application - is *conspicuous* when it becomes unusable. Unusability means in this context a situation when a thing no longer serves the use for which it was initially designed.[31] It is not just about breaking the seamless interaction and utility paradigm in partially working machines or software. The conspicuousness is a result of a complete failure of the computational, a situation in which a user is confronted with a broken piece of hardware, or an application that fails to launch. A thing becomes *obtrusive* when it is missing. As Heidegger argues, the thing is then not 'handy' but is not 'to hand' at all. The more we need what is missing to perform a task, the more intensive it enters into the state of obtrusiveness.[32] The problem of obtrusiveness occurs when for example a certain media file cannot be opened or processed due to lack of a specific codec, or when a cloud-based application cannot access data which is stored on the remote server. The state of obtrusiveness will become even more relevant as the interaction and functioning of computational technologies will be based on interconnected software and hardware ecosystems composed of various devices, software and data types. Any malfunction in such an ecosystem can result in an obtrusive piece of equipment (both material and immaterial) at the level of user-computational interaction. The last variation of unreadiness-to-hand is the state of *obstinacy*. The *obstinacy* is encountered when it 'stands in the way' of our concern and interrupts our activities. Anything which is un-ready-to-hand in this way is disturbing to us, and enables us to see the obstinacy of that with which we must concern ourselves first before we do anything else.[33] If we were to study glitch in the light of obstinacy, we could claim that a glitch is an unexpected deviation from the intended functioning of a computational system which prevents the user from completing the task (in a usual manner). However, the state of obstinacy does not mean a complete failure of the system - a compression artifact in a video content may introduce a different aesthetics, or may lead to a break

31   Heidegger, *Being and Time*, p. 102.

32   Heidegger, *Being and Time*, p. 103.

33   Heidegger, *Being and Time*, p. 103.

in continuity of narrative in the usually fluid continuity of the postdigital (cloud-based and real-time) media – but it does not make the file completely unusable nor make the content unwatchable. Similarly, glitches in the display of elements of graphical user interfaces or image artifacts in web-based services such as Google Earth, Apple Maps, do break the immediacy of a particular tool, challenging the seamless interaction and perfect visual representation paradigms, but the tool as a whole itself is still functioning. Many phenomena and artistic interventions associated with the New Aesthetic are manifestations of the state of obstinacy. They do interfere with a particular software or device to an extent that they cannot be ignored by the user (altering media aesthetics, modifying the scope of software's operations logic), but they do not lead to a complete failure of a system / machine understood as a tool. In this paradoxical, ontic condition we see a great critical and analytical potential of glitches and the New Aesthetic.

Where Should we Look for Glitches?

The oscillation creates the "glitch" that is a specific feature of computation as opposed to other technical forms (Berry 2011a). This is the glitch that creates the conspicuousness that breaks the everyday experience of things, and more importantly
breaks the flow of things being readily at hand.[34]

Following Heidegger's analysis we could conclude that glitches which occur in contemporary computational systems can be characterized as different instances of unreadiness-
to-hand, particularly as manifestations of conspicuousness and obstinacy in everyday
functioning and interaction with digital media and computational technologies. In order
to position glitches in a context of specific technologies, we should firstly deliver a clear
ontological backbone for understanding various ontological levels of the computational
which is rooted both in the material (networks, infrastructure, devices) and the immaterial (software, protocols, data).

David M. Berry argues that all manifestations of the computational, be it certain technologies, devices, software, data protocols etc. exist on different ontological levels. His
categorization structures the complex technological world into six different categories:

1 Physical: Material and transactional level (of the hardware)
2 Logical: Logical, network and informational transactional level (level of
software as diagram or platform)
3 Codal: Textual and coding logics (level of code as text and/or process)
4 Interactional: Surface/interface level (between human beings and non-humans
mediated through code)
5 Logistics: Social and organizational structure (at the level of institutions, econo-
mies, culture, etc.)
6 Individuational: Stratification of embodied personality (the psychology of actors,
the user, etc.) [35]

If we were to look again at the constellation of the various visual phenomena associated with the New Aesthetic – glitches in software and visual media, works of art based
on the pixelated aesthetics, interventions that challenge dominant HCI paradigms or
critically examine the autonomy of ubiquitous systems – we would see that they can be
positioned on various ontological levels of the computational, as advocated by David
M. Berry, and would see even further that some of them do exist in the actual physical
world. However, the most interesting levels for our analysis would be these where a user
meets the computational and consequently, where the computational enters into the
physical reality and begins to change it. Following that perspective, we argue that the

---

34   Berry, *Critical Theory and the Digital*, p. 99.

35   Berry, *Critical Theory and the Digital*, p. 58.

Interactional, Logistics and Individuational levels of the computational have become the realm of the New Aesthetic. Different New Aesthetic artifacts function and interact with themselves and users across these ontological levels, blurring the clear distinctions between the analog and the digital and the human and the machine.

Why do we need a clear categorization of media, tools, works of art and artifacrs associated with the New Aesthetic both at the micro-level (Heidegger) and in a broader context of today's technological milieu (Berry)? In order to grasp the critical potential of the New Aesthetic we should be aware of the very conditions of manifestation of these phenomena, to put it simply, we should know where to look for them in todays stream- and cloud-based software media and what is their place in the broad landscape of the computational. We conclude our discussion of the glitch with two examples showing the importance of critical glitch studies to our endeavor that aims to conceptualize the New Aesthetic. Many New Aesthetic products and objects that will be discussed in the following chapters do fall into the category of obstinacy that is encountered across 'ontological levels of the computational'.

Clement Valla, a New York-based artist, has critically analyzed glitches in Google Earth, which appear as distorted images of the earth's surface i.e. drooping roads and bridges. His analysis resulted in the 'Universal Texture' artwork presented in 2012.[36] According to Valla, Google uses the Universal Texture mapping system which applies hybrid images, a patchwork of two-dimensional photographic data and three-dimensional topographic data extracted from a slew of sources, data-mined, pre-processed, blended and merged in real-time in order to create this particular god-like fluid planetary navigation system – Google Earth.[37] {Fig. 41}

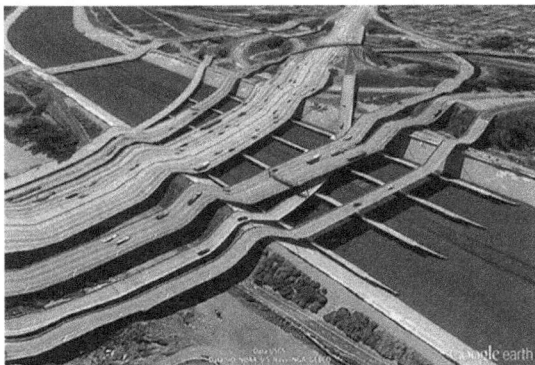

Fig. 41 Clement Valla, *Postcards from Google Earth* (2010–)

---

36   Clement Valla, 'The Universal Texture', *Clement Valla*, http://clementvalla.com/work/the-
      universal-texture-recreated-46423-50n-1202628-59w/.

37   Clement Valla, 'The Universal Texture'.

Valla argues that drooping roads and bridges, and distorted building facades in Google Earth are not in fact mere errors but rather anomalies within the inner logic of the computational system. Clearly, their existence does not lead to a complete breakdown of Google Earth. Consequently, they should rather be considered as noise, an anomaly or, as Heidegger would put it, an obstinacy within a functioning system.

Many glitches that appear in contemporary visual media are symptomatic for the technologies of the postdigital age. We would argue that that they reveal a new model of seeing and of representing our world. Software and tools of the postdigital era are based on dynamic, ever-changing data from a myriad of different sources, which are endlessly combined and constantly updated to create an illusion of seamless interaction and perfect automation. Google Earth is an example of such a system, an interface for the assemblage of data coming from various stakeholders and sources. The data is constantly updated, and Valla claims that many of these glitches have disappeared from the system due to improvements in the algorithms. The postdigital era is marked by the logic of constant, seamless and equally obfuscated updates, which do not longer take place at the interface level. Today's cloud-based and ubiquitous computing systems such as Google and Facebook algorithms, are being constantly rewritten and updated, often without the user's knowledge. Noticing, analyzing and archiving glitches in the ever-changing postdigital technologies is one of the few practices that enable us to critically reflect on the development of flux technologies of the postdigital age.

CHAPTER 4
SETTING THE STAGE:
THE NEW PRECURSORS
AND BOUNDARIES FOR A NEW
AESTHETIC ART

To the best of our knowledge, there is not a single sustained instance of critics or commentators using the parameters of the New Aesthetic to identify New Aesthetic objects as examples of art. Writing about the effect of technology on art practices is becoming increasingly sophisticated, but it's surprising how uneven the progression has been, and this has been especially true of New Aesthetic objects. Often, writings about art and the digital have focused on a limited range of considerations. In many cases, the use value and the impact on our lives is the primary focus, and if any consideration is given towards beauty, taste, impact or evaluative considerations of the objects as objects it's directed towards the design of the graphic user interface rather than on some underlying notion of an inherent status as art. In other cases, the technological and the digital are superficially acknowledged as merely tools leading to the creation of art objects, and the deeper implications of the use of digital and technological tools is ignored. The recent publications of *Postdigital Aesthetics* (2015), edited by David M. Berry and Michael Dieter, and *Postdigital Artisans* (2015), by Jonathan Openshaw, while excellent books (including Łukasz Mirocha's own essay in *Postdigital Aesthetics*), are good examples of these different but inadequate strategies at a theoretical level matched by the inadequacy of recent exhibitions such as *Crafted Objects in Flux* (2015-16) at the Museum of Fine Arts in Boston, USA; in the case of the work by the theorists there's been very little discussion of actual art while in the case of the exhibitions there's been almost no discussion of the theory.

Perhaps even more importantly, the New Aesthetic has not been treated in an *art historical* fashion but has existed as a topic for discussion and analysis almost solely amongst philosophers, critics, artists, designers and others who are interested in the effects of the digitalization of the world. Certainly art history as a discursive practice has always been a little slow to acknowledge contemporary artistic practices, and we hope that what follows will rectify that at least a little bit. More than just setting out our belief in the timeliness and importance of this book, we believe that our interdisciplinary approach is crucial to understanding the entirety of the effect of the New Aesthetic. An illuminating example is Christian Ulrik Andersen's and Søren Bro Pold's treatment of Aram Bartholl's *Dropping the Internet* (2014). {Fig. 43}

Borrowing uncritically from Bartholl's own website,[1] Andersen and Pold describe the photographic triptych in terms of the security concerns and sense of crisis in the post-Snowden era, placing an emphasis on the work's presentation of the 'internet' as inherently fragile. At the same time Andersen and Pold engage in a little aesthetic analysis that seems to go quickly awry.

Bartholl's work seems deliberately lightweight, pointing towards the banality through both its form and its iconography. Looking closely, one realizes that the high-teach

---

1　Aram Bartholl, 'Dropping the Internet', *Datenform*, 2014, http://datenform.de/dropping-the-internet-eng.html.

iconography consists only of cardboard, candlelight and people acting according to strange behavioral scripts: pointing to how the big utopias become banal and mundane, including how they control sharing, communication and perception.[2]

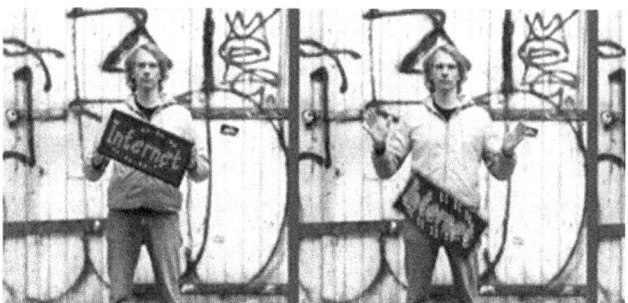

Fig. 43 Aram Bartholl, *Dropping the Internet* (2014)

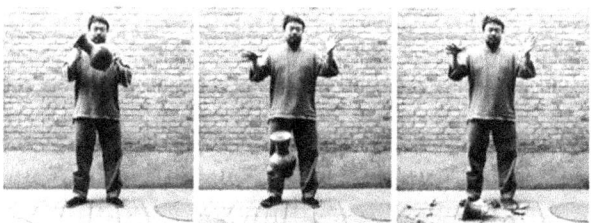

Fig. 44 Ai Wei Wei, *Dropping a Han Dynasty Urn* (1995)

In many ways, this is an illuminating analysis of the effect of the work, reading it as symbolic of the wrenching, almost existential transformation of the internet that occurred after Snowden revealed the extent to which our privacy and the secrets of governments had been compromised; almost immediately the general public's understanding of the internet as an interactive source of data and method of communication went from a blind acceptance of it as a freely used tool to thinking about it as an adversarial and nefarious intrusion into everyone's lives. Bartholl intended his work to evoke a sense of violent dislocation and excessive centralization, contrary to the early days of the internet with its engineered decentralization as a means of surviving nuclear war, but returning to Andersen's and Pold's description of the work it's clear that other things are going on, and that Andersen and Pold may be ill-equipped to acknowledge them. Bartholl readily acknowledges his appropriation of Ai Weiwei's famous work *Dropping a Han Dynasty Urn* (1995)[3] {Fig. 44} but why don't Andersen and Pold mention it?

---

2   Christian Ulrik Andersen and Søren Bro Pold, 'Aesthetics of the Banal – "New Aesthetics" in an Era of Diverted Digital Revolutions', in David M. Berry and Michael Dieter (eds) *Postdigital Aesthetics: Art, Computation and Design*, New York: Palgrave MacMillan, 2015, p. 286.

3   Aram Bartholl, 'Dropping the Internet'.

Ai Weiwei's work engages with China's difficult relationship to the past, shattering any expectations of reverence for ancient artifacts that substantiate China's image of itself as a nation while at the same time setting in motion a deconstructive turn that subverts Ai Weiwei's own powers as an artist to actuate change in Chinese society. Bartholl's iconography, though, is itself a subversion of the appropriation process, with what appears to be a digital picture frame symbolically and almost mischievously (despite Bartholl's saddened statement that the internet as he once knew it is gone) representing computational devices, and with a touch of irony in the color choices and the need to literally spell out 'internet'. In both Ai Weiwei's and Bartholl's works the iconography involves a radical break with the past, Ai Weiwei is 'post-Chinese' while Bartholl is 'postdigital,' that does far more than Andersen and Pold suggest: Bartholl's work is participating in a tradition of breaking with the past and is, therefore, less radical of a break than is implied. We will return to Bartholl's work later in the chapter – he is, after all, one of the most important artists working in in this context – but we wanted to make clear what is revealed through more than just an examination of the postdigital, and that this is only apparent in an interdisciplinary fashion. In this chapter to investigate New Aesthetic art becomes an important means of furthering the definition of this set of phenomena in its entirety.

Importantly, the very term 'New Aesthetic' implies a specific relationship to aesthetics as the philosophy of art. For much of its history, at least until recently, aesthetics has been focused on questions regarding such things as the nature and purpose of art, the means of identifying art objects as distinct from everyday objects, the definition of beauty, and the relationship between 'fine' art and craft (if there is a distinction between the two). Reading through the literature, however, it's been apparent that the use of the term 'aesthetic' in 'New Aesthetics' has been more akin to the way it was used prior to Alexander Gottlieb Baumgarten's transformation of its meaning. Beginning in 1735 and culminating in Baumgarten's *Reflections on Poetry* (1750), aesthetics shifted from a philosophical concern with the experience of sense perception to analyses of ideas of taste and beauty and concerns about ontologically driven questions on the nature of art. From our perspective, discussions of the New Aesthetics has a pre-Baumgartenian flavor. Most of the recent discussions of New Aesthetic objects have never been about their nature as art per se, even though this would be a fruitful line of inquiry; focusing on their digital existence, they seem less entangled in the past 250+ years and more concerned with the pre-Baumgartenian notion of aesthetics that focuses on how things are for our perception, how they feel, how they impact our comfort or discomfort in our relationship to the world. In many respects, Baumgarten's ideas have been taken up in phenomenological investigations but what is particularly valuable in making this connection between primarily 21st century phenomena and an 18th century philosopher's important but flawed modern interpretation of the term 'aesthetics' is Baumgarten's insistence that aesthetic appreciation functions within the locus of truth and the presentation of perfection, aiming towards an extensive clarity with various affects. The parallels to any discussion of the efficiency of a GUI are striking. Baumgarten writes in his *Meditationes*:

Since affects are more notable degrees of pain and pleasure, their sensible representations are given in representing something to oneself confusedly as good or bad, and thus they determine poetic representations, and *to arouse affects is poetic.*[4]

The effect of these affects is sensible cognition, not only as the physical embodiment of the presentation of ideas but as the aesthetic perfection of those ideas, an obvious driving force in apps like *Waze*. For Baumgarten: 'The aim of aesthetics is the perfection of sensible cognition as such, that is, beauty, while its imperfection as such, that is, ugliness, is to be avoided.'[5] Colin McQuillian describes Baumgarten's position nicely.

When the objects of sensible cognition agree with one another, then sensible cognition is perfectly ordered, so it is beautiful. The beauty of signification is also a perfection of sensible cognition, because we cannot represent the beauty of the objects of sensible cognition and their order without signs. When the signs we use to represent sensible perfection agree with one another, then sensible cognition expresses itself eloquently, and it is beautiful.[6]

What is interesting here is how appropriate this is when discussing New Aesthetic objects and, by extension, New Aesthetic art; Baumgarten's enlightened rationalism is outdated in so many different ways, but the notion that aesthetics is about the analysis of the perfection of the presentation of ideas, making them available for sensible cognition such that their truth is seemingly irrefutable, ties in nicely with New Aesthetic objects' presentation of their own autonomy and self-sufficient, self-generated and self-perfected state despite inherent and unavoidable glitches, errors and pervasive manipulations of the experiences and understanding of the consumers of the New Aesthetic objects.

Taking a Baumgartenian perspective complicates the very foundations of this chapter. If New Aesthetic objects are the presentation of their own self-determined perfection then the only criteria we could employ when critically engaging with them is the degree to which they achieve that sense of presented perfection, that sense of being natural objects that appear to be natural part of our environments. In fact, the only criteria that we could then use to distinguish between non-New Aesthetic and New Aesthetic objects, to take this line of thought to an absurd conclusion, would be to note that objects seemingly recognizable as the later are, in fact, not such objects, simply because their lack of perfection means that their inherent artificiality is apparent. Of course, that's ridiculous,

---

4   Alexander Baumgarten, Paetzold, Heinz (ed.) *Meditationes philosophicae de nonnullis ad poema pertinentibus/Philosophische Betrachtungen über einige Bedingungen des Gedichtes*, Hamburg: Felix Meiner Verlag, 1983. p. 24

5   Alexander Baumgarten, Aesthetica/Ästhetik, Dagmar Mirbach (ed), 2 vols.,Hamburg: Felix Meiner Verlag, 2007. (*Aesthetica*, §14)

6   J. Colin McQuillian, 'Baumgarten on Sensible Perfection' *Philosophica*, 44, Lisboa, 2014, pp. 53-54.

but it's instructive when thinking about them generally in that it is the manifestations, theoretical underpinnings, and the attitude which generates New Aesthetic objects that further a complicated and increasingly complicated reception while confounding our ability to accurately and critically engage with the world. This increasingly complicated means of seeing the world through the New Aesthetic can be seen readily in the digitalization of the art experience.

The Google Art Project states that it has three aims: 1) to provide the experience of art in museums and other cultural institutions digitally so that people can see them from a distance, see objects in greater detail (often in greater detail than they would if they were actually in the museums looking at the objects themselves), and share the experience of art; 2) to provide a means to safeguard and protect history and cultural heritage; 3) to serve as a lab to allow for cross-disciplinary creative activities between curators, historians, artists, designers and educators.[7] In all three cases, as much as it might seem like the Google Art Project is an effort to extend the opportunities to appreciate art in museums, in its narrowing of the aesthetic experience, it is far more an opportunity to appreciate the art at a distance, the objects transformed from their state as physical objects to being merely digital artifacts, to the point that Walter Benjamin's warnings about the loss of aura seems very much like reality. In particular, the second aim is the most difficult to come to terms with, in that the preservation of the objects cannot, by definition of the efforts as digital, be an actual preservation of the objects but only the preservation of their appearance. Notwithstanding Plato's admonishment against aesthetic experiences being twice removed as a danger to the very fabric of social structures, this just seems odd, a reification of the collecting impulse extended to the point that the physicality of objects disappears. This is not as absurd as it sounds, as evidenced in the artwork of João Enxuto and Erica Love and their ongoing art project *Anonymous Paintings* (2011-).[8] {Fig. 45}

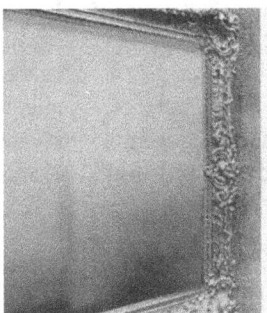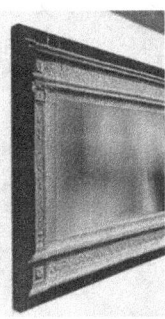

Fig. 45 João Enxuto, and Erica Love, *Anonymous Paintings* (2013)

7   Google Cultural Institute, https://www.google.com/culturalinstitute/about/.

8   João Enxuto and Erica Love, 'Anonymous Paintings (2011-)', *theoriginalcopy.net*, 2011, http://www.sept6.info/anonymous-paintings/.

Given the obvious copyright issues involved with the Google Art Project, Enxuto and Love have been producing inkjet prints on stretched canvases of blurred images appropriated from Google's website. Describing the work, as the artists do, as 'censored' might seem extreme but their artworks have a singular and stunning effect:

> The censored artworks are like the blurred individuals caught in the path of Google's omnipresent Street View camera where occlusion denotes an identity and subject-hood. Our Anonymous Paintings use abstraction as a code for autonomy and with-drawal from Google's comprehensive visual record.[9]

Making the analogy between the paintings and the blurred images of human faces in Google Street View pushes this sense of a complex autonomy to the forefront of aesthetic issues. Such autonomy is now couched almost in nefarious terms, with the press release from the Carriage Trade Gallery's exhibition of Enxuto's and Love's work stating:

> With the growth of Internet activity producing previously unimaginable amounts of personal data that has recently been revealed to be freely accessible to government agencies, the convenience associated with online activity has increasingly been shad-owed by the surveillance of its users [...] Derived from the remnants of pixelated art works that have returned to the world of objects, the *Anonymous Paintings* seem to exist between an artwork as memory, and an assertion of the indispensable nature of a tangible space, where meaning is derived from a conscious encounter between subject and object.[10]

What left's is nothing but the distortion of a work, perhaps almost an apocalyptic mani-festation of Benjamin's loss of aura. Or perhaps we're being too drastic here? These are enlarged reproductions of the images found on Google, after all, and further the images are themselves often works on loan or less frequently exhibited pieced of contemporary art, meaning that the legal ramifications of breaking copyright are what drives their man-ner of presentation. Is negotiating the conceptual space sufficiently valid as art or as the New Aesthetic? In our opinion, absolutely. Enxuto and Love point out that 'Google is single-handedly redefining the public sphere of art spectatorship in much the same way that it is redefining the mapping of public space.'[11] The unquestionable positive artistic value notwithstanding, we only disagree on an aesthetic level with one thing in this state-

---

9   Enxuto and Love, 'Anonymous Paintings (2011-)'.

10   'Enxuto & Love, Anonymous Paintings', (Press Release), Carriage Trade Gallery, October 2013, http://www.carriagetrade.org/article82,82.

11   Peter Brook, 'See Some Art While You Can – Google Will Eventually Replace Museums', *Wired. com*, September 2013, http://www.wired.com/2013/09/see-some-art-whir-you-can-google-will-eventually-replace-museums/.

ment, but we disagree with it strongly. For us, it's not Google that is single-handedly redefining the experience of art but the very parameters, the paradigmatic and almost metaphysical shift that is doing so. The Google Art Project is not the cause but merely one of many symptoms.

Given the strange nature of the New Aesthetic, its products and its objects, it might seem difficult if not impossible to imagine it as more than a category of digital manifestation but as a category of actual instances of art. To that end, we've divided our discussion of the related art across two chapters and into four sections: 1) a discussion of artists working in the early history of digital art whose work is a prelude to the development of New Aesthetic art; 2) a detailed presentation of artists whose work is clearly aligned with the principles of New Aesthetic art but which is, in the final analysis, insufficiently autonomous to be full examples; 3) a presentation of artists whose work we do consider examples of the New Aesthetic, often exhibiting autonomous elements and aesthetic strategies and results that are markedly a manifestation of the paradigm; and 4) most controversially, a small set of aesthetic objects that have arisen out of the paradigm without the direction of human agency that we believe can be labeled 'art'. To this end we've decided to take a concentric rather than a linear approach; pure, autonomous, self-generating examples of New Aesthetic art objects are at the center of our exploration, with each section of this chapter shifting from one layer to the next closing in on that target. It's our belief that the New Aesthetic didn't just appear as an end result or a product of specific set of necessary technological innovations but that it's been nascent in the very of idea of the digital for a long time, perhaps even embryonic in the very idea of mathematics and the beauty of mathematics.

Setting the Stage for New Aesthetic Art: Early Figures in the History of Digital Art

It might seem strange to start with Malcom Morley's painting *The School of Athens* (1972), if for no other reason that in many ways it appears to be a painting in a very traditional sense and especially because of it's subject matter, namely a reproduction of Raphael's *The School of Athens* (1509-11), but we promise there's a good reason. {Fig. 46}

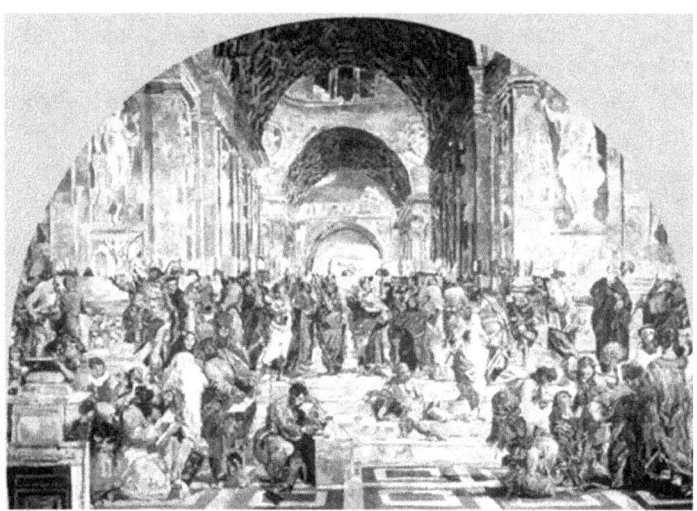

Fig. 46 Malcolm Morley, *School of Athens* (1972)

Raphael's painting is a masterpiece of the Italian Renaissance, the 'perfect embodiment of the classical spirit of the Renaissance'[12] marking the dialectical relationship between Aristotle's theories and the ideas of Plato. Malcolm Morley's painting is a reproduction of photograph of Raphael's painting; that second step is important - Morley is copying a photograph rather than the actual painting - because it highlights Morley's career as a photorealist painter, his use of technology in his specific technique of using projected grids of the Raphael in the reproduction process, and the fact that Morley mistakenly shifted the grids one space over thus creating a glitch in the reproduction.

Morley never makes corrections - once it's done it stays done - and every bit leads to the next. "Even if a mistake gets made, I turn it into something positive. For example, I made a painting of Raphael's 'School of Athens' and I got one grid in the wrong place. So for Plato and Aristotle the skull is over here and the rest of the head here; I said I

12   So much so that Scott wrote that without realizing he was using the same exact phrase quote on the Wikipedia article about the painting (https://en.wikipedia.org/wiki/The_School_of_Athens), which quotes Janson's *History of Art: The Western Tradition*. Which itself is a quotation from various other sources.

lobotomised Greek philosophy. The wit comes from the unconscious. As somebody put it to me, you make friends with your unconscious life, as a collaborator."[13]

It may be a simple point, but it bears repeating that Morley used a glitch in his reproduction of a photograph of Raphael's painting in an almost teleological fashion, with the subsequent effects generating specific aesthetic impacts. Given Morley's artistic strategies in a long, fascinating, and masterful but often unjustifiably overlooked career, the fact that he's embraced 'mistakes' as part of the creative process falls in line with both modernist traditions and postmodern assimilations and reconfigurations of modernism. At the same time, we would argue that Morley's passively embraced concession to the faults produced by the margins of error connected to the technology is evidence of the impact that the New Aesthetic will have in subsequent years.

In a similar fashion, certain recent examples of infographic art also conceptually set the stage for New Aesthetic objects to have a genuine artistic existence and function. In 2014 graphic design artists and illustrators Tom Whalen and Kevin Tong held a joint exhibition at the Phone Booth Gallery in Long Beach, California.[14] {Fig. 47}

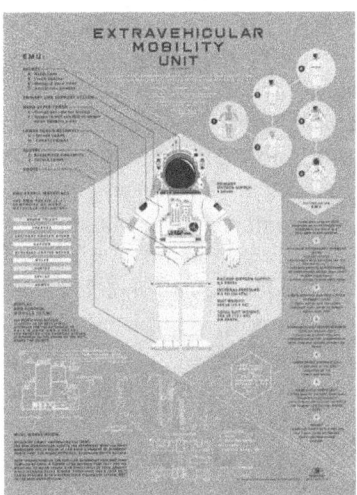

Fig. 47 Tom Whalen and Kevin Tong, *Spacesuit* (2014)

---

13   Andrew Lambirth, 'Welcome home, Malcolm Morley', *The Spectator*, 26 October 2013, http://new.
      spectator.co.uk/2013/10/malcolm-morley-the-last-wild-man-of-modern-art/.

14   Ben Marks, 'Art in the Infographic Age', 22 August 2014, *Boing Boing*, http://boingboing.
      net/2014/08/22/art-in-the-infographic-age.html.

The content of the work ranged through a disparate set of subjects such as leaf cutter ants, the P-51D Mustang fighter plane, Nikola Tesla and an example of an extravehicular mobility unit or, simply, a spacesuit; the consistent and organizing force of the exhibition was evidently the utilization of broad stylistic similarities that hark back to utopian flavored 1950s science fiction and a clear impetus to utilize the aesthetic potential of infographic methodology. While producing visually very interesting work, Whalen's and Tong's prints are nostalgically indebted to an era in the history of graphic design in which high modernism's impulses to guide and correct social development were themselves understood as fundamental design considerations, practices and aesthetic strategies; Whalen cites Jan Tschichold, Saul Bass and Milton Glaser as influences on his website[15], figures who unquestionably strove to use graphic design in a transformative fashion. A first response – or a second response, since the rich, lush colors and bold layout of Whalen's and Tong's work are the first aspects of their images that catch the viewer's attention – is to think of these designs as evidence of the continuation of postmodern impulses, particularly in light of the evident, if consciously and effectively contrived, nostalgia running through all of the design decisions; regardless of the state of the debate about postmodernism's definition and continuing existence (if it ever existed at all), a general tendency is to identify the apparent appropriations, quotations and evocations from an earlier era in these works as an active but parenthetical engagement with modernist longings. Still, there's something different going on here, fitting these works almost into a New Aesthetic status, and that's the use of infographics as a technology. Infographics is a well-established means of representing complicated information; Charles Minard's 1861 representation of Napoleon's invasion of and retreat from Russia is one of the most well known examples, and Otto Neurath's development of the Vienna Method in the 1920s and 1930s, Edward Tufte's *The Visual Display of Quantitative Information* (1983), and Peter Sullivan's use of infographics in the New York Times from the 1970s to the 1990s were instrumental in establishing its viability and shifting its conceptualization towards data visualization. Today, infographics and data visualization have become so diverse and powerfully implemented that we cannot fully discuss their impact here, but one aspect is crucial: the assumption, often made uncritically, that the best presentation of data is an aesthetic presentation. In some respects, that may seem indisputable, in that it seems logical that aesthetic visual content drives, for instance, best practices in the communication of information in the context of social media, but at the same time something else is going on. There's a fine line between infographics and data visualization, precisely because they are both methods presenting data visually, converging towards the same goals, but in both cases there's an underlying assumption regarding the veracity of the data sets and the effectiveness of the presentation methods; infographics and data visualization put the viewer into the role of a passive consumer of information, and even more insidiously puts the graphic designer into the role of a passive accomplice. What makes Whalen's and Tong's work intriguing in the context of this intertwined perspective

---

15   Strong Stuff, Tom Whalen Illustrations-Design, http://www.strongstuff.net/about-flatiron/.

on infographics, data visualization and the New Aesthetic is their use of visual nostalgia, which has two effects. First, it eases the presentation and consumption of the information in such a way that the effect becomes less about the actual information per se and more about the process of learning. Second, the visual nostalgia facilitates a historicized context of the data itself, as if the methods of presenting establish a continuity of data, substantiating the methodology's manifestation much to the expense of the veracity of the data itself. There is a striking conceptual similarity between the work of Otto Neurath and Whalen's and Tong's images, despite the glaringly obvious differences in appearance, in that the underlying methodology, the encoded pathways of presentation that are pre-arranged similarly to programmed instructions, are treated in a fashion that assumes a natural form of appearance. We will return to two projects by Lev Manovich – *Selfiecity* (2015) and *On Broadway* (2014-2016) – later in this chapter to pick up on the pervasive presence of data, its relationship to its own interpretative methodology and how these issues can specifically emerge in artistic production.

If painterly glitches and infographics set the stage for a preliminary consideration of New Aesthetic art, a consideration of artists who have been producing digital art that uses software and hardware, programming and data visualization with a clear aesthetic goal of producing art is even more important. In 1965, Frieder Nake, A. Michael Noll and Georg Nees may have been the first artists exhibiting drawings that were entirely computer-generated in art galleries, and the similarity of their work reveals not only shared working methods and concerns but also the limitations of their aesthetic explorations. Georg Nees is a German pioneer of computer and art and generative graphic, and was probably the first artist to display art that was entirely dependent on digital technology in Stuttgart, where he was educated and had been a student of Max Bense, an important pioneer in the field of information aesthetics and the integration of the humanities and natural sciences. Importantly, Nees served as the scientific advisor for *SEMIOSIS*, an international journal devoted to issues of semiotics, technology and aesthetics, whose title is derived from Charles Sanders Peirce describing a process (potentially artistic) that understands signs as self-referentially operative. Nees' work began at Siemens:

> In 1959, he began to program digital computers. In 1965, he procured for his department at Siemens a table-sized, punched tape-operated drawing automaton constructed by Konrad Zuse, the "Zuse-Graphomat", which could move a descendible drawing pencil in two right-angled axes over a page of drawing paper. Nees recalls: "There it was, the great temptation for me, for once not to represent something technical with this machine but rather something 'useless' – geometrical patterns."[16]

---

16   ZKM Exhibitions, August 2006, 'Georg Nees – The Great Temptation: Early generative computer graphics', *ZKM*, http://on1.zkm.de/zkm/stories/storyReader$5255.

Nees' work is innovative simply because of the new medium that he started using, but equally so because it was simple in its visual appearance. {Fig. 48}

In part this is because of Nees' development of generative design, wherein a set of parameters would be provided to the software and the image was created as the software controlled the hardware, a process that in the early 21st century seems rather primitive but in the 1960s would have been astonishing. What's interesting about generative design is that there are two different sets of aesthetic choices an artist can make when using this method. First, they can choose between providing predetermined values for the software or randomly generated numbers, a choice that firmly places Nees' ideas in the same context as the types of decisions being made by Jasper Johns and Robert Rauschenberg in the early years of their careers, particularly when they were making art at Black Mountain College in North Carolina when a predetermined and programmatic approach was central to their experimentation deeply influenced by Marcel Duchamp, as well as different aesthetic strategies employed by performance and conceptual artists across the world in the 1960s. In this respect, Nees' work bears a strong resemblance to Karl Otto Götz, a German artist whose paintings were based on '"statistic-metric modulations" with grids filled with black and white rectangles'.[17]

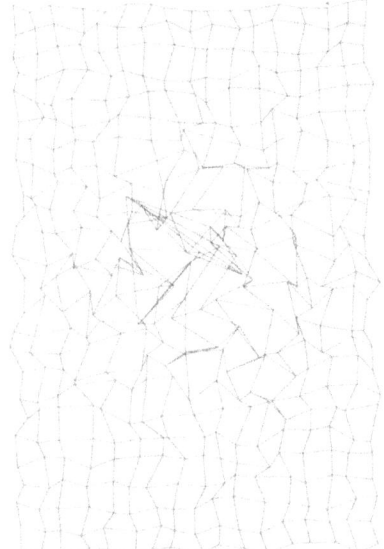

Fig. 48 Georg Nees, Computer art produced between 1965–1968

17   Thomas Dreher, 'Computer Graphics', *History of Computer Art*, September 2013, http://iasl.uni-muenchen.de/links/GCA-III.2e.html#Computergrafik.

Second, and much more importantly for us, Nees' generative design method sets into place an aesthetic decision, evaluative and judgmental in nature, regarding the output; given that the imagery was produced on a flatbed graphing machine, which at the time had instructions provided by punch card and which was primarily designed for scientific and military purposes, it is without question that some images would be produced with unintended effects, whether through error in the instructions, in the hardware's implementation of those instructions or simply in a lack of familiarity with the flatbed drawing machine. It's clear that Nees must have had to choose to accept the possibilities and the limitations of his methods, but it's also clear that Nees didn't think of the technology merely as a tool that he could fully control. At the 1965 exhibition in Siemens, he states:

> A number of artist-professors from the Stuttgart Staatliche Akademie der Bildenden Künste attended the opening. One of them asked Georg Nees whether he could make his computer (a program) to draw the same manner the artist was drawing ('Duktus'). Nees' answer is a classic. After a short hesitation he replied: 'Yes, of course, I can do this. Under one condition: you must tell me how you draw.' – In the ensuing irritation, Max Bense spontaneously coined the word 'Artificial Art'.[18]

This has two implications: Nees is obviously recognizing that an artist's draughtsmanship could be reproduced through computer technology, but Nees is also implying (or, perhaps, was prompted by Bense) that the programming itself could be taught to draw, in the active sense of the word, in a way that was more than just reproduction. While acknowledging the practical limitations involved with the technology, we also want to strongly disagree with the Victoria & Albert Museum's explanation for the limited content in Nees' art:

> Many of the earliest practitioners programmed the computer themselves. At this time, there was no 'user interface', such as icons or a mouse, and little pre-existing software. By writing their own programs, artists and computer scientists were able to experiment more freely with the creative potential of the computer.

> Early output devices were also limited. One of the main sources of output in the 1960s was the plotter, a mechanical device that holds a pen or brush and is linked to a computer that controls its movements. The computer would guide the pen or brush across the drawing surface, or, alternatively, could move the paper underneath the pen, according to instructions given by the computer program.[19]

---

18   compArt database Digital Art (daDA), 'Georg Nees: Computergrafik', http://dada.compart-bremen. de/item/exhibition/164.

19   Victoria & Albert Museum, 'A History of Computer Art', http://www.vam.ac.uk/content/articles/a/ computer-art-history/.

Writing about the computer 'guiding' the pen, brush or even the paper betrays a subtle, almost unspoken notion that the process was entirely controlled by the artist. To what extent this represents a high modernist faith in an infinite set of capabilities of technology is indeterminable, but that Nees at least seemed to agree with if not advocate for the notion of an artificial art production is without doubt.

A. Michael Noll is an American engineer and professor emeritus with the University of Southern California who has been active in the development of everything from security protocols to the invention of video conferencing, a biography that would make him seem an unlikely candidate to the second computer artist except for the fact that his was the second exhibition of computer art, taking place in New York City just two months after Nees' exhibition (though he claims, with some evidence, to have produced computer art as early as 1962).[20] Whereas Nees' work seems to have been focused on the potential of the hardware, Noll's work was always focused more narrowly on the aesthetic value of the output. (Fig. 49)

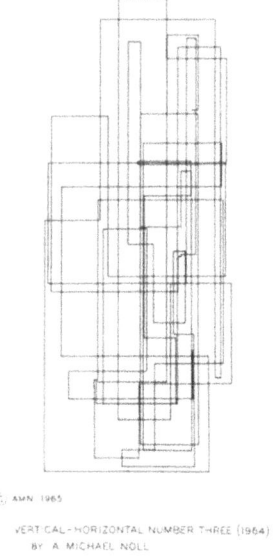

VERTICAL-HORIZONTAL NUMBER THREE (1964)
BY A MICHAEL NOLL

Fig. 49 Noll, A. Michael, *Vertical- Horizontal Number 3* (1964)

Consisting of images whose visual appeal is based on contrasting vertical and horizontal relationships or Gaussian-Quadratic equations, Noll's work is less random and more premeditated but still bears all the hallmarks of an attitude exploring and finding value in art that is distinctively digital in its appearances. Even more than Nees, some of Noll's art and his writings show a sense of faith in technology as an equivalent source of aesthetic value;

---

20   A. Michael Noll, http://noll.uscannenberg.org/.

in 1964 Noll produced a computer generated image that mimicked closely *Composition with Lines* by Piet Mondrian which was preferred by viewers over the actual paintings as well as mistakenly identified as a drawing by Mondrian himself. This resulted in Noll's paper 'Human or Machine: A Subjective Comparison of Piet Mondrian's 'Composition with Lines' and a Computer-Generated Picture'[21] in which he described the methods used to produce the image as well as the psychological experiment gauging the responses of a hundred people, and in which he also asserted that the 'randomness' was determinative in the aesthetic response. In short, despite claiming that 'an indistinguishable pair could be achieved', there's the implication that there's something superior about the art that is computer-generated.

Frieder Nake's work is derived primarily from his research as a mathematician; a work like *Hommage à Paul Klee 13/9/65 Nr.2* (1965) {Fig. 50} displays concerns and influence similar to Noll's interest in Mondrian but at the same time it is far more conceptually assertive of the distinct nature and independence of computer art in relation to its inspiration.

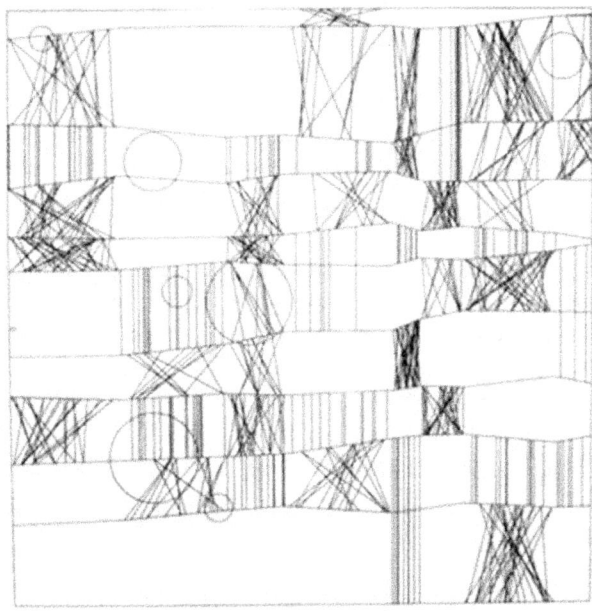

Fig. 50 Frieder Nake, 13/9/65 Nr. 2 (*"Hommage à Paul Klee"*) (1965)

---

21   A. Michael Noll, 'Human or Machine: A Subjective Comparison of Piet Mondrian's 'Composition with Lines' and a Computer-Generated Picture,' *The Psychological Record*, Vol. 16. No. 1, January 1966, pp. 1-10.

Continuing to add further levels of complexity to his work, Nake has explored series of matrix multiplications as a means of generating imagery, detailing in his book *Ästhetik als Informationsverarbeitung* (1974) a belief in the inherent aesthetic relationship between aesthetics and mathematics. Nake has also been upfront about trying to find a shared communality amidst the explosion of different art forms in the 1960s; 'it seems to me what they share is, starting with Marcel Duchamp, going beyond the confines of tradi-tional art. Each one of these movements in some other way denied art as it was known'[22] even if he stopped making art in the 1970s after writing an article titled 'There Should Be No Computer-Art'[23] for *Page*, the bulletin of the Computer Arts Society, and later accusing other computer artists of being technocratic Dadaists. Such a position places Nake firmly in the realm of the art world, unlike Nees and Noll who seem to have been engineers and programmers first and artists second. His exit from making computer art indicates even further an awareness of the increasingly pervasive nature of the digital realm into artistic practice; Nake, like Nees and Noll, had accepted a research position to use computing devices that were also booked by military and corporate entities, at a time when computing power was expensive and access was limited, and he had decided that it was immoral to participate in a method of art production that paralleled these entities' destruction of society. The editors of Wikipedia have summarized Nake's position nicely:

> The involvement of computer technology in the Vietnam War and in massive attempts by capital to automate productive processes and, thereby, generate unemployment, should not allow artists to close their eyes and become silent servants of the ruling classes by reconciling high technology with the masses of the poor and suppressed.[24]

Other artists have pioneered computer art in ways that set the stage for New Aesthetic objects. Hiroshi Kawano, who may have been the first programmer to produce computer art in 1964 (though not exhibited, and unrecognized perhaps because he wrote about his work in Japanese) studied aesthetics at the University of Tokyo and later taught it at the Metropolitan College of Air Technology. His first forays into computer art varied in output – lyrics, music, sculpture and two-dimensional visual art – but influenced by Max Bense's *Programmierung des Schönen* (1960) he began focusing on the use of algorithms,

---

22   DAM Berlin, 'Artist's Statement: Frieder Nake in conversation with Wolf Lieser at the DAM GALLERY Berlin, November 2010', November 2010, http://dam.org/artists/phase-one/frieder-nake/artist-s-statement.

23   *Page* No. 18, October 1971, pp. 1-2. Reprinted in Arie Altena, Lucas van der Velden (eds) *The anthology of computer art*, Amsterdam: Sonic Acts 2006, pp. 59-60.

24   Wikipedia contributors. 'Frieder Nake', 26 February 2016, https://en.wikipedia.org/w/index.php?title=Frieder_Nake&oldid=688732078.

cybernetics and artificial intelligence to develop a position that sought increasing degrees of autonomy in computer art production. {Fig. 51}

Fig. 51 Hiroshi Kawano, *Design 3-1*, Color Markov Chain Pattern, 1964

While the result of this is that Kawano's work often looked more like facsimiles of Mondrian's paintings than original work, nevertheless there was an effort to work within the limitations (for the time) of digital creative processes. For Kawano 'a computer artist should be a programmer who can teach his computer to produce works of art by itself, and furthermore know about the digital computing behavior of his computer in detail. It is never a computer artist, but a computer itself that produces works of art; a computer artist only helps his computer acting as a programmer.'[25] Clearly, for Kawano, the human imagination was still of primary importance as an originating point, but how long could this last when his programmatic abstraction would, inevitably, be susceptible to the internal consistency of the programming?

Jean-Pierre Hébert is our final important figure from these early years. Born in France, and exposed to art at an early age when summering in Vence, Provence where he was given access to the Galerie Alphonse Chave's collection as well as seeing work there by Matisse, Chagall, Picasso, Man Ray, Léger and many others, Hébert started programming in Fortran in 1959 and worked on some of the first Hewlett-Packard lab computers in the 1970s but he maintained an interest in producing art.[26] Moving to California, Hébert became the founder of the Algorists, a loose association of computer artists and pioneered the use of code to produce images in a range of materials beyond paper such as sand, water and as installations that would be proofed by algorithms. He explains:

---

25   compArt database Digital Art (daDA), 'Hiroshi Kawano', http://dada.compart-bremen.de/item/
      agent/234.

26   Index for jean-pierre hébert, 'Biography', http://jeanpierrehebert.com/docs/bio1209.pdf.

'The principle behind my work has always been pretty simple [...] It consists of putting together a process that creates instructions for a tool. It's all computer-driven motion of a tool on a surface.'[27] {Fig. 52}

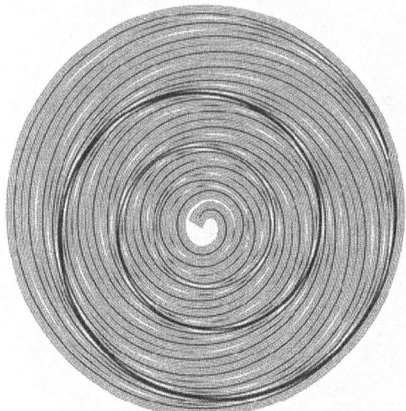

Fig. 52 Jean-Pierre Hébert, computer art, 1970s

What's especially interesting from our perspective, is Hébert's emphasis on drawing: 'I draw because I love to draw and always had a passion for drawings [...] the seventies, I have been working with the conviction that to gain power and beauty, drawing should become a pure mental activity, rather than a mere gestural skill. I have endeavored to make it so by banning the physical side of drawing.'[28] In essence, Hébert is advocating a rational approach to drawing, a notion that algorithms in and of themselves are sufficiently aesthetically valid, especially if they function as mediators between natural origins and natural output as evidenced in his recent use of spirals as prevalent and, seemingly, independently and universally artistic;[29] while Hébert may not be pushing for the eventual complete expulsion of the physical artist, what he has established is that programming is potentially sufficient at a fundamental level at the cost of drawing as a practice based on direct observation or free association.

Where we've ended up is with a group of artists who've embraced the use of digital technology but haven't called it into question, with the exception of Nake, or have utilized it

27   compArt database Digital Art (daDA), Jean-Pierre Hébert', http://dada.compart-bremen.de/item/agent/549.

28   'The Work of Jean-Pierre Hébert', *Juxtapoz*, May 22 2015, http://www.juxtapoz.com/current/the-work-of-jean-pierre-hebert.

29   Thoma Foundation, 'There Are Spirals Everywhere,' Says Computer Artist Jean-Pierre Hébert', (Press release), July 25 2015, http://thomafoundation.org/there-are-spirals-everywhere-says-computer-artist-jean-pierre-hebert/.

so seamlessly that its presence is subsumed under the primary medium or disregarded in favor of digital output. Over the course of the last fifty years digital art has become increasingly sophisticated but the digital as a medium hasn't gone through the same reflective evaluation the other mediums have over the course of modernism. There have been a few exceptions. Artists such as Vera Molnár, one of the founders of the Groupe de Recherche d'Art Visuel (GRAV) in 1961, advocated a computational approach based on Victor Vasarely's notion that the individual artist was outdated. Claude Shannon, Ken Knowlton, Leon Harmon, Lillian Schwartz, Charles Csuri, A. Michael Noll, Edward Zajec, Desmond Paul Henry, Billy Klüver, Paul Brown, Kenneth Snelson, Joseph Nechvatal and James Faure Walker have all taken leading roles in pushing what could be done (often out of Bell Labs, when Klüver and Rauschenberg created E.A.T. (Experiments in Art) in 1967). {Fig 53}

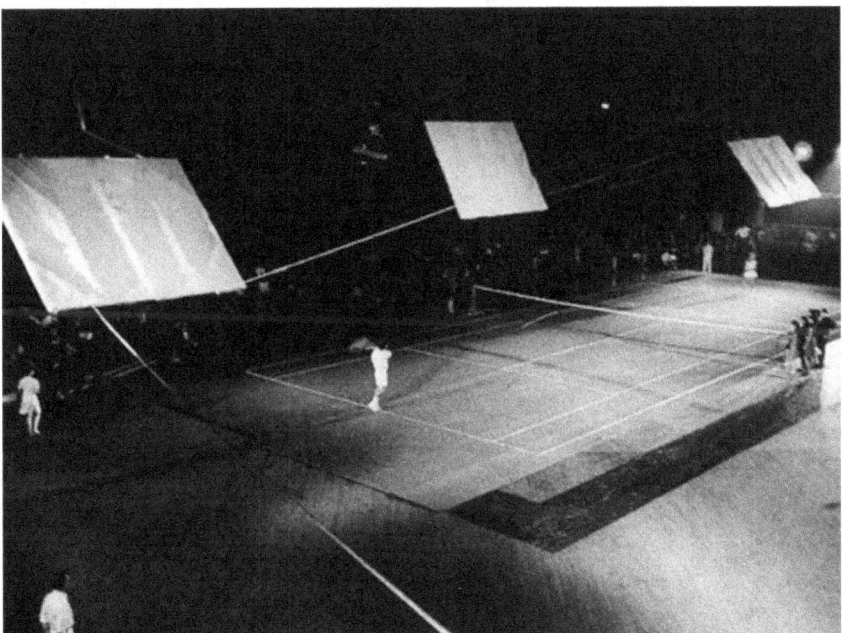

Fig. 53 Robert Rauschenberg, Open Score (1966), with Frank Stella and Mimi Kanarek, performance at the E.A.T. (Experiments in Art and Technology) forum, Bell Laboratories, Murray Hill, NJ

The increasingly dominant presence of the digital, however, has started to become natu-ralized. Along with the digital means of reproducing the appearances of traditional art forms, which has been continually accelerating to the point that handcrafted objects are, in some instances, seen as almost a rebellion against the use of digital technology, digital art has become accepted as normal or equivalent to other art forms. At the same time, as a number of artists have taken digital tools in a different direction, shouldn't we be questioning the digital's pervasive presence while at the same time refusing to eschew their usefulness? Frieder Nake's position is once again illuminating here, particularly his position that

> it was not before the first exhibitions of computer produced pictures were held (1965) that a greater public took notice of this threat, as some said, – progress, as others thought. The threat and the progress being the use of an extremely complicated, sophisticated, expensive and rational machine in the arts, i.e. in one of the last refuges of the irrational.[30]

A representative set of these artists were included in the exhibition *Painting After Technology* at the Tate Modern in London in 2015, among them Christopher Wool, Albert Oehlens and Laura Owens.[31] The exhibition takes as its starting point a brief view into the effect of technology on the practice of painting, with the central premise that 'rather than simply celebrating such technologies, however, the artists in this room are often interested in the errors, glitches and misregistrations that can result from them.'[32] Wool's *Untitled* (2009) is representative of his use of computer technology. Working with digital photographs of his own paintings, Wool rearranges them and then silkscreens the imagery onto the paper that is then fixed onto canvas. Oehlens' *Loa* (2007) {Fig. 54} quotes phrases and lyrics from Scooter, a German techno band, and is a good example of his own description of his practice as 'post-non-representational'.

Owens' *Untitled* (2012) {Fig. 55} is part of her series 'Pavement Karaoke', a set of seven 'paintings' first created in Photoshop and then projected onto the canvas in a manner similar to the Photorealists but with a continual sense of deconstructing the very process of image making.

Described by curator Mark Godfrey as a 'selection of work [reflecting] one of the urgent conversations around painting today'[33] the exhibition certainly had a sense of urgency about it, albeit a laconic one, that suggested that the intersection between traditional media and digital technology is increasingly becoming an uneasy place. In many respects Godfrey's curatorial choices, equally reflected in his Artforum article 'Statements of Intent'[34] that serves as an external curatorial statement for the Tate exhibition, compli-

---

30 *Page* No. 18, October 1971, pp. 1-2. Reprinted in Arie Altena, Lucas van der Velden (eds) *The Anthology of Computer Art*, pp. 59-60.

31 Tate, 'Painting After Technology', March, 2015, http://www.tate.org.uk/whats-on/tate-modern/display/painting-after-technology.

32 Tate, 'Painting After Technology'.

33 Tate, 'Painting After Technology'.

34 Mark Godfrey, 'Statements of Intent: Mark Godfrey on the Art of Jacqueline Humphries, Laura Owens, Amy Sillman, and Charline von Heyl', *Artforum*, April 2014, http://owenslaura.com/wp-content/uploads/2014/11/LO_2014_Apr_Artforum_small.pdf.

cates the matter further with its emphasis on abstract art. The artists included in the exhibition and discussed in the article are presented as clearly negotiating a position between the inherent value of pure formal elements in abstraction, vis-à-vis Abstract Expressionism, and the facility that digital technology brings in the production of images; quite simply, it's almost as if the contemporary shift to abstraction is a regressive, if also revealing, effort against the seduction of technology itself, with these artists trading one set of autonomous aesthetic values for another. We would argue, however, that the autonomy of digital art production is more seductive and stubborn and that regressive strategies have limited efficacy.

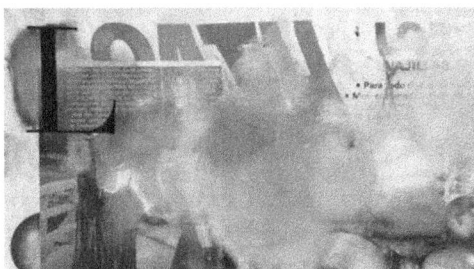

Fig. 54 Albert Oehlen, *Loa* (2007)

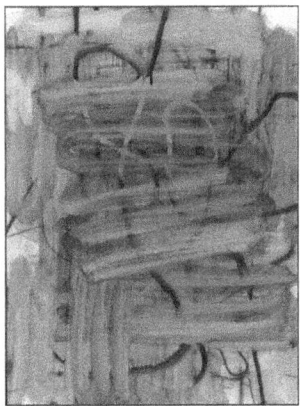

Fig. 55 Albert Oehlen, *Loa* (2007)

Almost, but not Quite, New Aesthetic Artists and Artworks

Right from the beginning, let us be clear that this second section isn't about artists who have tried to be New Aesthetic artists and failed. Nothing further could be from our minds, as every one of the artists we will subsequently discuss are ones whose work we admire and appreciate, that we've shared with each other through text messaging links and on social media in our efforts to understand these new forms and phenomena as a cultural shift and metaphysical paradigm, and that has given us many an occasion to think about what the New Aesthetic is as both an attitude and a strategy. Rather, each of the artists discussed in this section have been producing work that feels like a New Aesthetic object, which exhibits many of the characteristics of these digital forms, but in the final analysis their artistic output is not sufficient to be considered as actual objects and are, at best, products. This isn't a failure of the art (far from it) but the implementation of a criterion that involves a multiplicity of necessary elements. In some respects the work of these artists has been setting the stage, with increasing potential, for New Aesthetic art to fully emerge, and for that reason we've dealt with these artists in a progressive fashion, with their work getting closer and closer to a New Aesthetic object status. What follows is a presentation of artists whose work is unquestionably worth extended and serious con-sideration as a valuable or crucial layer in our concentric exploration towards our target.

Kohei Nawa[35] is a professor at Kyoto University of Art and Design, and has been produc-ing fascinating works that are manipulations of the intersection of material and digital means. Nawa's first appearance in a specific New Aesthetic context emerged out of his association with the *Sandwich* space in Kyoto.[36] *Polygon Double Deer #2* (2011)[37] {Fig. 56} is a work that obviously draws on the growing translation of real world objects into polygonal forms for game design and digital simulations and was featured on Bridle's blog, but other works by Nawa are even more fascinating and breath-taking.

For example, works in his *Pixcell* (2009-2011) series and his *Liquid* (2007-2011) pieces utilize a range of chemical and physical effects to simulate the digital in fascinating ways; his *Trans* (2012-13) work applies surface manipulation techniques to 3D scanned models, resulting in fluid and otherworldly figurative apparitions; and *Biota* (2013) and *Manifold* (2013) {Fig. 57} are massive representations in sculptural form of simulations of evolution, mysticism and gravity.

---

35   Kohei Nawa, http://kohei-nawa.net/.

36   Sandwich: Creative Platform for Contemporary Art, http://sandwich-cpca.net/.

37   artnet, 'Kohei Nawa, SCAI The Bathhouse', http://www.artnet.com/artists/kohei-nawa/polygon-double-deer-2-a-iODzN9ohK0_WbjhUoeM5OQ2.

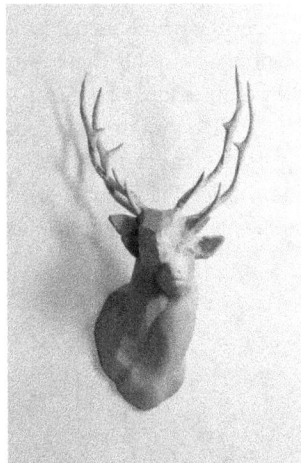

Fig. 56 Kohei Nawa, *Polygon-Double- Deer #2* (2011)

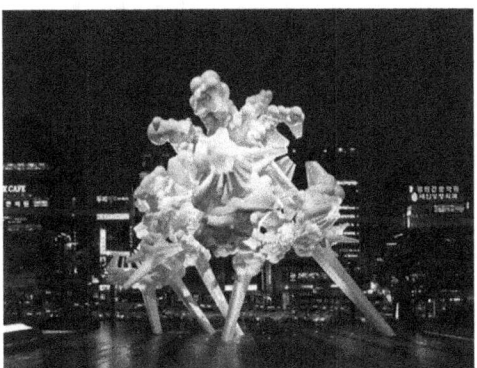

Fig. 57 Kohei Nawa, *Manifold* (2013)

This primacy of the simulation is important because of the inherently seductive nature of simulations; what Nawa's work does is set up the apparent integration of data across sensuous and embodied forms which are seemingly evolving as an opportunity for aesthetic appreciation but at the same time confounding the viewer's ability to make a free aesthetic judgment through their coherence as an environmental system. To put it another way, it's just as much the nature of the systems that Nawa employs that direct the aesthetic experience as are the artistic choices, and it's the system itself that begins to become aesthetically self-sustaining through Nawa's aesthetic strategies.

Matthew Plummer-Fernandez[38] is a British-Columbian artist who has also been mentioned in the context of the New Aesthetic. Like some of Nawa's work, Plummer-Fernandez

---

38   Matthew Plummer-Fernandez, http://www.plummerfernandez.com.

has been borrowing digital techniques to respond to conditions of the world, particularly the artificiality of the conditions of our experience of the world. One of his most well-known artworks *is sekuMoi Mecy* (2012), {Fig. 58} a 3D modeling of the shape of the iconic Mickey Mouse (the title is an anagram) that has been deconstructed randomly so that it has returned to being a digital model merely recollecting its original form. *sekuMoi Mecy*, as a result of the custom software Plummer-Fernandez has created for 3D printers, has been described as a liberator for future work entangled with the complexities of intellectual property law.

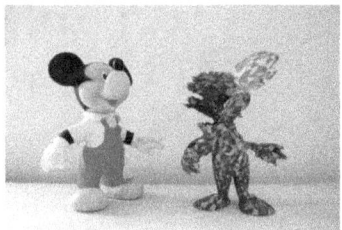

Fig. 58 Matthew Plummer-Fernandez, *sekuMoi Mecy No. 2* (2012)

Stephen Fortune writes:

> Matthew Plummer Fernandez holds the honour of firing the first shot at those who would seek to control what files can and can't be shared. His free software, Disarming Corruptor, is what he terms 'circumvention software'. It scrambles a 3D printed file, encrypting it in such a way that the user will be greeted with a glitched-out visual treat if it is loaded into any 3D editing software. If you've got the decryption keys, you get to see the object's true form. It's hiding in plain sight, thumbing its pixel-bled nose at the Mary Whitehouses of physible culture.[39]

More than just an engagement with a character, this work tears into the notion of intellectual property, copyright and trademark law, suggesting an alignment with the growing perspective that outdated legal structures are broken in the digital age. Plummer-Fernandez notes:

> The Disney Corporation fascinates me for paradoxically pioneering remix culture by creating their own versions of public domain characters such as Snow White and Cinderella, and yet the company take a hostile approach against any attempts to copy their own creations. In 1976 Disney and others sued Sony for developing the betamax video tape recorder for being a device that could be used for copyright

---

39   Stephen Fortune, 'Disarming Corruptor will encrypt your 3D creations', *Dazed*, 2014, http://www.dazeddigital.com/artsandculture/article/18019/1/disarming-corruptor-will-encrypt-your-3d-creations.

infringement. Mickey has been trademarked as well as copyrighted to ensure it will never have the freedoms of a public domain character, and the corporation have strongly lobbied and secured the Copyright Term Extension Act (known as the Mickey Mouse Protection Act). A Disney insider also revealed that the design of Mickey is constantly updated (such as the disappearance of the tail) to continually reset the copyright timer.[40]

Plummer-Fernandez's point is an intriguing one – by noting that there's a history or an evolution to the form of Mickey Mouse that 'necessitates' new intellectual and trademark filings Plummer-Fernandez is elucidating an almost biological set of flowing relations between an outdated legal structure and its mismatched digital encompassment – at the same time the reciprocal, dialectical relationships between legal concepts and digital formatting doesn't quite achieve New Aesthetic object status but remains a product in its incorporation of various digital transformations of the original subject matter. This is glitch art, and even more so this is glitch with a serious purpose, but it's not quite New Aesthetic art per se.

The shift towards a heightened awareness of the presence of the digital is clear in the work of both Nawa and Plummer-Fernandez, but there have been many other artists who have brought out this characteristic of their work and made it a defining part of their stylistic strategies. In line with this, Bridle noted in his 2012 presentation at SWSX that:

> One of the core themes of the New Aesthetic has been our collaboration with technology, whether that's bots, digital cameras or satellites (and whether that collaboration is conscious or unconscious), and a useful visual shorthand for that collaboration has been glitchy and pixelated imagery, a way of seeing that seems to reveal a blurring between 'the real' and 'the digital', the physical and the virtual, the human and the machine. It should also be clear that this 'look' is a metaphor for understanding and communicating the experience of a world in which the New Aesthetic is increasingly pervasive.[41]

As interesting as this was, we find it problematic, excusably so in the context of the early history of the New Aesthetic but still problematic especially when it comes to New Aesthetic art. Bridle is suggesting a few specific things. First, New Aesthetic objects are collaborations with technology; what Bridle means by this is that designers work with the underlying structure of digital tools and methods of analysis as partners, whether consciously or not. Given the propensity of many of the objects we've presented so far, it's clear that the digital is far less collaborative than wished for. Second, Bridle is sug-

---

40   Plummer-Fernandez, 'sekuMoi-Mecy', http://www.plummerfernandez.com.

41   James Bridle, 'Report from Austin, Texas, on the New Aesthetic panel at SXSW', booktwo.org, March 15 2012, http://booktwo.org/notebook/sxaesthetic/.

gesting that glitchy and pixelated imagery is collaborative while also being a means of productively denoting a blurred distinction between the real and the digital, an experiential breakdown between the two; what's become increasingly clear is that a complete different process has taken place, whereby the digital assumes the nature of the real rather than being situated in a liminal relationship with the real. Third, Bridle suggests that New Aesthetic objects conform to a 'look', apparently meaning that they are simply pixelated and blocky in appearance, like something out of Minecraft; in some cases, this is correct, but Bridle's other notion of the New Aesthetic as an attitude is even more accurate, in that a style is often insufficient to determine the New Aesthetic nature of an object, particularly an artwork. A number of specific examples illustrate the point we're trying to make.

The work of Ferruccio Laviani,[42] specifically his cabinet *Good Vibrations* (2013),[43] {Fig. 59} has become a rather famous example of work that stylistically similar to what one might anticipate New Aesthetic objects would appear like, showing up in many print publications and exhibitions over the last few years, being a fascinating example of craft at the highest level.

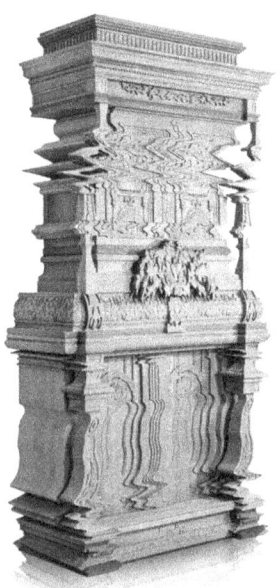

Fig. 59 Feruccio Laviani, *Good Vibrations* (2012)

---

42   Studio Laviani APFL, http://www.laviani.com/.

43   Studio Laviani APFL, http://www.laviani.com/#!good-vibrations/cq2s.

At first glance, as every writer notes, it looks like a distorted photograph, an example of a glitch. It's only after you recognize that it's been made to look that way that its artistry really becomes strikingly evident. At a superficial level it seems to be a perfect representation of the New Aesthetic, but we're inclined to differ with that response at a more critical level; in many ways, perhaps it's one of the best examples representing Bridle's theories of New Aesthetic art at a stylistic level, in the way that we've described as product, but its inadequacies as a digital artifact (not, we would clarify, its superlative nature as a physical object) or as an example of an autonomous digital process precludes it from being an example the New Aesthetic. Designed for the Italian company Boffi, it's appearance as a distorted object is merely a simulation of glitch distortions, purposively imitating an apparent breakdown of the object's integrity, but it's also a crafted object with the effect that its use value, its practicality, quickly disables the continuation of an appreciation of or interaction with its digital origins. Many pieces by Laviani are amazingly clever, and *Good Vibrations* is a virtuosic masterpiece of woodcarving, craft and design, but its glitchiness is only imitative rather than an engaged response to the digital presence.

This sense of finding a space between the real and the digital is present in an equally interesting fashion in the work of Matthieu Tremblin,[44] a French street artist. Seemingly borrowing certain artistic strategies from a tradition of artists going back to Kurt Schwitters coupled with an acute sense of the functionality of the urban environment, Tremblin's work can best be described as urban interventions. *Rainwater Popsicles* (2014) uses discarded popsicle sticks and collected rainwater in a lyrical fashion to return the pleasure back to the environment; *Sourires Volés (Stolen Smiles)* (2014) consists of smiles removed from ubiquitous political posters redisplayed in a more congenial fashion; *Copying Van Gogh* (2013) and *Hakim* (2015) are re-appropriations of found graffiti tags that simultaneously question and assert the authenticity of street art. For our purposes, however, Tremblin's most important work is *Watermark* (2013).[45] {Fig. 60}

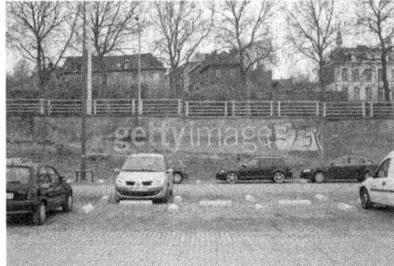

Fig. 60 Mathieu Tremblin, *Watermark* (2013)

---

44   Matthieu Tremblin, Demo De Tous Les Jours, http://demodetouslesjours.free.fr/.

45   Matthieu Tremblin, Demo De Tous Les Jours, http://demodetouslesjours.free.fr/watermark/.

An initial observation sees the image appearing as a watermarked digital photograph, similar in style to that found in the Getty Images library, but further investigations reveals that the watermark is carefully spray-painted onto the wall of the car park. Tremblin has noted that most of his interventions have had an almost curious banal quality to them, as if any ordinary citizen could have arranged the objects involved in a way that wouldn't be art at all, but *Watermark* is obviously something different; the image on Tremblin's website, the appearance of the graffiti in the photograph, all speak to a carefully planned execution that exemplifies what Tremblin refers to as 'a certain dynamic using photography, graffiti and site-specific installation to end up with this attitude where we're making forms of art in symbiosis with the context of its creation or diffusion, turning everyday life spaces in experimental art spaces'.[46] Almost every artwork by Tremblin can be understood within the context of this statement, but *Watermark* is something more; as Tremblin noted, the work came out of his criticism of the city of Mons' attempt to control its imagery in anticipation of its designation as a 'European Capital of Culture' in 2015, which Tremblin saw as being contrary to the representation of the identities of its ordinary citizens. The sense that this is close to the New Aesthetic lies readily in this last point: Tremblin's work not only highlights the growing usurpation and economic colonization of the public sphere (and literally of public spaces) through increasingly draconian interpretations and applications of copyright and intellectual property laws, in the confusion generated by the seeming dichotomy of its appearance there's a clear sense that the primary means of such encroachment into the lives of ordinary human beings is not only facilitated by the digital but driven by the digital. Therein lies the even greater impact of *Watermark*: Plato's artist, imitating the world and thereby making art simply by holding up a mirror to everything around him or her, doesn't just imitate the world but ends up owning the images and, thereby, owning the world; the lyrically horrifying effect of *Watermark* is rooted in a heightened awareness that the digital presence visible here, in an almost ghostly fashion, is a means of taking possession of the world in the same fashion in a way normally unseen but still, as an unseen watermark, very much present in its representation. In effect, everything that can be digitally photographed is now owned by the possibility of those photographs being digitally watermarked by Getty Images.

In contrast to the fascinating work above - fascinatingly contrasting precisely because of its radical sense of reversion to traditional craft, rather than usurpation of craft into the digital - one of the most interesting artists that is a part of this setting of the stage for New Aesthetic art is Faig Ahmed. Coming from Azerbaijan, Ahmed's education in the Azerbaijan State Academy of Fine Art in Baku exposed him not only to contemporary means of artistic production but also to the rich tradition of Azeri art, most importantly

---

46   Mark Byrnes, 'This Is Not a Watermark: Meet French Street Artist Mathieu Tremblin', *The Atlantic,
      Citylab*, 15 July 2013, http://www.citylab.com/design/2013/07/not-watermark-meet-french-street-
      artist-mathieu-tremblin/6083/.

the long history of intricate rugs and other forms of fiber art. Ahmed's work is a result of the relationship between the past, in a deeply rooted traditional sense that he notes as extending back to the 'beginning of times', and the present as an opportunity for poignant fractures and reconfigurations.[47] Looking at Ahmed's work it's immediately obvious why it's relevant here: with work like *Ledge* (2011), *Oiling* (2012), *Liquid* (2014) and, especially, *Tradition in Pixel* (2010), {Fig. 61} the fields of liminality he explores between traditional carpet design and digital effects and patterns are evidently experimental ventures broaching normally opposing forms of art practices.

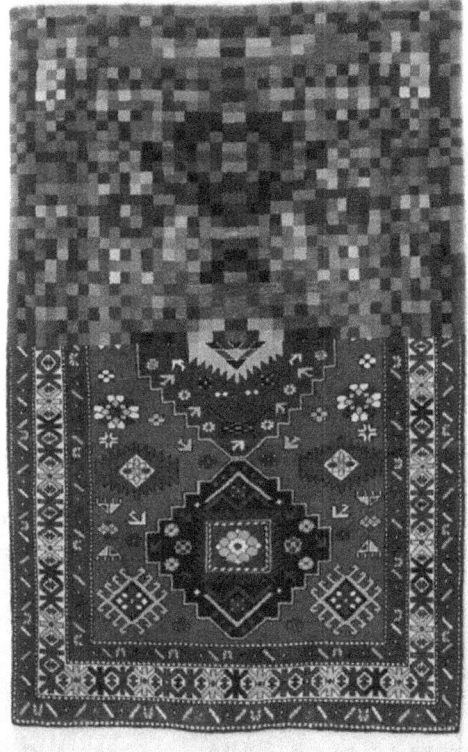

Fig. 61 Faig Ahmed, *Tradition in Pixel* (2010)

Much of Ahmed's carpets are woven in a traditional fashion, but the alterations that make them appear as if they were expanded through a digital loupe in a digital photo library organizer, manipulated into a design that looks like it's been smeared in an image editor on an iPad, expanded and strained to create an object almost sublime in its deconstruction of the traditional carpet format and transformed by reducing sections of the carpets

---

47   Faig Ahmed, http://www.faigahmed.com/about/info/.

into pixelated fields colors, all speak to the necessity of Ahmed's artistic practices being situated at the intersection of craft and technology. In many respects, Flusser's ideas are appropriate as a guide when thinking about Ahmed's wonderful art, in that it's clear that technological innovations are driving these crafted manifestations, and Ahmed's own statements back this up:

> I explore ancient traditions, cults and cultures, I make my own research and as I communicate with it, I create art. My carpets, installations and embroideries are the result of this interplay. It is fascinating to observe the process of such an easy transformation of such ancient and stable objects.[48]

It is Ahmed's assertion of the ease of the transformation that's just as intriguing as the objects themselves. Why is it easy? Not just because of the evident mark of the digital tools that Ahmed is using in the design of his art but also in their appearance as pixelated rather than pixelized. Pixelated is usually understood as the unwanted appearance of pixels, often betraying the digital nature of the image, while pixelized is the intentional use of pixels to obscure details of the image. *Tradition in Pixel* operates in both processes in a powerful way. Ahmed writes:

> The carpet is a symbol of invincible tradition of the East, it's a visualization of an undestroyable icon. In my art I see the culture differently. This is more of expectation of a reaction because it's exactly the change of the points of view that changes the world. Slight changes in the form of a carpet dramatically change it's structure and maybe make it more suitable for the modern life. The Eastern culture is very rich visually. I cover it all in minimalistic forms, destroying the stereotypes of the tradition and creating new modern boundaries. A man can widen the borders and change them but no one has ever dare to break our spirit.[49]

Understanding the carpet as a symbol of invincible tradition, Ahmed's pixelating reinforces its digital transformation as an alteration, forcing a reconsideration of the original source tradition, while at the same time the pixelization of the work conceptually censors the rigid effect of tradition as a stereotype in a refusal to avoid the modern. What makes Ahmed's work so interesting is the dialectical interplay between a determinative and reflective position, sourced in the intractable foundations of the history of Azeri carpets and the equally unavoidable transformative power of the digitalization of the world. The influence of the New Aesthetic is clearly affecting the work; the pixels are not slight changes that set into motion the recollection of tradition but activated elements redefining the invincibility of tradition.

---

48   Faig Ahmed, http://www.faigahmed.com/about/info/.

49   Faig Ahmed, *artworks catalog,* http://www.faigahmed.com/site/assets/files/1017/faig_ahmed_ artworks_catalogue.pdf.

The appearance of a glitch aesthetic does not necessarily indicate the use of the New Aesthetic in an artist's work but certainly represents an attitude or an awareness of the significant shift at an almost epistemic level. One of the best examples of this is the use of glitch effects in the photography of Sabato Visconti, a Brazilian born artist trained and working in the United States. According to Visconti's website it was a defective memory card that prompted his experimentation with glitch photography in 2011.[50] Visconti's art puts him at the forefront of glitch photography; using deliberately executed errors which Visconti refers to as 'breaking the image', he tries to strike a balance between a complete collapse of the image into digital errors and incomprehensible artifacts and straight photography, 'trying to find this really fine balance where something doesn't break fully, but breaks just to the point that you can see it breaking'.[51] {Fig. 62}

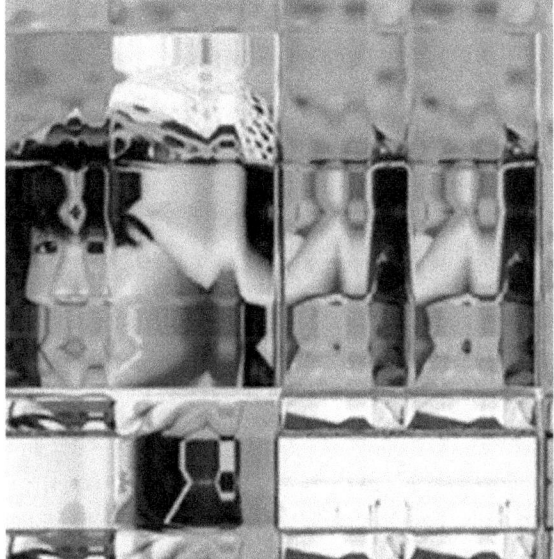

Fig. 62 Sabato Visconti, *Peeper (11th Iteration)* (2014), from the *Little Monsters* series

More than just nostalgia for 8-bit graphics, Visconti's art clearly takes the glitch as a starting point for manipulating the image almost to the point of surrealism, a connection that is evident in the control that he tries to maintain over the final product. In fact, it's clear that there is a thread of art historical referentiality, particularly with certain images

50   Sabato Visconti, http://www.sabatobox.com/about.

51   Douglas Bierend, 'Breaking Things On Purpose, Glitch Art's Pixel-mixing Algorithms', *Medium.com*, 26 August 2014, https://medium.com/re-form/breaking-things-on-purpose-14f413bdf2ce#.sdbpsxsmt.

that show a strong influence from other artists like René Magritte[52] and André Kertész, even if art history permeates only at the most superficial level. {Fig. 63}

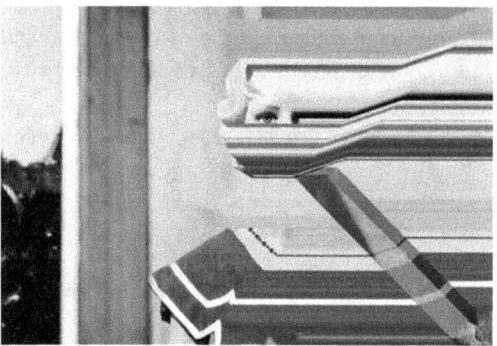

Fig. 63 Sabato Visconti, *Untitled* (2011), from the *Images Adrift* series

For Visconti, an awareness of the code that drives image manipulation programs is what sets his parameters.

> You get an idea more or less of what you're going to get, but you can't really predict it. And that's part of the charm – you don't have control over what you're doing, you kind of rely on the machine [...] If I wanted to do a lot of squares and fractal squares I'll probably want to do a 'cash smash' glitch, because those tend to produce squares. If you want to have a kind of wavy distortion that's almost like a super warped-out VHS effect, you're going to want to use an audio program for that [...] It's definitely more satisfying sometimes when you get down and dirty with the code and kind of just finesse something out.[53]

The balance that Visconti is trying to strike here is clearly twofold: on the one hand his efforts are directed towards producing an image that is aesthetically interesting, with a sufficient level of recognizable references to fix a viewer's focus, while on the other hand there's also an effort to encode the visuality of the image precisely to reveal its digital origins through the manipulation, both controlled and uncontrolled, of its appearance.

Visconti's work, however, isn't fully New Aesthetic art. Reading through various interviews and articles about his photographs, it becomes clear that his process is a combination of deliberate utilization of various image manipulation tools coupled with a limited degree of randomness, all the while primarily driven by an expressionist and symbolic intent. What's amazing about Visconti work is the variety of techniques he uses:

---

52   Liz Stinson, 'Wonderfully Twisted Photos from a Glitch Art Guru', *Wired.com*, 10 September 2014, http://www.wired.com/2014/10/wonderfully-twisted-photos-glitch-art-guru/#slide-8.

53   Bierend, 'Breaking Things On Purpose, Glitch Art's Pixel-mixing Algorithms'.

In the last few years, Visconti has created static-filled images by editing a photo with audio equipment. He's opened raw files through WordPad and saved them so the encoding would produce strange characters in the final image. He's embraced cachemashing, and distorted photos by converting them to vectors then databending the file. The point being: There are plenty of ways to glitch a photo.[54]

At the same time, what brings Visconti's work back into the realm of normal art production is the virtuosity with which he uses the digital tools he's familiarized himself with most. In the end, the result is that 'glitch photography transcends the idea of simply altering something and becomes a medium in its own right, replete with a digital toolbox of tricks and best practices'.[55] Clearly there's a concern on Visconti's part to produce the best possible image, the most successful example of art, and to that end he's quite upfront about continuing to have control over the final images.

I'm not sure if focusing on unpredictability is the most meaningful way to critically engage with glitch art. I think it feeds this misconception that glitch artists simply stumble on these happy accidents without any thought or effort. Creating glitch art can be as labor intensive as any other art form. Glitching is the careful simulation of malfunction. It's an absurd scheme that requires some finesse, because some glitches will break a file beyond recognition and other glitches will have no effect at all.[56]

Visconti uses Pixel-Drifter,[57] a program written by Dmitriy Krotevich, in much of his work. Pixel-Drifter works by taking the 'power' of each pixel, gauged by its luminosity and screen position, and putting it into conflict with its neighboring pixels in parameters set into place by the user. As much as we like Visconti's art, this need to control the final outcome, to successfully wrestle with the algorithms, and to labor in a productive and ordered fashion towards an intended final product indicates that Visconti's work is only related to the New Aesthetic. As noted by Margaret Rhodes:

In the beginning, glitch art was the appreciation of how software hiccups can distort an image. Depending on who you asked, glitch art only qualified as glitch art if the aesthetic cracks happened by accident. Then the medium evolved, and some digital artists began to force those errors by editing code and manipulating pixels.[58]

---

54   Liz Stinson, 'Wonderfully Twisted Photos From a Glitch Art Guru'.

55   Liz Stinson, 'Wonderfully Twisted Photos From a Glitch Art Guru'.

56   Lital Khaikin, 'The Radical Capacity of Glitch Art: Expression through an Aesthetic Rooted in Error', REDEFINE, 5 February 2014, http://www.redefinemag.com/2014/glitch-art-expression-through-an-aesthetic-rooted-in-error/.

57   Dmitriy Krotevich, Pixel-Drifter, http://pixeldrifter.tumblr.com/.

58   Margaret Rhodes ,'This Glitch Art is Made of Pixels Powered by Their Own AI', Wired.com, 7 August 2014, http://www.wired.com/2014/08/this-glitch-art-is-made-of-pixels-powered-by-their-own-ai.

It is here that we draw a distinction between art informed by the New Aesthetic as product and actual New Aesthetic art objects as artistic embodiments.

Antoine Geiger's work is also heavily dependent on the aesthetic strategy that image manipulation revealing the digital origins of the work transforms our perception of the work itself but also effects reconfigured social awareness. With a quote from Walter Benjamin's 1935 essay 'The Work of Art in the Age of Mechanical Reproduction', Geiger's series of manipulated photographs *Sur-Fake* (2015) seems to be a flag-bearer for the impending apocalypse. {Fig. 64}

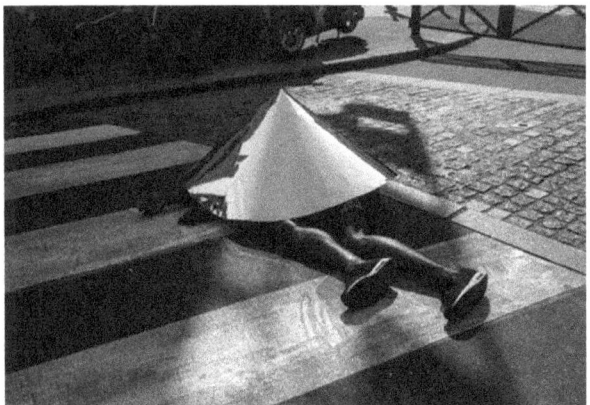

Fig. 64 Antoine Geiger, from the *Sur-Face* project (2014)

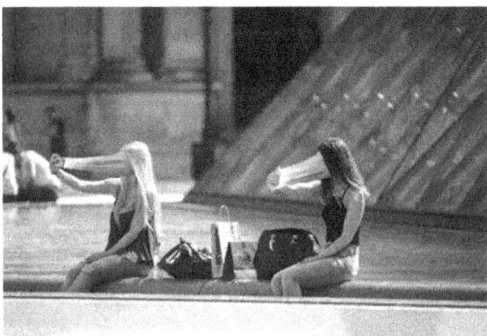

Fig. 65 Antoine Geiger, from the *Sur-Fake* project (2014)

Benjamin's words – 'Mankind, which in Homer's time was an object of contemplation for the Olympian gods, is now one for itself. Its self-alienation has reached such a degree that it can experience its own destruction as aesthetic pleasure of the first order' – bear out in Geiger's images of people willingly sucked into the screens of their smartphone. {Fig. 65}

Geiger notes about the project that it's a continuation of *Sur-Face* (2014), wherein his images of people with their head covered by mirrors evoked a need for privacy in our

ever-present state of facial recognition, but what makes *Sur-Fake* even more interesting is the apparent willingness of the participants to relinquish their identities to their
technological mediators.[59] Geiger writes: 'What interests me in this texture of sucked
faces, is that the over-exposure gradually allows a very organic dimension, as well as
digital, to render something quite disturbing.'[60]

Ralf Brueck's work bears some resemblance to that of Geiger, but there are crucial dif-
ferences that only come out through a closer inspection. A German artist, Brueck trained
at the Kunstakademie Düsseldorf and belongs to what has been sometimes referred to
as the Düsseldorf School of Photography, a group of artists that includes Andreas Gursky,
Candida Höfer, Thomas Ruff and Thomas Struth. These artists not only share similar
backgrounds, influences and educations but their work often necessitates an increased
sense of participation of the viewer to acknowledge their complicit role in creating a
completed aesthetic experience. While the other photographers, particularly Gursky,
use digital tools, Brueck includes the presence of the digital to such an extent that it
overwhelms the presence of his subjects in his compositions. In 2011 Brueck started his
Distortion series, a set of photographs whose subjects, ranging from the interior of Gothic
cathedrals and urban landscapes to highways and desert vistas, are heavily manipulated
through the extraction of tonal elements in order to enhance the presentation of their
digital origins by premeditated manipulations; images such as *Golden Cage* (2011) and
Twin Peaks (2011) {Fig. 66} contain sufficiently recognizable details with specific aspects
drawn out to set a dynamic visual contrast that redirects the viewer back to the production and manipulation or editing methods.

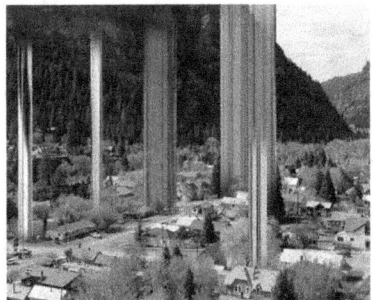

Fig. 66 Ralf Brueck, *Twin Peaks* (2011)

Often noted as appearing to be bar codes, the work of the *Distortion* series perhaps
looks more like extensions of DNA testing markers, which is more in line with some of

59   Kate Sierzputowski, 'The Attention-Sucking Power of Digital Technology Displayed Through
     Photography by Antoine Geiger', *Colossal*, 11 November 2015, http://www.thisiscolossal.
     com/2015/11/cellphone-attention-antoine-geiger/?src=footer.

60   Antoine Geiger, *Sur-Fake*, http://files.cargocollective.com/440813/SUR-FAKE--translated-.pdf.

Brueck's statements attesting to his consistent interest in the fundamental elements of the photographic medium. By 2015, with his *Dekonstruktion* (2015) series, the level of recognizable elements has been dramatically curtailed, so that images like *Home sweet home* (2014) {Fig. 67} and *Shopping with grandma Elisabeth* (2015) are startling in their evocation of the implied but non-existent presence of the viewer, an obfuscation built into the necessary cooperative aesthetic engagement.

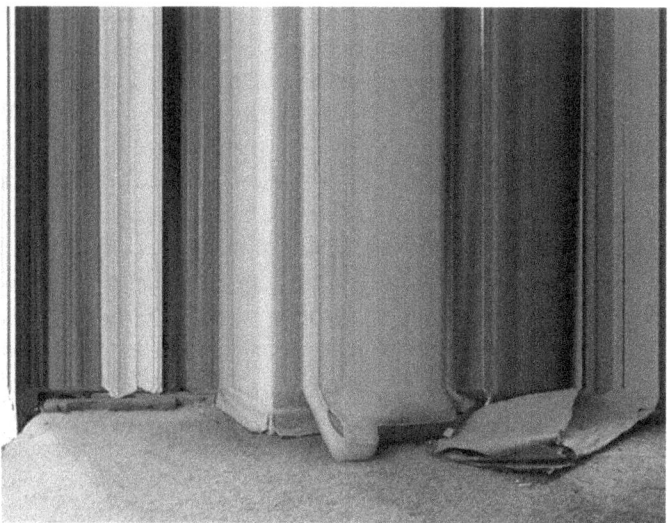

Fig. 67 Ralf Brueck, *Home sweet home* (2014)

Like in so many instances of postdigital analysis, there are often strange interpretations of Brueck's work, with one article in *Wired* describing the *Distortion* series thus:

> IT'S FINALLY HAPPENED – ALIENS are among us.
> Ralf Brueck's images transform daily life into a sci-fi wonderland. Distorted shapes and glitches disrupt otherwise normal landscapes, making it easy to imagine para-normal activity or a good old-fashioned beaming up. In his series Dekonstruktion and Distortion, Brueck brings the unnatural closer to home.[61]

We're not sure where the aliens are – Brueck notes that there's been almost a constant tendency to look at this work in a science fiction context[62] – but the disjunctive relation-ship between the familiar and the otherworldly presses our aesthetic sensibilities into a

61   Alyssa Coppelman, 'Distorted Photos Show the Alien Side of Suburban Life', *Wired.com*, 1 March 2015, http://www.wired.com/2015/03/ralf-brueck-distortion/.

62   Michael Corbin, 'Ralf Brueck: Surreal Distortion', *ArtBookGuy*, http://artbookguy.com/ralf-brueck-surreal-distortion_433.html.

consideration of the medium. Brueck works with a 4x5 analog camera and is self-taught in the use of digital manipulation software. He notes: 'One of the ideas behind my work is to manipulate the DNA of the picture, to let it mutate. Every detail you see originates only from the one sole photo.'[63] From this, we would suppose that, despite the initial analog origins, the presence of digital manipulation is almost teleological, a position substantiated by Amani Olu's and Jon Feinstein's curated photography website, which states: 'Ralf Brueck manipulations of images are not geared towards pointing out that contemporary digital photography is deficient in its representation of reality but argues that a photograph constitutes its own reality.'[64]

The use of distortions by digital manipulation software has often been noted as a readily identifiable manifestation of the influence of the New Aesthetic, if not an example in its own right. Artists like Mishka Henner have produced work like *Dutch Landscapes* (2011)[65] {Fig. 68} that explore the concessions that Google makes to government censorship and its 'need' for secrecy, and Helmut Smits' *Dead Pixel in Google Earth* (2008-10)[66] {Fig. 69} borrows from Land Art techniques to aesthetically contrast our expectations and experiences in the digitizing of our landscapes.

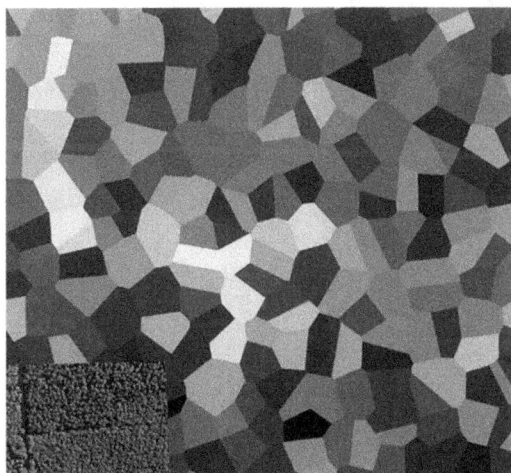

Fig. 68 Mishka Henner, *De Peel Patriot Missile Site*, Dutch Landscapes (2011)

---

63   Alyssa Coppelman, 'Distorted Photos Show the Alien Side of Suburban Life'.

64   group show 42: *Occultisms* The Artists, Humble Arts Foundation, http://hafny.org/group-show-42-occultisms-statements-and-bios/.

65   Mishka Henner, 'Dutch Landscapes', *mishkahenner.com*, February 2011, http://mishkahenner.com/filter/works/Dutch-Landscapes.

66   Helmut Smits, 'Dead Pixel in Google Earth', *helmutsmits.com*, 2010, http://helmutsmits.nl/work/dead-pixel-in-google-earth-2.

Similar to the work of Visconti and Geiger is that of Kim Asendorf, though the similarities are set off by the different directions these artists have taken. Asendorf is one of the first digital artists to start using pixel sorting, a technique wherein pixels in an image are sorted along certain parameters, and Asendorf's release of his own programming code for pixel sorting quickly sparked a wide range of emulators and imitators.[67] With images like those in the series *Mountain Tour* (2010)[68] {Fig. 70} and an example of his work processing source code,[69] Asendorf is clearly subverting the conventions of landscape while at the same articulating divergent aesthetic parameters.

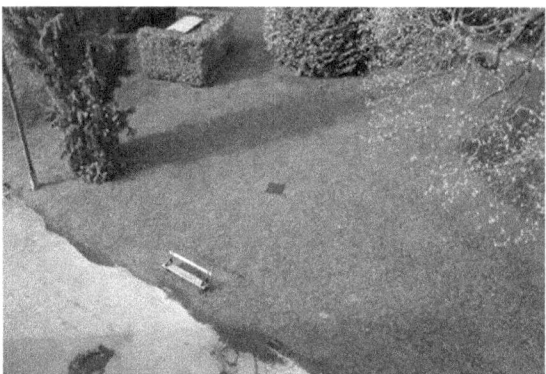

Fig. 69 Helmut Smits, *Dead Pixel in Google Earth* (2008–2010)

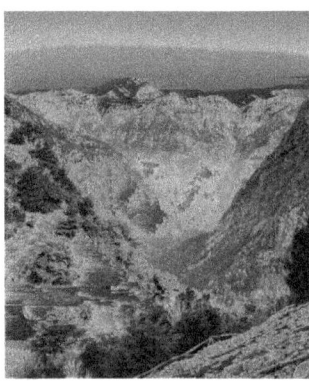

Fig. 70 Kim Asendorf, from the *Mountain Tour* series (2010)

---

67   Kim Assendorf, *Kim Assendorf Up and Running*, http://kimasendorf.com/www/.

68   'Mountain Tour (2010) by Kim Asendorf ', *Prosthetic Knowledge blog*, 25 August 2012, http://prostheticknowledge.tumblr.com/post/30196185509/mountain-tour-2010-by-kim-asendorf-one-of-the.

69   Kim Asendorf, 'Processing Source Code', 5 October 2012, *kimasendorf blog*, http://kimasendorf.tumblr.com/post/32936480093/processing-source-code.

More than just glitch art, Asendorf's artistic efforts explore the assumptions users make when employing digital tools at a level that is more like conceptual art. *KIM ASENDORF TTF* (2013) is exactly what it sounds like – a TrueType font family – but with disruptive consequences, since it substitutes 'Kim Asendorf' as the only visible characters.

Sandbox (2009), by Erwin Driessens & Maria Verstappen, is another example of a power-ful and interesting artwork that brings up a sense of the New Aesthetic but is not fully participating in its attitude. {Fig. 71} Installed at *The Power of Things* exhibition at the DEAF (Dutch Electronic Art Festival) in 2012, *Sandbox* is an elaborate skillful recreation of a desert environment, with a diorama enclosing only sand and wind.[70]

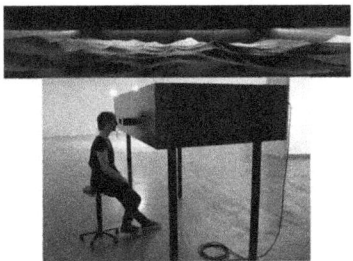

Fig. 71 Erwin Driessens and Maria Verstappen, *Sandbox* (2009)

Looking at the imitation of natural forces as they are mimicked inside of the diora-ma, a viewer might be inclined to think of this as no more than an elaborate science project or display typically found in a science museum, but this work by Driessens & Verstappen does far more than that; V2, the 'Institute for Unstable Media' describes the team of artists as producing 'e-volved' imagery based on scientific principles, resulting in an exploration of 'the possibilities that physical, chemical and computer algorithms offer for the development of image-generating processes'.[71] What differentiates the work by Driessens & Verstappen from a being merely a display of scientific principles is the governing, systematic structure of control digitally implemented in their work; as they note about their own work:

> They attempt an art in which spontaneous phenomena are created systematically. Art that is not entirely determined by the subjective choices of a human being, but instead is generated by autonomously operating processes. In addition to work-ing with natural generative processes, the couple develops computer programs for artificial growth and evolution. An important source of inspiration at this are the self-organising processes in our natural surroundings: the complex dynamics of all

---

70   Erwin Driessens & Maria Verstappen, 'Sandbox', 2009, http://notnot.home.xs4all.nl/sandbox/sandbox.html.

71   V2_Institute for the Unstable Media, 'Sandbox', http://v2.nl/archive/works/sandbox.

kinds of physical processes and the genetic-evolutionary system of organic life that continuously creates new and original forms.[72]

The emphasis on natural growth puts their work very close to being New Aesthetic, but at the same time we're not so certain about the naturalness in that there's little apparent autonomy to the programming. The series of images *E-volved Cultures* (2005-2011) {Fig. 72} and *Formulae E-volver* (2015)[73] get even closer – perhaps genuinely closer to the New Aesthetic than anything we've discussed so far – but their dependency on complex mathematical formulas, with the predetermined pathways of visual development that maintain a viable structure imposed on the objects by the artists, puts them more in parallel (in an updated manner) to the work of 1960s computer artists.

A final consideration in this section appears in two different examples and involves an approach that is more installation-oriented: *Project Blinkenlights* (2001-02) and Ryoji Ikeda's *supersymmetry* (2015). At first it would seem that the works are very mismatched. *Project Blinkenlights* {Fig. 73} was a project executed by the German Chaos Computer Club, whose members can rightfully be described as hackers in the broadest sense.

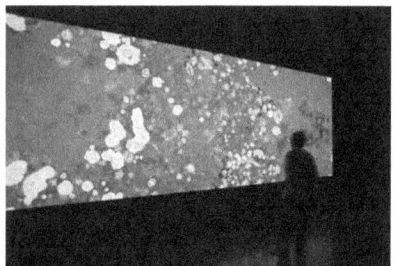

Fig. 72 Erwin Driessens and Maria Verstappen, *E-volved Cultures* (2005-11)

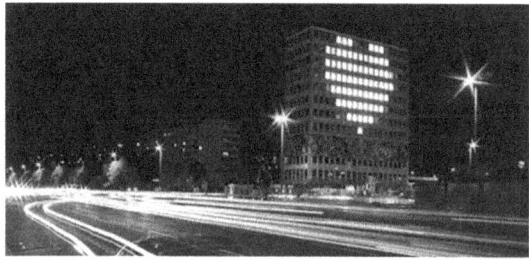

Fig. 73 Chaos Computer Club, *Project Blinkenlights* (2001-2002)

---

72   Erwin Driessens & Maria Verstappen, 'Bio', http://notnot.home.xs4all.nl/text/shortBio.html.

73   Erwin Driessens & Maria Verstappen, 'E-volved Images', http://notnot.home.xs4all.nl/evolvedimages/evolvedimages.html.

It started on September 11th 2001 at the Haus des Lehrers in Alexanderplatz, Berlin, and lasted until February 23rd 2002. Consisting of 144 lamps arranged behind the windows of the Haus des Lehrers, it displayed various patterns that increased in complexity over the course of the installation as planned but also incorporated love letters, the classic video game Pong, and submitted patterns from users through the Blinkenpaint software program written specifically for user to participate in and contribute to a growing social occasion as its popularity increased almost nightly. Was *Project Blinkenlights* art? That's debatable, especially given its hacker origins with an emphasis on engineering rather than artistic success. Nevertheless, the effect of *Project Blinkenlights* clearly was artistic at a very deep level, especially given the title's origin in the hacker neologism for diagnostic lights used in old computer mainframes and the ironic effect of the lack of failure in the project's display. Ryoji Ikeda's *supersymmetry* {Fig. 74} is a project of a very different nature from *Project Blinkenlights*, but certain similarities do exist.

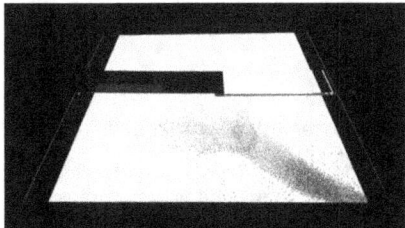

Fig. 74 Ryoji Ikeda, *supersymmetry* (2014), Studio A

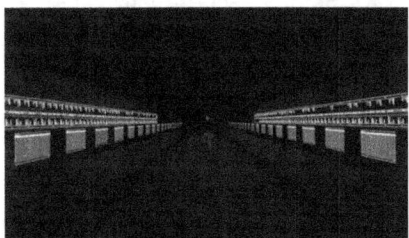

Fig. 75 Ryoji Ikeda, *supersymmetry* (2014), Studio B

Taking as its starting point the theory of particle physics that attempts to reconcile the incompatible models of quantum mechanics and general relativity, Ikeda's installation, atop the Brewer Street Car Park in London, as part of a series supported by The Vinyl Factory, was a disorienting experience divided into two sections and that is 'an artistic vision of the reality of nature through an immersive and sensory experience to the visitors'.[74] In the first section of *supersymmetry*, large numbers of balls roll across moving platforms that are sometimes illuminated by strobe lighting and scanned *in situ*; in the

---

74   Ryoji Ikeda, 'supersymmetry', *Ryoji Ikeda*, 2014, http://www.ryojiikeda.com/project/
      supersymmetry/.

second section, the data produced by the balls is projected onto forty computer screens, with correlations and divergences in the data that is mapped and analyzed emphasized visually. {Fig. 75}

In an unjustifiably dismissive review, Jonathan Jones provided some a clear starting point to understanding Ikeda's intentions:

> There's a giveaway when the pulses are replaced by streaming text: the words flowing across batteries of screens are deliberate nonsense. I see this as the artist's view of physics, just a different language that makes no sense at all.

> Art and science, we feel, should have something to say to each other. But perhaps they speak different languages after all. I don't speak the language of science too well, either, but I do know one thing: it is concerned with the wonder of nature. There is a depressing lack of wonder in this technically sophisticated but intellectually and emotionally empty art.[75]

Regardless of Jones' inability to see the wonder, his observation that Ikeda is focusing on the language of science and is conflating it with the language of art is quite astute. The theory of supersymmetry is an attempt, still unproven, to explain why particles have mass, and both *Project Blinkenlights* and *supersymmetry* have artistic goals that are very analogous to each other: namely, the visible presentation of the effect of mass, in both social or cultural and physically experimental ways. Both projects visually consist of blinking lights, but it's more important to recognize that these utterly different projects still retain a faith in the systems that sustain their manifestations; it's not just that a digital language is necessary to realize the works, but even more so it's inherent that the pervasiveness of that language be employed while simultaneously going unrecognized. This attitude - uncritically embracing the digital as almost a natural language, thereby giving it an autonomous function determining artistic productivity - is not fully realized in either *Project Blinkenlights, supersymmetry* or any of the other projects mentioned in this section, but we believe that they set the stage for other artists to fully work within the restrictions and opportunities of the New Aesthetic and create New Aesthetics artistic objects.

These last embodiments, delineations and demarcations in their particular form are what mark, for us, examples of art that are so close to being New Aesthetic that they in turn help us define what New Aesthetic art is. Curiously, the common characteristic (the only one, in fact) that unites all of them - Erwin Driessens & Maria Verstappen, *Project Blink-*

---

75   Jonathan Jones, 'Should art respond to science? On this evidence, the answer is simple: no way',
     The Guardian, 23 April 2015, http://www.theguardian.com/artanddesign/jonathanjonesblog/2015/
     apr/23/art-respond-science-cern-ryoji-ikeda-supersymmetry.

enlights, and Ryoji Ikeda - is the immersiveness of their projects, the use of installations and the creation of environments that fundamentally alter the experience of the viewer. *Sandbox* creates unseen vistas firmly grounded in our understanding of the world which are continually being renewed as otherworldly, *Project Blinkenlights* took a public space and made it even more public while at the same time transforming participation into an entirely private matter, and Ikeda's work transforms our understanding of our place in the universe into a sequence of lights and sounds that reduces our ability to differentiate our experiences, our lives and our language into the mathematical and thereby into something immensely depersonalized. Tremblin's *Watermark* achieves the same effect, though in a lyrical rather than immersive fashion. It's when these and other examples of art, immersive and all encompassing, affect us that the categorical conditions of existence of New Aesthetic art are revealed.

CHAPTER 5
LETTING GO:
NEW AESTHETIC ARTISTS AND
THE NEW AESTHETIC ART
THAT WORKS

Although Walter Benjamin had posited a loss of aura in the reproduction of physical objects in almost apocalyptic terms, couched in his further analysis of the rise of fascism, and Arthur Danto posited the death of art[1] on the basis of art's capacity to indistinguishably reproduce real objects in a way that parallels Benajmin's decrying of modernist transformations of art almost to a level of apotheosis (though in a manner later disavowed but still retaining a certain feel of authenticity), it's clear that auras and life both have remained in art. Benjamin and Danto were expressing the collapse of confidence marking the end of modernism, a shift that was more than just a radical rejection of modernist trends but a wholesale undermining of the conviction that had permeated modern art since the middle of the nineteenth century, a conviction that was driven by an increasingly evident unwillingness to participate in a artificial and false teleology based on a Hegelian notion of historical necessity; it's not so much that Benjamin and Danto were participating in this endgame, more that they were some of the final pieces on the board as new players chose to move onto other games. Taking the form of postmodernism at first and, when that new but shallow paradigm was shown to still be consistently linked to modernity, developing a sense of the contemporary that shattered any notion that centralized narratives or art worlds still existed, artists have spun themselves away into new games, new sets and subsets of games, so that hyper-individualism has become the new norm. It's in this context that New Aesthetic art objects have appeared. This chapter is focused on artists whose work are examples of such objects, often exhibiting autonomous elements and aesthetic strategies and results that are markedly a manifestation of the New Aesthetic paradigm: autonomous objects, most often digital or at least digitally formed, that are the results of intentional or unintentional glitches and imperfections which paradoxically give them an aesthetic presence or weight in a fashion that forms an entirely new paradigm. New Aesthetic art is, for us, a presentation of a new type of work as one of many antidotes to the crisis of modernism that both Benjamin's and Danto's positions represented, a full participant in this new decentralized art world precisely because each work operates as the embodiment of its own self-sustaining teleological drive.

---

1   A witty and intelligent summary of this can be found in Tiernan Morgan and Lauren Purje, 'An Illustrated Guide to Arthur Danto's "The End of Art"', *Hyperallergic*, 31 March 2015, http://hyperallergic.com/191329/an-illustrated-guide-to-arthur-dantos-the-end-of-art/.

A transition is necessary, however, and an illustrative work to this end that appears to be New Aesthetic but is decidedly not serves as a good illustration of our point: Liza Lou's *Color Field* (2015). {Fig. 76}

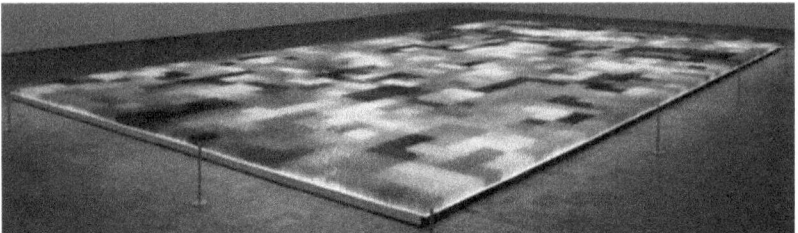

Fig. 76 Liza Lou, *Color Field* (2010-2013)

Liza Lou is an American artist whose work has increasingly been recognized and gained respect following the exhibition of *Kitchen* (1991-1996) at the New Museum of Contemporary Art in New York City, a work that recreated a modern kitchen with appliances, counters, various food items and running water in glass beads. Glass beads have since become her signature artistic form, with work like *Backyard* (1999) using thirty million of them, but nothing quite reached the point of the sublime in a manner reminiscent of Abstract Expressionists like Mark Rothko or Barnett Newman than the 2015 installation of *Color Field* in the Neuberger Museum, NY. Consisting of eleven beads of glass on all of 576 blades positioned on 1,196 tiles, its approximately 7.5 million beads are arranged in a color scheme reminiscent of much of the art we've discussed that emphasis a pixelated visual structure; opening and closing patterns emerge in this site-specific work, but the grid remains in such a fashion that each tile takes on the approximate appearance of a pixel as if the entire work is a massively expanded close-up of a digital image that is no longer available at a resolvable level. Yet, this isn't quite correct; as noted in articles,[2] the artist's website[3] and the curatorial statement of the Neuberger Museum where it's installed,[4] Lou's work has increasingly shifted such that 'I became really interested in seeing what would happen if I took away subject matter and just had it be about process'.[5] For a number of years Lou lived part of the time in the KwaZulu-Natal province in South Africa where she employed a team of local Zulu women to help produce the work; in this case, and in related work, it is precisely the physical activity that changes and enhances the material into its final artistic form.

2   Susan Hodara, 'Liza Lou's Handmade Sea of Sparkling Glass', *The New York Times*, 2 January 2016, http://nyti.ms/1OBekoq.

3   *Liza Lou*, http://lizalou.com/.

4   Helaine Posner, Chief Curator, 'Liza Lou: Color Field and Solid Grey November 8, 2015 - February 21, 2016', *Neuberger Museum of Art*, https://www.neuberger.org/exhibitions/current/view1/314. html?width=660&height=500.

5   Susan Hodara, 'Liza Lou's Handmade Sea of Sparkling Glass'.

Color Field is most definitely not a work based on digital principles, even if it appears to be that way. The sublimity of this amazing work is present in the material of the work itself rather than the design, in the shared physical activity that's gone into making the art, in a manner extending beyond the rough, solitary idiosyncratic independence of the abstract expressionists to whom the work is indebted at least in title. So why discuss *Color Field* in the context of the New Aesthetic, and specifically in the context of teleology? Or, rather, as an object that can be teleologically assessed? We will turn to this in more detail in the next chapter but suffice it to say, at this point, that *Color Field* represents the exact opposite of a conceptualization of an autonomous, self-sustaining teleology in a very narrow and peculiar Kantian or biological sense, wherein objects are observed as self-sufficient and independently existing. Don Garrett provides an excellent description of what it means to judge or assess an object teleologically:

> a teleological explanation explains why something is so by indicating what its being so is for. Somewhat more precisely, a teleological explanation is one that explains a state of affairs by indicating a likely or presumptive consequence (causal, logical, or conventional) of it that is implicated in the state's origin or etiology. Such consequences often, if not always, take the form of ends, goals, or goods.[6]

The important thing that we add to Garrett's description is the sense of autonomy, of independence, to the object; it's not just that there's an observable set of causal relations but also that those causal relations are fixed in the single object. To make a teleological judgment about an object is to see its purpose, and for us to see its purpose contained within itself without the need for external justification. Precisely because *Color Field* involved so many studio assistants, at all stages of its physical development, its dependence on external input means that it functions as a negative example illustrating the boundaries of the New Aesthetic objects that appear entirely independent even if they actually aren't. *Color Field* occupies a position of liminality, its digital origins just as clearly evident as its collective construction methods, that allows us to observe the permeation of the digital into *Color Field* to gauge how important its presence is, and how important its negation is sustained through the intense and obvious craft of Lou's work.

The boundary between artwork that seems to be New Aesthetic and actually is New Aesthetic is very thin, and seemingly permeable, but there are some specific criteria that are involved. Perhaps the most important criterion is not the fact that the work often is digital but that the work is driven by the technology itself amidst a postdigital condition. This has two corollaries. First, the work doesn't necessarily have to be digital but at least reflect the digital in its manifestation. Second, art of the New Aesthetic must be just as

---

6   Don Garrett, "Teleology in Spinoza and Early Modern Rationalism" in Gennaro, Rocco and Huenemann, Charles (eds), *New Essays on the Rationalists*, New York : Oxford University Press. 1999, p. 310.

much a product of technology, the digital and/or the postdigital as it is a product of the artist; the technology involved must be more than an opportunity or inspiration to make new art but should be a fundamentally generative component independent from the imaginative capacity and artistic skills of the artist. Benjamin Grosser, an American artist and composer working in new media, is an excellent example of this, especially in his series of art works that are part of the 'Flexible Pixels' project. Grosser writes:

> The pixel is the fundamental unit of digital imaging, a square representation of a single color. Pixels are always the same size, and always arranged in orderly grids. This project ['Flexible Pixels'] looks at what happens when you change these universally agreed upon standards. More broadly, I'm interested in how the construction of digital images alters our perceptions of reality. Does computer-mediated vision change how we see without computers?[7]

Grosser's *Variable Mirror* (2009), {Fig. 77} one of the works that are part of this series, shows how changes can take place in the standard relationship between pixel and image, transforming the normative paradigm that has been in place in the first digital images from the late 1950s into something that is more organic in nature.

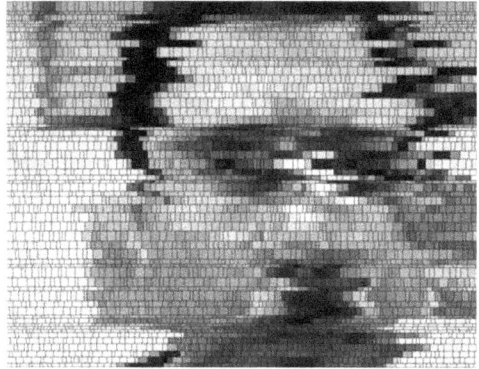

Fig. 77 Ben Grosser, still image capture from *Variable Mirror* (2009)

The result of *Variable Mirror, Self-Portrait 1x4x9* (2009) – an oil on canvas representation of the digital art work *Self Portrait (animated)* (2009 – and other works is, as Grosser indicates, that the general nature of our vision changes once pixels become increasingly independent entities. Through his art Grosser asserts that the way we see the world is fundamentally transformed not just when images are pixelated but when the resulting pixelization assumes a natural presence. This is the second most important criterion: the art must achieve a degree of autonomy in appearance and effect. In many ways, this

7   Benjamin Grosser, 'Flexible Pixels', 2009-11, *Benjamin Grosser*, http://bengrosser.com/projects/
     flexible-pixels/.

is the perfect starting point to distinguish between artists whose work resembles New Aesthetic objects by being products and artists whose work can be seen as evidence of the presence of the New Aesthetic attitude through a set of productive strategies. What Grosser is proposing is a deconstruction of the pixel as a standard structure of digital perception, but because the pixel remains such a fundamental element the deconstructive process shifts. Deconstruction is a term that's been misused and poorly applied since Derrida's *Of Grammatology* (1967), so much so that we're reluctant to use it, but here it seems appropriate in that the structure being investigated – the fundamental language of digital visual representation – begins to turn back on itself and takes apart its sense of a fixed function; the existence of its idea as an underlying notion embodied in *Variable Mirror* indicates more than just an 'unpacking' of the pixel, as a fundamental elementary aspect of the visualization of the digital work, but a relationship of the pixel to itself wherein the repetition reveals that the role of the pixel is no longer just a part of the representation but has an active identity. The perception of the visual presentation of digital information to human experience is revealed at an even more poignant and insightful level when it breaks into the real and achieves in its presentation a state that Manovich refers to as hybridity, where 'software simulation substitutes a variety of distinct materials and the tools used to inscribe information (i.e., make marks) on these materials with a new hybrid medium defined by a common data structure'.[8]

Variable Mirror, and the other examples of work from the 'Flexible Pixels' project, is an interactive work, during which the pixels used to represent the viewers as they look at it change dynamically and randomly but it's clear that its status as an example of New Aesthetic lies in the fact that the pixels are *actively representing* the viewers rather than the artist doing the representing. Typically, a viewer's reaction to a video presentation of themselves looking at the art would take place with the assumption that the fundamental units of the presentation would be fixed; instead, what Grosser's statement indicates is an artistic positioning and an exploration that creates a heightened awareness of the autonomy of the aesthetic agents involved – namely, the digital object as an autonomously functioning agent in relationship to the viewer – and the subsequent development of the pixel, at a fundamental level, as a continuously mediating and deferring referent that continually challenges any notion of certainty of identity, position and function. To put it another way, Grosser's *Variable Mirror* is a perfect instance of the effect of the New Aesthetic in art, in that the means of its production are not only an embodied reminder for the viewer of its digital origins and its continuing digital manifestation but also a reminder of the underlying uncertainty in the confrontation with the postdigital that is a growing characteristic of our world as it is driven by the specifics of its digital existence.

Grosser's work has developed a strong and variable approach to the New Aesthetic as an artistic strategy, representing a move beyond a form of art that participates to one

---

8   Manovich, *Software Takes Command*, p. 203.

that drives the production of the New Aesthetic by creating art objects that are fully New Aesthetic in their autonomy. One thing that's important to note about Grosser's career is that the work he has produced has been remarkably variable; some instances of it are very traditionally 'art' (e.g. his work from the late 1990s consists of abstract paintings) while other works break the boundaries of what art is often to the point of potentially, and erroneously, being labeled simply 'programming'. We will return to Grosser's oeuvre in the next section, but it's important to note here that we believe diversity, in all of its myriad connotations, is a key factor in identifying New Aesthetic art. By this we don't simply mean a diversity of forms but a diversity of references, models and paradigms. In every example of New Aesthetic art that we've looked at our first reaction has ranged from immediate and intuitive understanding of the intention and the effect to a deep appreciation of the beauty of the gestures and assertive aesthetic strategies, but all of this has been coupled with a sense of confusion as to how we are supposed to categorize New Aesthetic art. It couldn't be that we should just call it all 'New Aesthetic art' and be done with it, could it? At this stage, that will have to do, but we also want to emphasize that one primary element of all New Aesthetic art is diversity in form, function, intent, interactivity and effect.

Emphasizing that an important part of our consideration of the New Aesthetic is a recognition of the pervasive influence it has across the variety of human experience leads to us to look at different forms of art, which necessitates not only seeing evidence of the New Aesthetic effects in the visual arts but seeing them across a variety of different arts that have fallen outside of the scope of typical studies of art historical investigation. The creative projects of a team of artists working in dance and theatre, the Adrien M/Claire B Company, directed by Adrien Mondot and Claire Bardainne in Lyon, France[9], is one of the best examples of its presence across artistic disciplines. Since 2004, the company has been producing work that ranges across various artistic disciplines, but it would be fair to say that there's always been a performative, theatrical element driven by a virtual orientation in software or manifested as installation art. What makes the work of the Adrien M/Claire B Company interesting in the context of the New Aesthetic is the direct incorporation of software, designed and customized specifically for them, facilitating the interaction of the artists' activities with animated lighting and the projection of digitally developed visual textures. Regarding the company's artistic intentions:

> They place the human body at the heart of technological and artistic challenges and adapt today's technological tools to create a timeless poetry through a visual language based on playing and enjoyment, which breeds imagination.[10]

---

9   Adrien Mondot and Claire Bardainne, *Adrien M / Claire B*, http://www.am-cb.net/.

10   *Adrien M / Claire B.*

Different examples of their work reflect this exploration of the conjunction of the human presence and digital constructions in an imaginative fashion. *Convergence 1.0* (2005)[11] is a notable early work, in which a juggler uses virtual balls and interacts with phantasmal figures in ways that seemingly undercut physical laws of time and space. It is an exploration of the human presence of the performer while simultaneously being bound, in a suggestive fashion, by the restriction of the technology. *XYZT, Les paysages abstraits* (2011) {Fig. 78} already indicates in its title a concern for both a Cartesian and a relativistic geography, which the artists describe as follows:

Horizontal X

Vertical Y

Depth Z

Time T

These four letters are used to describe the movements unfolding at one point in space to reveal an imaginary territory. It is an exhibition landscaped by mathematical paradoxes, typographical illusions and metaphors in motion. Strolling through a luxuriant digital space, touching algorithms, sensing matter of light; some of the manifold imaginary fields are to be explored.

A pathway, as if traversing, revisiting nature; a coincidence between geometry and the organic: between real and virtual.[12]

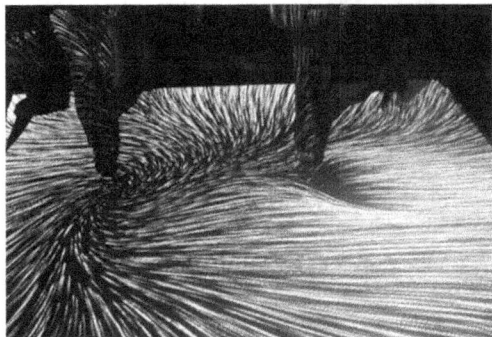

Fig. 78 Adrien M / Claire B Company, XYZT, *Les paysages abstraits* (2011)

---

11   Adrien Mondot and Claire Bardainne, 'Convergence 1.0', 2005, *Adrien M / Claire B*, http://www. am-cb.net/projets/convergence-1-0/.

12   Adrien Mondot and Claire Bardainne, 'XYZT, Les paysages abstraits', 2011, *Adrien M / Claire B*, http://www.am-cb.net/projets/xyzt/.

The very idea of digital space as luxuriant is fascinating, as is the notion of 'touching' algorithms, and through this conceptualization of a physicality in the digital, the Adrien M/Claire B Company is effectively presenting a notion of the digital as more than just an appearance of data fields but as a manifest presence in our world. This is most effectively realized in two different works: *Hakanaï* (2013) {Fig. 79} and *Le mouvement de l'air* (2015). {Fig. 80}

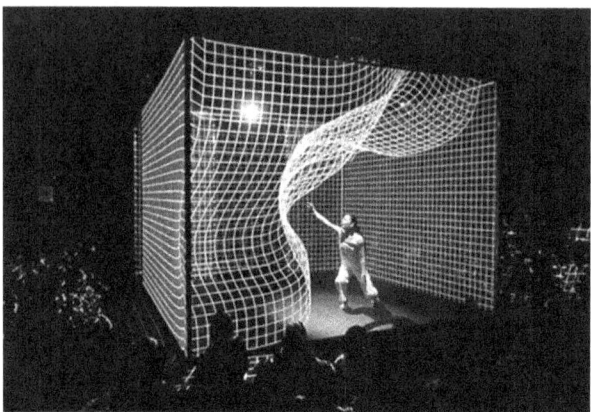

Fig. 79 Adrien M / Claire B Company, *Hakanaï* (2013)

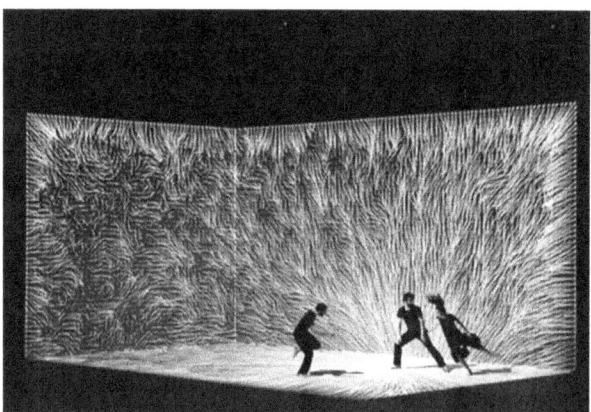

Fig. 80 Adrien M / Claire B Company, *Le mouvement de l'air* (2015)

With *Hakanaï*, which means fleeting, ephemeral or transient in Japanese, the 'performance's outcome is the revelation of a digital installation to its audience'[13] as the software responds to sounds generated by the dancer as she moves through the space and responds to imagery digitally projected around her by the software. In *Le mouvement*

---

13   Adrien Mondot and Claire Bardainne, 'Hakanaï', 2013, *Adrien M / Claire B*, http://www.am-cb.net/projets/hakanai/.

de l'air, three dancers move through an immersive environment of projected images; an important element of this performance is the physical space which is shaped responsively by the software. The designers hope this will be understood as more than just a 'technical achievement, what matters is the attempt at creating a motion dreamscape by way of images'.[14] This sense of digital presence in a cooperative, responsive partnership makes both *Hakanaï* and *Le mouvement de l'air* particularly strong candidates as examples of New Aesthetic art. *Hakanaï* is, according to the artists, a transposition of a term normally associated with processes in the natural world, but which here reflects the transience of the interactive experience between the human and the digital as separate artistic agents. *Le mouvement de l'air* takes this even further, using aerial dance and other movements in an interactive fashion that is never rehearsed nor previously animated.

> This "living light" is produced by video projectors and generated in real time by a set of algorithms [...] It is a mix of control room operated human interventions and on-stage data sensors that outlines a precise writing of motions and generative behaviors. Thus, the images are never pre-recorded for a rigid show on an imposed rhythm: on the contrary, they breathe and move with the dancers and organize a new space for them to explore.[15]

It's this notion of a 'living light' that breaks the company's performances out of the normal modes of theater or performance art and makes them examples of the New Aesthetic. The notion that the light and images are released freely to function collaboratively with the performers implies a conceptualization of these effects that originate and manifest themselves in and through the digital, which could be disconcerting but isn't; given the emphasis in theater and performance art on the human element as the aesthetic agent or vehicle, when the props become actors then something should seem amiss but it isn't. Adrien Mondot's and Claire Bardainne's work is beautiful and also incredibly interesting because it signals a syncretic partnership between two contrasting elements wherein one, the digital, signals its increasing independent presence into the human performative components. Ultimately, the overall effect exhibits many of the characteristics of New Aesthetic art.

An important characteristic of New Aesthetic art is a level of interactivity that is decreasingly seamless and increasingly apparent, contradicting many of the tenets of modernist design. The independence of the digital objects in the work of the Adrien M/Claire B Company exemplifies this. Interactivity has long been an important aspect of digital

---

14   Adrien Mondot and Claire Bardainne, 'Le mouvement de l'air', 2015, *Adrien M / Claire B,* http://www.am-cb.net/projets/air/.

15   Christopher Jobson, 'The Movement of Air: A New Dance Performance Incorporating Interactive Digital Projection from Adrien M & Claire B', 11 November 2015, *This is Colossal,* http://www.thisiscolossal.com/2015/11/movement-of-air-dance/.

objects, a paradigm that shifts through different GUIs and appears in various physical forms often accompanied by a great deal of debate as to the level of skeuomorphism necessary to insure an efficient experience. Thinking about the level of interactivity as a part of New Aesthetic art might seem obvious – the whole point of software design is, at times, a facilitation of users' interaction and manipulation of data, and artists using digital tools have gravitated to interactive art precisely because the technology encourages it – but something different takes place when the digital objects become New Aesthetic digital objects. In terms of an aesthetic evaluation, a duality emerges in postdigital and New Aesthetic objects, so that what we mean by interactive isn't quite the same anymore; rather, for our purposes, interaction in New Aesthetic art is the seamless integration of digital activity into the artistic process that occurs while simultaneously having the digital aspects be autonomously responsive to the artist's choices and actions. We're taking this notion of interaction directly from Lev Manovich, who writes:

> After the novel, and subsequently cinema, privileged narrative as the key form of cultural expression of the modern age, the computer age introduces its correlate – the database. Many new media objects do not tell stories; they do not have a beginning or end; in fact, they do not have any development, thematically, formally, or otherwise that would organize their elements into a sequence. Instead, they are collections of individual items, with every item possessing the same significance as any other.[16]

This is a remarkably interesting thing to state. Manovich is strongly asserting that interactivity is increasingly unavailable, that most digital objects are merely means of facilitating access to databases of information, meaning interfaces, or are predetermined in a standardized modularity, meaning that they exist not only as interfaces but also as building blocks, rather than offering genuine forms of interaction with the objects themselves. Furthermore, Manovich's implication in suggesting the primacy of standardized modularity is the basis for his disavowal of traditional narrative structures that are normally considered an essential aspect of non-digital, traditional art. Manovich's disavowal of narrative is an exclusionary theoretical strategy favoring an autonomous agency to digital objects that don't create experiences but shape data sets. Amidst the increasing efforts of governments to control their populations through security devices like facial and pattern recognition, this reduces the participation of citizens to dehumanized and inactivated information references. Movies like *Metropolis* (1927) and *Minority Report* (2002) and television shows like *Person of Interest* (2011-present) may represent a dystopic vision of computer programs (or human 'programs') observing our every moment, a prospect most people find a frightening invasion of privacy; far more dehumanizing is the fact that most people are classified as too uninteresting to warrant any extended attention while they are, still, continually subjected to this surveillance. Manovich's art counters this by mimicking it, trying to make the datafication of our lives in his art the means to understand and respond to its negative effects in our daily lives.

---

16   Manovich, *The Language of New Media*, p. 218.

The Individual Politicalization of New Aesthetic Art

A number of New Aesthetic artistic responses explore this situation and we want to high-light three of them: the work of Adam Harvey, Zach Blas and the collective Metahaven. Symptomatic of this response to the agency of interactivity is the work of Adam Harvey.[17] Harvey's art has become well known for being at the forefront of the artistic exploration of security and privacy issues, in particular focusing on the imbalance and power asym-metries between surveillance technology and basic human rights. Three recent projects starkly project Harvey's clear understanding of the insidiousness of surveillance tech-nology and its negative effects: *CV Dazzle* (2010) {Fig. 81},[18] *Stealth Wear* (2013) and the *Privacy Gift Shop* (2013)[19] that was on display in the New Museum, New York City, in 2016.

CV Dazzle is our primary focus, as it's clear that the other two projects share their origins and concerns with it; inspired by the camouflage patterns used by British and American navy ships during WWI that were based on modernist art styles of geometric patterns,[20] *CV Dazzle* simi-larly is an effort to obscure or defeat pattern and facial recognition algorithms used by security services across many levels of contemporary society from national government organizations to local shopping malls; moreover it is a conceptual reaction to OpenCV,[21] an open sourced software used for facial recognition, and a clear response to the Janus program's efforts to utilize social media to improve facial recognition with algorithmically driven databases.[22]

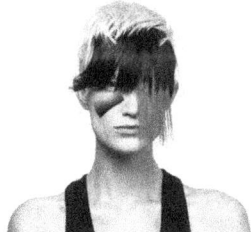

Fig. 81 Adam Harvey, *CV Dazzle* (2010)

---

17   Adam Harvey, *Adam Harvey Projects*, http://ahprojects.com/.

18   Adam Harvey, *CV Dazzle*, https://cvdazzle.com/.

19   Adam Harvey, *Undisclosed*, https://undisclosed.cc/.

20   Which, we must point out, are generally regarded as entirely ineffective. Designed by the English artist Norman Wilkinson, it was intended less to hide and more to confuse the targeting technology of the day. Further, no evidence exists that it was inspired by Cubism except Picasso's own claim. C.f. Wikipedia contributors, 'Dazzle camouflage'.

21   Eugene Kurutepe, 'Face Recognition with OpenCV', *objc.io*, February 2015, https://www.objc.io/issues/21-camera-and-photos/face-recognition-with-opencv/.

22   Terry Adams (project manager), 'Janus', Research Programs, Office of the Director of National Intelligence, http://www.iarpa.gov/index.php/research-programs/janus.

Much of current thought regarding surveillance is extremely pessimistic, rightly so in regards to most concerns, with Metahaven recently noting:

> The preemptive electronic surveillance of potentially every global subject can be thought of as a way for governments to weaponize themselves against the capacity of every person or group in society to change spontaneously – expanding the state's monopoly on violence into precognitive policing of all thought and action [...] Today, every person's capacity to evade surveillance is determined by their position in a feudal matric of technological and institutional dependencies. Almost all antidotes to this patronizing system of global surveillance go under shades of black.[23]

CV Dazzle is one of those exemptions, an almost aggressive artistic response to governments' efforts at creating a self-justifying program of policies and technological tools designed to dismantle individual privacy. Whereas Metahaven is absolutely correct to describe these intrusive efforts as the violent weaponization of surveillance – we're adding to their description that the process of weaponization itself has been violent, adding to the violence in an exponential fashion, something we believe is not out of line with their thinking – *CV Dazzle* is an effort to weaponize individual appearances in an effort to oppose governmental incursions into privacy. Utilizing makeup, hair styling, clothing and accessories in a manner that parallels high concept fashion, Harvey is addressing the need to avoid not just detection but constant observation: it's not so much that the average citizen needs to camouflage themselves but that the continual identification, location and tracking of their persons is more than just intrusive in that it establishes a continual condition of suspicion; we are being observed not to protect us from threats but because it is believed any one of us might become a threat. The result, and the artistic value of *CV Dazzle*, is in the active confrontation that the user employs against surveillance; by using makeup, hairstyle and fashion design in a manner that is excessively visible to the ordinary people the 'dazzled' individual now hides in plain sight.

This last point is where *CV Dazzle* enters the realm of the New Aesthetic as art, as noted in the curious remark in *dis* magazine that 'CV Dazzle is an unobvious style of camouflage because its eye-catching patterns and colors draw attention instead of hiding from it'[24] along with the paraphrased instructions, borrowing from Harvey's own website, that enhancing makeup should be avoided, the nosebridge should be obscured, the area around the eyes needs to appear altered and, perhaps most importantly, 'Remain inconspicuous [...] For camouflage to function, it must not be perceived as a mask or disguise. NB: Wearing masks or disguises can be illegal in some cities, including here in

---

23   Metahaven (Daniël van der Velden and Vinca Kruk) *Black Transparency: The Right to Know in the Age of Mass Surveillance*, Berlin: Sternberg Press, 2015, p. 3.

24   Adam Harvey, 'How to Hide from Machines: The Perilous Glamour of Life Under Surveillance', *dis magazine*, http://dismagazine.com/dystopia/evolved-lifestyles/8115/anti-surveillance-how-to-hide-from-machines/.

NYC.'[25] What's curious about these instructions revolves around the contrasting char-acterization of these strategies to both remain unobvious and to not demand attention, which is almost an impossibility. To put it another way, it's clear that there's a difficult balance between not being identified and not being noticed, a difficulty that *CV Dazzle* virtuously fails at and, in a way, it's precisely at that point of failure that *CV Dazzle* becomes art. This contrast appears also in the article 'Reverse-engineering Artist Busts Face Detection Tech' that notes that *CV Dazzle* 'combines hipster fashion aesthetics with hardcore reverse engineering of face detection software. The goal: to give individuals a low-cost and visually stimulating means to prevent their likenesses from being detected and cataloged by face-recognition monitors.'[26] *CV Dazzle* is dependent on a heightened awareness of being observed with a desire or need to avoid being observed precisely by being almost excessively observable, an attitude based entirely on a heightened aware-ness that digital surveillance is far more threatening than human surveillance. Our focus on this contrast is based on our own awareness of the conditions that make Harvey's art possible, equally evident in the work from the series *Stealth Wear* {Fig. 82} that is described thus: 'Collectively, Stealth Wear is a vision for fashion that addresses the rise of surveillance, the power of those who surveil, and the growing need to exert control over what we are slowly losing, our privacy.'[27]

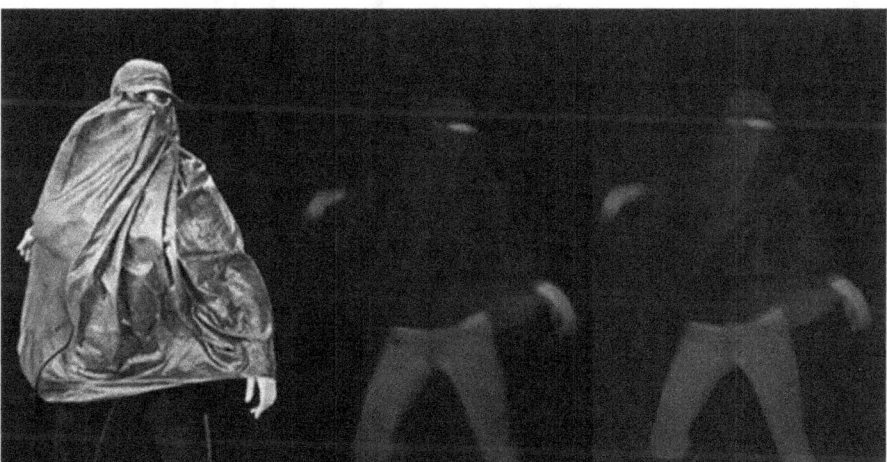

Fig. 82 Adam Harvey, *Stealth Wear* (2013)

Without the increasingly effective digital technology driving facial recognition, without the generation of ever larger databases, there's no need for *CV Dazzle* and *Stealth Wear;*

25   Harvey, 'How to Hide from Machines'.

26   Dan Goodin, "Reverse-engineering artist busts face detection tech", *The Register*, April, 2010, http://www.theregister.co.uk/2010/04/22/face_detection_hacking/.

27   Adam Harvey Projects: Stealth Wear, https://ahprojects.com/projects/stealth-wear/.

it is precisely the conditions they seek to counter that define the validity of its efforts, but it's also precisely the impossible success of these efforts that define their artistic value. As the description of the Janus program notes: 'Data volume now becomes an integral part of the solution instead of an oppressive burden.'[28] It's as if the volume of data has taken on a life of its own, self-determinatively driving initiatives in an autonomous fashion, with CV Dazzle reflecting an unconscious concession on the part of its participants that their participation is a foregone conclusion. Not only does this drive CV Dazzle and Stealth Wear into the category of New Aesthetic art but because the first is itself merely the product of research that consists entirely of a set of programmed instructions interfacing with algorithmically driven surveillance programs, because the second are 'fashion' items with a strong political effect, and because both are sets of non-digital products whose effects are entirely digital because the need they address is digital makes them almost gloriously and interdependently substantiated at an artistic level through the repetition of their own aesthetic conditions. Because the artistic material's subversive effect is dependent on its programmed response to its subject matter, whereby the subject becomes the grounds for the subversion of the subject, CV Dazzle and Stealth Wear are two of the best examples of New Aesthetic art, as is much of the work of Harvey, because they negotiate the increasingly complex and irresolvable relationships of the digital and the ordinary. Once the repetition is there, once the aesthetic programming takes place self-referentially, an important shift is evident.

In line with Édouard Glissant's notion of opacity, that focuses on breaking the divisions between hierarchies in the art world through a reconsideration of postcolonialism that emphasizes a lack of transparency against the continual demands of social and cultural structures to account for oneself, Zach Blas' work addresses many of the same issues as Harvey's. For one, it also addresses the complex issues of facial recognition as an intrusion into privacy rights, but his Facial Weaponization Suite (2013)[29] {Fig. 83} takes a different and more intriguing artistic strategy.[30]

As noted by Blas, Facial Weaponization Suite was created in part as a response to the New York City Police Department's invocation of the 1845 law banning two or more people congregating together while wearing masks during the 2011 Occupy Wall Street movement; not only did the NYPD arrest protestors for wearing Guy Fawkes masks, they then subjected them to iris scans for inclusion in a database of offenders as a condition of bail or release. Blas asks:

---

28   Terry Adams (project manager), 'Janus'.

29   Zach Blas, https://www.flickr.com/photos/zachblas/.

30   Zach Blas, 'Escaping the Face: Biometric Facial Recognition and the Facial Weaponization Suite',
      Journal of the New Media Caucus, 2013, http://median.newmediacaucus.org/caa-conference-
      edition-2013/escaping-the-face-biometric-facial-recognition-and-the-facial-weaponization-suite/.

Why does the masked protestor pose such a great threat to the state, resulting in the police's willingness to deploy a 168-year-old law originally designed to prevent Hudson Valley tenant farmers from dressing in disguise and rioting over debt and eviction? Why does facelessness fuel the state of New York to surreptitiously construct incentives for protestors to willingly agree to biometric scans?[31]

The answer to that question seems obvious – there isn't much difference between the aims of 19th century rioters and the Wall Street protestors, especially as both of them had very legitimate grievances and aims – but Blas' inquiry after the value of facelessness is itself very interesting. Protestors' identities are clearly valued by those trying to control the apparatus of social structures. {Fig. 84}

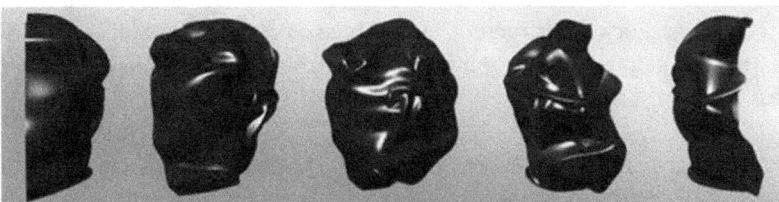

Fig. 83 Zach Blas, *Facial Weaponization Suite* (2013)

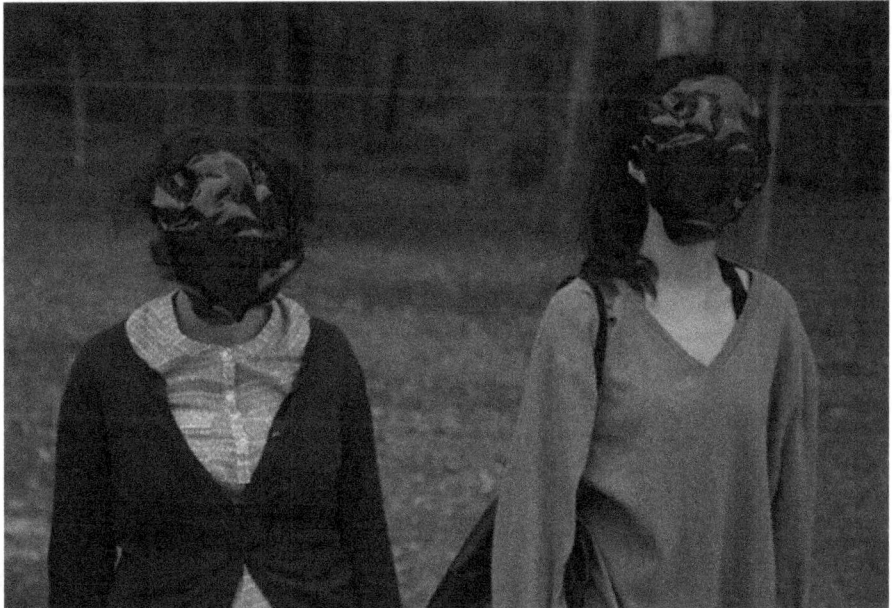

Fig. 84 Zach Blas, *Facial Weaponization Suite* (2013), 'Protest Line / Face Off' Tableau Vivant

---

31   Zach Blas, 'Escaping the Face'.

For Blas 'the face becomes a site of ever increasing control and governance' and his *Facial Weaponization Suite* is specifically a means of arming individuals against those efforts at control in a manner similar to Berry's articulation of 'obfuscated code'[32] resulting in 'data exhaustion'.[33] At the same time, *Facial Weaponization Suite* is more than just an experiment but is an elegantly aggressive artistic response to a crucial issue of our contemporary world, like Hito Steyerl notes:

> While a lot of contemporary technologically oriented art tries to resuscitate the wreckage of Futurism, or overidentifies with strategies of surgical marketing and apple polishing, Blas's work insists that one doesn't need to brand oneself into voluntary servitude or to eagerly identify with the aggressor. It may well suffice to fuck him. Or her. Or it. It's such a reasonable idea and possibly much more fun too! Fuck military technology. Fuck infrastructure. Fuck drones. Fuck protocol 'til it hums with pleasure. Throw in glitter and some shiny sensors. And after a few million years, there might be a smashing progeny![34]

In response to Shoshana Amielle Magnet's argument that biometric recognition is a failure because human identity cannot be reduced to a data set, and working through Agamben's idea of exposure vis-à-vis Levinas, the *Facial Weaponization Suite* is a set of masks made in community workshops that deny facial recognition software algorithmically applicable data. While functioning as masks, the objects of the *Suite* 'are weapons of defacement, modes of escaping the recognition-control of the face, a queer illegibility that disallows easy calculations and categorizations of the face'.[35] This makes them dramatically different from Harvey's work (though both are equivalent aesthetically, in our opinion), not simply because Blas' work consists of actual objects rather than aesthetic strategies of concealment but also because their overt nature as objects is a demonstrative and declamatory response to the intrusion into privacy; driven by communal production methods that incorporate discussion of the related issues, participants are scanned by a Kinect and a single mask is generated in a non-averaged manner of all of the participants, making the communal statement even more substantial because it is heightened by a public intervention. Where the New Aesthetic comes into the work isn't simply at the level of the object's production or its motivation but, similar to Harvey, out of the necessary conditions of the increasingly digitalized nature of the world and our place in it. While Harvey's work might be unfairly construed as a fashion statement of

---

32   Berry, *Critical Theory and the Digital*, p. 192.

33   Berry, *Critical Theory and the Digital*, p. 209.

34   Hito Steyerl, 'Zach Blas Future Great 2014', *ArtReview*, March 2014, http://artreview.com/features/2014_futuregreats_zach_blas/.

35   Blas, 'Escaping the Face'.

sorts, and is complicit with the conditions its protesting to a degree, Blas' *Suite* is about the creation of art as weapons with a singularity to their appearance that is unmistakably one of denying the value of identification even to the point of denying social reciprocity through defacement. As Blas names them: 'interfaces in other modalities that are not readable to those that aim to control but rather communicates to all those that strive to liberate'.[36] In short, Blas' *Suite* is an artistic acknowledgement, through rejection, of the existence of the New Aesthetic as a pervasive influence in our lives; it is a rejection of digital modalities as agents that had found their conceptual reification already in the NYPD's valuation of the protestors' identities, a condition which most certainly did not originate in the human agents of the police but out of its ever changing nature as an institution.

---

36   Blas, 'Escaping the Face'.

The Collective Politicalization of New Aesthetic Art

In a way with which we completely agree, the collective Metahaven[37] has been described as 'one of the most theoretically informed, strategically adept and articulate groups of thinkers operating in graphic design'.[38] As noted by Sarah Hromack in *Frieze* magazine, Metahaven's work can be identified as a response to the specific conditions generated by the introduction of web 2.0 around the turn of the millennium, and it's worthwhile summarizing her position. For Hromack, a major shift starting taking place in the internet in the 1990s – described in two important essays: Michael Rock's 1996 'The Designer as Author'[39] and Ellen Lupton's 1998 'The Designer as Producer'[40] and related to Walter Benjamins' 1934 essay 'The Author is Producer' – that signals not only an increasing level of interactivity through the internet as a medium but also an increasingly fraught level of a politicized driven denial of the central and authoritative voice of the author. Hromack writes:

> The fallout from Web 2.0 has been nothing short of astounding. The internet that once seemed open and free has been transformed into a dystopia of double meanings and commercial and political dealings. Ingrained psychological dependencies have developed out of brightly blinking "user friendly" experiences, monitored by businesses and government agencies.[41]

She traces this fallout as a direct catalyst for the formation of Metahaven. Metahaven has been described insufficiently as an international collective of graphic designers, and it might be more accurate to describe them as a group of artists whose work draws from the changing graphic nature of the world in a way that is disruptive and disconcerting, but at its roots it consists of the Amsterdam based artists Vinca Kruk and Daniel van der Velden. Their largest publication to date was *Uncorporate Identity* (2006), a monumental treatment of the relationships between databases, national identity, networks as social objects driving social norms, branding and the very idea of readability about which one Amazon customer wrote:

> it is a very bizarre book.

---

37   Metahaven, http://www.metahaven.net/.

38   Rick Poynor, 'Borderline: Metahaven makes visual proposals that suggest a new role for graphic design in public life', *Eye Magazine*, no. 71 vol. 18, 2009, http://www.eyemagazine.com/feature/article/borderline.

39   Michael Rock,'The designer as author', *Eye Magazine*, 1996, http://www.eyemagazine.com/feature/article/the-designer-as-author.

40   Ellen Lupton, 'The Designer as Producer,' *The Education of a Graphic Designer*, (ed.) Steven Heller, New York: Allworth Press, 1998, pp. 159-62, http://elupton.com/2010/10/the-designer-as-producer/.

41   Sarah Hromack, 'What is Metahaven?', *frieze* magazine, issue 175, 2015, http://www.frieze.com/issue/article/what-is-metahaven/.

The typography is okay, the printing and binding is good [...] but the design is shockingly awful: there are weird effects that you shouldn't use if you want to communicate trustworthiness and confidence such as amateur effects like drop shadows, hyperactive gradients and also seems to be on trend with this "exposed content style" – I would go so far to say it looks like very bad 90s Flash websites with all these superfluous elements that generate a feeling of schizophrenia and anxiety almost. I read the texts but they don't really offer any practical advice or useful analysis about branding and corporate identity useful to a branding designer – for example how to deal with the internet and social media, what good form and harmony in application is and so on.[42]

In a way, this review is absolutely telling: the book is bizarre, it does break many of the assumed rules of good design, it eschews trustworthiness and reeks of a bad use of Flash in printed form, and ultimately drives a sense of distrust into a dialogue focused on branding and corporate identity.

Metahaven's aesthetic impulses are driven by a striking awareness of artists' complicity in the increasingly overwhelming nature of the digital in the world, and are neatly encapsulated in a statement from the trailer for their film project *The Sprawl* (2015): {Fig. 85} 'We were very likely spreading fictitious information ourselves, but couldn't help it.'[43]

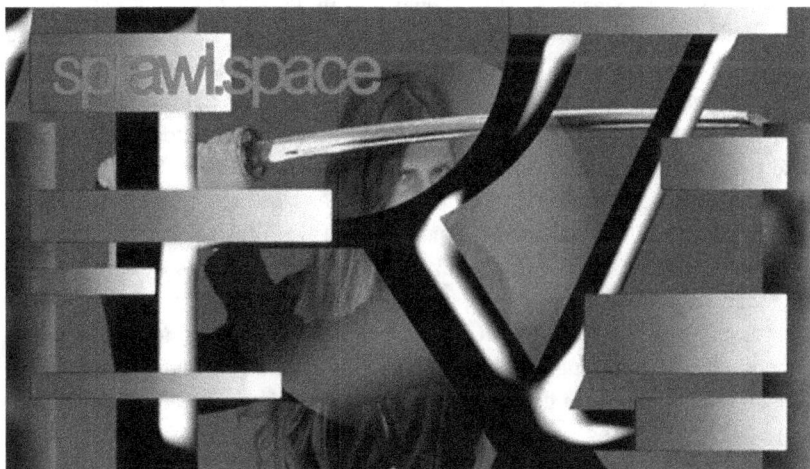

Fig. 85 Metahaven, *The Sprawl* (2015)

---

42   Big_Fisted_BB, Amazon Customer Review, 'Weird and disappointing', January 6 2014, http://www. amazon.com/Uncorporate-Identity-Daniel-van-Velden/dp/3037781696.

43   Metahaven, The Sprawl (Propaganda About Propaganda). 'THE SPRAWL (PROPAGANDA ABOUT PROPAGANDA) – Official Trailer'. Filmed [2015]. Youtube video, 2:58. Posted January 2016, https:// youtu.be/Bs7NFbE2NS8.

Metahaven's work takes exception with the internet's general status as a neutral medium by challenging our complicity with it. For most users, the internet has not become a medium by which we interact with others nor a generative new field of social discourse but instead has simply become a utility, with the consequences being that we unthinkingly, uncritically accept the parameters of its usage because we've become habituated and conditioned to its manipulations. For Metahaven, this situation needs to be transformed, and the best means of doing so is through the use of methods that borrow from the internet's own means of manipulation, with the aim 'to explore how fantasy and propaganda have now gained prominence over transparency and accountability [...] The relationship between social media and geopolitics is not just about liberal democracy anymore but about the fashion of spectral totalitarianism.'[44] Through a changing membership and a constant shift in the forms of production, the group has taken on ephemera-like visual objects of corporate identity, webpage design, GUI forms, barcodes and URL addresses in a manner which appears directionless at first but, on further examination, quickly is understood as an attenuation to nationalist digital iconographies and their inherent conflict with multinational and even hypernational ones (by which we corporate entities that have assumed the status of international sovereign entities). Metahaven gives more than a simple aesthetic response but rather creates an active aesthetic running counter to prevailing tendencies, distinguished by its incorporation of corporate representational forms that appears to be sustained by the visual link to those corporations while questioning the underlying persuasiveness of the neutrality of those same entities amidst the supposed 'equality' available to all entities in the capitalist system. In a manner similar to the Neue Slowenische Kunst group's appropriation of National Socialist imagery that was mixed with propaganda from the Tito era of Yugoslavia, Metahaven has produced objects whose use-value is both questionable and secure in a self-contradictory dialectic; the scarves and t-shirts sold as part of the *Dark Store* (2012) installation in the Artists Space at the Berlin Contemporary Art Fair were both collectable luxury items and being covered in camouflage and the Wikileaks logo were simultaneously protests against government privacy intrusions.[45] Metahaven's recent book *Black Transparency: The Right to Know in the Age of Mass Surveillance* (Sternberg Press, 2015) raises similar issues while equally being a confounding text that is far from a traditional book but that functions as a reading experience while at the same time serving as a manual to counter the effects of the digital age. One review captures its intense contradictory effect, a governing feature of Metahaven's aesthetic strategies:

> Part essay, part zine, the Amsterdam-based design studio's book focuses on the "how" as opposed to the "what" of transparency, zeroing in on the paradox that the fight for accessible knowledge (by groups such as WikiLeaks) is often carried out through

---

44   The Space Commission, 'The Sprawl', October, 2014, http://www.lighthouse.org.uk/programme/
      the-space-commission-the-sprawl.

45   *Metahaven blog*, http://mthvn.tumblr.com/post/13736369881/wikileaksscarf04.

necessarily opaque and propagandistic means. *Black Transparency* swallows its own tail in pursuit of its subject, following the un-coiling and re-coiling of ideology and information at the hands of whistleblowers and organizations.[46]

It's as if Metahaven is proposing that the only effective counter to the complete erosion of our private lives, our individuality and the means of our own self-determinativeness is to set up a reified antithesis in the Hegelian sense, opposing the dominance of the digital world as a thesis. In line with Marshall McLuhan's idea of a 'counter-environment' in his 1967 essay 'The Invisible Environment: The Future of an Erosion',[47] Metahaven's *Facestate* (2011) is a complicated installation at the Walker Art Center consisting of various objects apparently produced as examples of graphic design in line with the corporate identity of Facebook but clearly opposed to its aims. 'We are interested in the ways in which Facebook and government, Facebook and employers, Facebook and friends, Facebook and enemies constitute a power arrangement, and the way in which this constellation might influence politics, currency, and the social contract.'[48]

Metahaven's concerns for the totalitarian effect of increasingly autonomous digital objects of control is shared worldwide, though most often only in a nascent form in comparison to their sophisticated approach on a multiplicity of levels, and their targeting of Facebook is emblematic of the concerns of many other artists. It's been pointed out that their work 'questions the purpose and value of design in a neurotic and treacherous era of geopolitical instability, economic recession, environmental crisis, cultural and moral confusion'[49] but just as importantly their work questions the value of our existence as end users, bringing up the notion that we are nothing but components of the technology that give it a functioning life rather than individuals able to utilize our digital devices freely to our own ends; responding to this art leads to the inevitable conclusion that we don't constitute the network of power but are merely components of the network's power. Metahaven's strategy of countering corporate propaganda with appropriated propaganda seems as effective as any other strategy these days, but is it capable of being effective outside of a 'westernized' context? What happens when the invasion of the digital is so rapid, when changes in technology are so swift, as they have been in developing countries of the 'non-western' world that no response is even possible because the territories have

46   Thom Bettridge, 'Coup de Net: METAHAVEN's "Black Transparency"', *032c*, 20 November 2015, http://032c.com/2015/coup-de-net-metahavens-black-transparency/.

47   Robert Wiesenberger, 'METAHAVEN: Somewhere Near You, Soon', *032c*, Summer 2014, http://032c.com/2014/metahaven-somewhere-near-you-soon/.

48   Quoted in Andrea Hyde, 'Metahaven's *Facestate* Social Media and the State', *Walker*, 13 December 2011, http://www.walkerart.org/magazine/2011/metahavens-facestate.

49   Alice Rawsthorn, 'A Quest for Meaning in a Dystopian Era', *The New York Times*, 16 May 2010, http://nyti.ms/1LyRL8W.

already been claimed and secured? Typing in 'non-western new aesthetics' gets you zero relevant results on Google, but anyone who has travelled to Africa, South America, India and 'less-developed' parts of Asia has experienced the widespread impact of internet culture. Perhaps more so than in the westernized social and cultural structures, where the increasing inclusion of the digital has been relatively gradual, the effect of the internet and its subsequent disappearance into the portals of smartphone apps as a means of navigating, defining and shaping human experience has been remarkably profound; whereas many in the developed world experienced the shift from dial-up modems (and the joy of moving from 14.4k to 56k!) to dedicated ISPs through cable, most people in the developing world have experienced the digital transformation through smartphone simply because it was more economical to build centralized cell phone towers than to try and implement land lines to every home. When digital content is provided exclusively through smartphone apps, with the individualized specificity of that experience governing the use-experience, then the shift from a non-digitized world to a digitized world is even more abrupt. This has resulted in some interesting effects. Very recently the Telecom Regulatory Authority of India forbid zero-rating mobile internet plans because they violated net-neutrality,[50] thereby denying Mark Zuckerberg's plan to provide free internet through mobile phones across India through a Facebook portal called 'Free Basics', after having prompted protests[51] and an organized campaign.[52] What's strange, however, is that the debate isn't quite settled; while many in India and elsewhere oppose Zuckerberg's plan because it violates net neutrality, the very idea of net neutrality may no longer exist in part because the internet no longer exists. The notion that 'smart villages' would be a means of relieving the burden of crowded urban centers seems fanciful at best, as does the notion that 'increased' access to information will invariably lead to improvements in people's lives regardless of whether or not this information is filtered through portals like Facebook or Google. Digital organisms, institutions, or functional objects (however you want to identify them) have shifted from being automatons within the internet to autonomous agents defining the internet.

This position is evidently symptomatic of the effect of the New Aesthetic across a broader range of cultures. The majority of artists discussed in this book are European, American or Japanese, presumably because the work by these artists is more readily accessible through the internet and art exhibitions in major Western cities where funding and a critical mass of technological means makes it easy. But what's happening in the rest

---

50   Daniel van Boom,'Why India snubbed Facebook's free Internet offer', *CNET*, 26 February 2016, http://www.cnet.com/news/why-india-doesnt-want-free-basics/.

51   TNN, 'Students, techies protest Facebook's Free Basics', *The Times of India*, 3 January 2016, http://timesofindia.indiatimes.com/city/bengaluru/Students-techies-protest-Facebooks-Free-Basics/articleshow/50424303.cms?utm_source=twitter.com&utm_medium=referral&utm_campaign=TOIBangalore.

52   *Save The Internet*, https://www.savetheinternet.in/.

of the world? Is the New Aesthetic a phenomenon or an attitude that is confined to a Western setting? Even the briefest of consideration of these questions would correct the tendencies to be absorbed with just one location, and a recent article in *The Guardian* sent us looking at African art and the presence of the New Aesthetic in a politicized social context.[53] A prime instance of this is Urban FabLab's project African Fabbers,[54] an effort to bring together European and African maker communities with an emphasis on open source software and alternative approaches to 3D printing. Run in two sessions – in Marrakesh (2014) and Dakar (2014), both associated with art fair events in those cities – its aim was to create 'an opportunity to creative clusters from different continents and backgrounds to meet up and share knowledge, to investigate the interaction between African material systems and computer aided manufacturing technologies, to create ecological prototypes through an advanced craftsmanship approach for sustainable living'.[55] Two interesting elements of the African Fabbers projects are noteworthy: first, there's an emphasis on the collaboration between levels of technology, with the implication being that older forms must necessarily be paired with newer, digital forms for their continued survival; second, such a collaboration itself necessitates an inherent valuation of advanced technology and its associated cultural forms or, to put it another way, despite the best of intentions this is still a form of cultural colonialism driven by technology. The Venn diagram on the main page for African Fabbers shows it as the intersection between local technologies, digital fabrication and computation design but the imbalance is plainly evident. How to counter this? The Afropixel[56] festival at Ker Thiossäne, Dakar certainly represents one effort. Begun in different forms in 2002, with the first official Afropixel event taking place in 2008, it's based on the idea that 'Technology doesn't prevent tradition from existing, it's the encounter between the two that is interesting'[57] but at the same time it exhibits all of the hallmarks of New Aesthetic art with assertions like 'Any designer will tell you that a pixel is the smallest element of a picture; a dot on a page. On its own, a pixel doesn't give much away. But when it joins other pixels it forms a whole, contributes to a mass, and gives meaning to whatever it is it represents'[58] on

---

53   Contributions from the African Digital Art (http://africandigitalart.com/), 'Africa Remix: The Artists Subverting Colonial Imagery', *The Guardian*, 11 February 2015, http://www.theguardian.com/world/2015/feb/11/africa-remix-artists-reinvent-colonial-imagery.

54   Urban FabLab, 'African Fabbers Project', 2016, http://www.urbanfablab.it/african-fabber/23-non-categorizzato/projects/53-african-fabbers.html.

55   Urban FabLab, 'African Fabbers Project'.

56   Kër Thiossane, http://www.ker-thiossane.org/.

57   Marion Louisgrand-Sylla, 'Interview: The Story of Ker Thiossäne, Villa for Art and Multimedia', 2010, http://www.ker-thiossane.org/spip.php?article10.

58   Moleskine, 'Afropixel: Using Evernote Notebooks to Spread Knowledge', 2014, 'http://www.moleskine.com/us/news/afropixel4.

the website of its sponsor Moleskine, who provided all of the participants with Evernote ready notebooks in 2014.

It's clear that a collective response is occurring in a New Aesthetic context, but individual artists are also working in a similar fashion. Folasade Adeoso has become well known both as a model from Nigeria and as an artist in her own right; her digital work consists of juxtaposed images that are often haunting, nostalgic, and jarring in their contrast between references to an older way of life and to digital artifacts. Especially in her series 'Kinfolk' (2014) {Fig. 86} there is an indication of Adeoso articulating a sensibility informed by technology, utilizing it for aesthetic purposes, aware of the temptations for its overuse, but deeply resistant to its intrusive and pervasive influences.

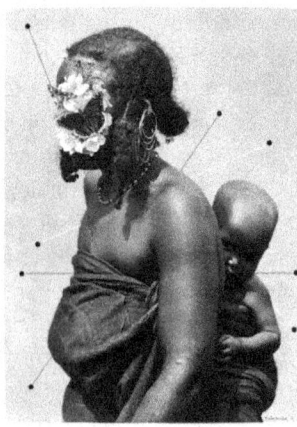

Fig. 86 Folasade Adeoso, *Motherhood,* from the series *Kinfolk* (2014)

Alexander Ikhide's work functions in a similar manner as Adeoso's but is more informed by an urban sensibility; originally from Nigeria and now working in London, Ikhide's collages mix the old and the new but in a way that's strikingly more contemporary, evidenced especially in his collaboration with the photographer Seye Isikalu on the project *Don't Police My Masculinity* (2015)[59] that incorporates the beautiful phrase 'Love Yourself As Much As Kanye Loves Kanye' by asserting: 'In a world where Hyper-masculinity is unfailingly sold to us on a daily basis, "Don't Police My Masculinity" playfully explores ideas of self-love, self-acceptance & general care-freeness of the Black Male in particular. Happy valentine's day people! love yourselves first!'[60] {Fig. 87}

---

59   Fashionably Male, 'Don't Police My Masculinity – Alexander Ikhide by Seye Isikalu', *Fashionably Male*, 14 February 2015, http://fashionablymale.net/2015/02/14/dont-police-my-masculinity-alexander-ikhide-by-seye-isikalu/.

60   Fashionably Male, 'Don't Police My Masculinity'.

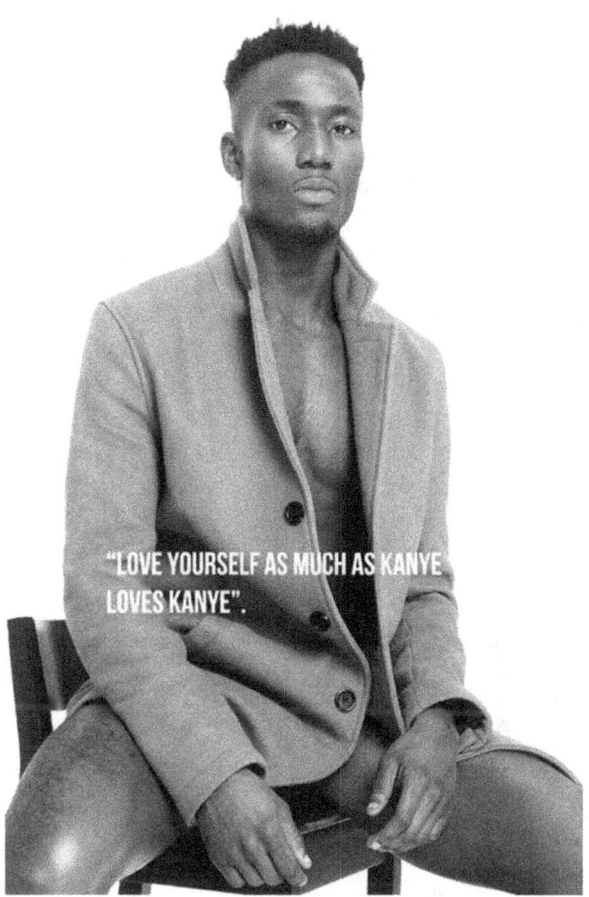

Fig. 87 Alexander Ikhide, *Love Yourself as Much as Kanye Loves Kanye*, (2015)

Sociological Interactionist Impacts of New Aesthetic Art

The German artist Aram Bartholl[61] has been one of the major figures to emerge within the context of the New Aesthetic. Educated at the Berlin University of the Arts with an engineering degree in architecture, Bartholl first came to notice with his project *Bits on Location* (2001)[62] which investigated the possibilities involved in the spatial repositioning of information sources, by attempting 'to connect, through a series of examples, the digital content from locationless global data networks to physical space'[63] and signaling a primary concern Bartholl's work has had ever since; much of his work exaggerates the tensions that exist between specified and despecified localization and articulates the continuous functions of contrasts and overlays between digital realities and the normal world. Two projects have introduced Bartholl's work into the broader art world: *Maps* (2006-10)[64] and *Dead Drops* (2010-12).[65] *Maps* {Fig. 88} has been a series of large scale sculptural reproductions of Google map pins used in a digital context to mark out highlighted locations and search results; Bartholl has created a series of life-sized versions of these pins to call into question the relationship between the real and the digital world with a clear assertion that this relationship is increasingly mutually dependent.

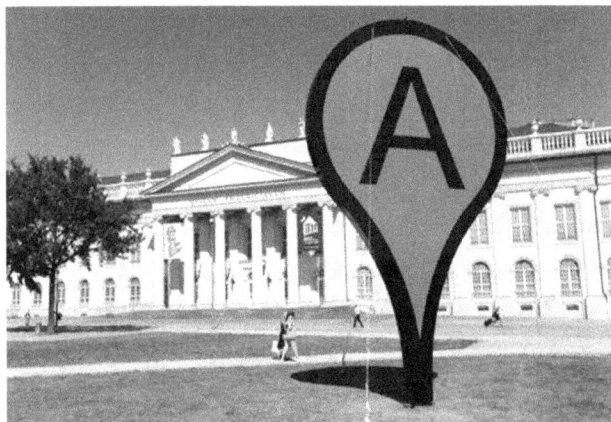

Fig. 88 Aram Bartholl, *Map* (2013)

61   Aram Bartholl, http://www.datenform.de/.

62   Aram Bartholl, 'Bits on Location', 2001, http://datenamort.de/eng/indexe.html.

63   Régine Debatty, 'Bits on Location', *We Make Money Not Art blog*, 23 February 2005, http://we-make-money-not-art.com/bits_on_locatio/.

64   Aram Bartholl, 'Map', 2014, http://datenform.de/blog/tag/map/.

65   Aram Bartholl, 'Dead Drops: Un-cloud your files in cement! 'Dead Drops' is an anonymous, offline, peer to peer file-sharing network in public space', 2011, http://deaddrops.com/.

The Google Maps pin, designed by Jens Eilstrup Rasmussen in 2005 as an integral part of the launch of Google Maps, has become so ubiquitous that it was acquired in physical form by MOMA in 2014; in Bartholl's use, {Fig. 89} it's become a sculptural intersection that highlights the complicated overlapping relationship of the way the world is represented with what is represented.

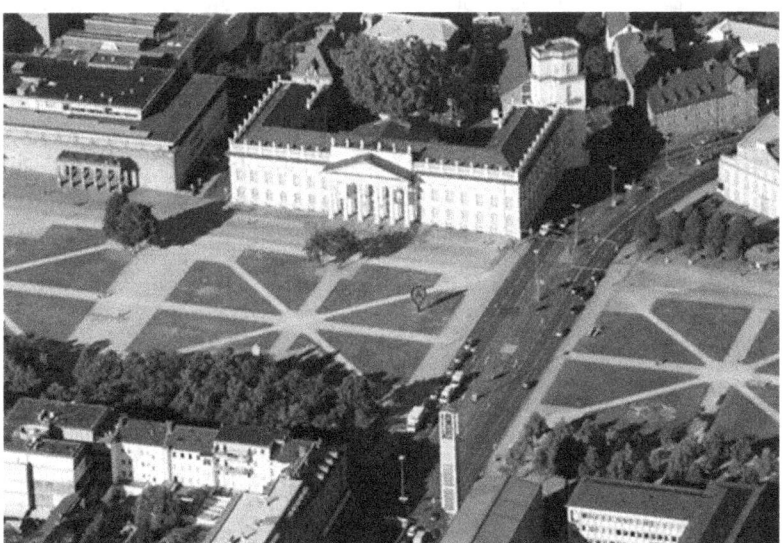

Fig. 89 Aram Bartholl, *Map* (2013)

While 'Google's maps have revolutionized how we interact with the world, how we perceive space and even how we navigate through it'[66] Bartholl's work questions the revolution itself by reversing the supposed continuousness of the relationship between the pin and the actual location, causing a heightened sense of a discontinuous relationship between the Google map pin and Bartholl's pin. *Dead Drops* {Fig. 90} has taken this even further, as described by Bartholl:

"Dead Drops" is an anonymous, offline, peer to peer file-sharing network in public space. USB flash drives are embedded into walls, buildings and curbs accessible to anybody in public space. Everyone is invited to drop or find files on a dead drop. Plug your laptop to a wall, house or pole to share your favorite files and data. Each dead drop is installed empty except a readme.txt file explaining the project. "Dead Drops" is open to participation. If you want to install a dead drop in your city/neighborhood follow the "how to" instructions and submit the location and pictures.[67]

---

66   Hilary Greenbaum, 'Who Made Google's Map Pin?', *The New York Times Magazine*, 18 April 2011, http://6thfloor.blogs.nytimes.com/2011/04/18/who-made-googles-map-pin/.

67   Aram Bartholl, 'About Dead Drops', *Dead Drops*.

Whereas *Maps* is an intervention, *Dead Drops* is a much more participatory art project that Bartholl has allowed to be copied, pasted and hacked worldwide, both metaphorically and literally, so that the idea itself has taken on a life similar to many instances of conceptual art from the 1960s which eschewed object production and commodification. Creating a peer-to-peer network that is more physical rather than virtual, like in the form of bittorrents, *Dead Drops* have served not only as locations to download files from but also to upload to because the USB drives are always public; borrowing a term from an information sharing method used by spies, Bartholl's project has become a set of sites that are either remarkably banal or dangerous, as in the case of one Cologne instance where plans for bombs were discovered on the USB drive,[68] but their artistic intent is still clear. More than just creating a community, though it has certainly done that with thousands of dead drops appearing worldwide, it embodies an artistic opportunity to share and communicate information, 'a unique space for uncensored public conversation into the physical structure of the city'[69] counter to any digital network's reach.

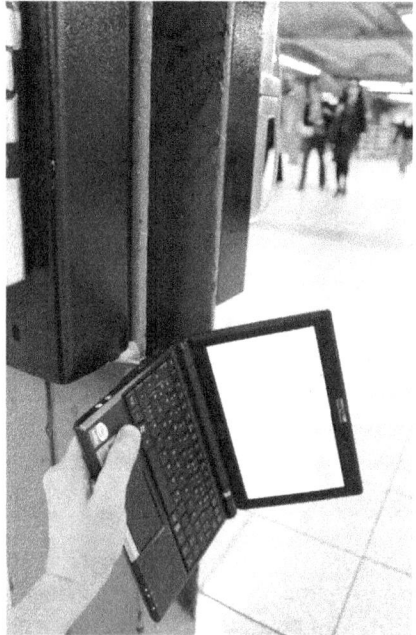

Fig. 90 Aram Bartholl, *Dead Drops* (2010)

---

68   Carsten Rust and Philip Buchen, "Eingemauert in einer Fassade Bomben-Bauplan auf öffentlichem USB-Stick in der Kölner Südstadt", *Express*, 23 February, 2015, http://www.express.de/koeln/eingemauert-in-einer-fassade-bomben-bauplan-auf-oeffentlichem-usb-stick-in-der-koelner-suedstadt-2031168.

69   MOMA, 'Dead Drops', Museum of Modern Art Interactive Exhibitions, http://www.moma.org/interactives/exhibitions/2011/talktome/objects/146365/.

Bartholl's career has consistently been an exploration of the way the real and the digital overlap, even when its use of spontaneity has verged on an almost ridiculous level of fandom and opportunism. In 2009, while having coffee, Bartholl spied a Google Street-view car driving outside and proceeded to chase it down the street; almost a year later he appeared in a series of images on Google Streetview, which were subsequently appropriated as *15 Seconds of Fame* (2010).[70] {Fig. 91}

Creating a further level of critical depth to his work, Bartholl's *Full Screen* (2014)[71] {Fig. 92} was a curated project with a number of well-known artists contributing works that were displayed on Samsung Galaxy Gear smartwatches.

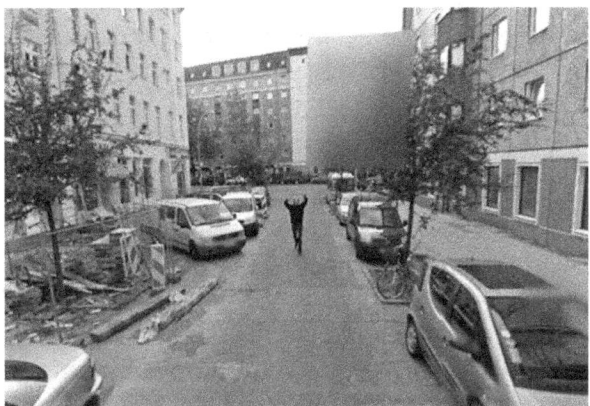

Fig. 91 Aram Bartholl, *15 Seconds of Fame* (2009-2010)

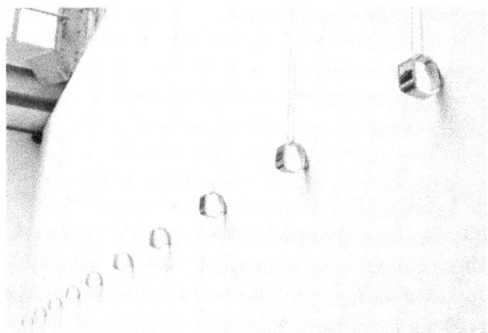

Fig. 92 Aram Bartholl, *Full Screen* (2014)

---

70   Aram Bartholl, 'Full Screen', 2014, http://www.datenform.de/15-secs-of-fame-eng.html.

71   Artists in *Full Screen* included Vincent Broquaire, Jennifer Chan, Petra Cortright, Constant Dullaart, Oliver Laric, Sara Ludy, Raquel Meyers, Evan Roth, Rafaël Rozendaal, Paul Souviron, Addie Wagenknecht, Ai Weiwei.

Viewers were invited to wear the art and interact with it in a limited fashion, driving the questions that Bartholl has been examining in his art even further. In an interview Bartholl asks 'The underlying question is, in what ways we can represent digital art?'[72] and his answer is a direct rejection of the continuing relevance of the screen as a medium. It's not just that over the course of the last fifty years the digital world has shrunk to the size of a watch and the interface has transitioned from room-sized objects with tiny monitors whose only representation of data consists of low resolutions text; the physical manifestation of the objects has changed and with it our conception of what data and its provider the 'internet' is. This providing has shifted in space and time; in more ways than just by making data available no matter where the user is, new devices (themselves quickly outdated in terms of technological capability) make the consumption of data literally timeless and spaceless, disconnected from the physical realm, and especially ironically so when in the form of wristwatches. While acknowledging that screens will continue to exist for a long time, often in a nostalgic capacity, and emphasizing that point with the reduplication of imagery from small screens to a huge LED screen, nevertheless Bartholl points out that 'There will be screens where you don't have the rectangle anymore. It's hard to tell, and it's going to take quite a while, but the next paradigm shift is going to happen soon.'[73] We are so used to the idea of 'seeing' the internet through screens, but once haptic interfaces, voice commands and gestural forms of interaction were introduced the point of contact shifts from a specific referential interface to a decentered form of interaction that is positionless precisely because of its fluid nature. This move away from screens as a mediating but limited form of interactive structure is something that appears in an even stronger sense as an aesthetic strategy in the work of Hito Steyerl.

In many respects, the artwork produced by Hito Steyerl is one of the best examples of art of the New Aesthetic. In fact, Hito Steyerl as both an artist and an art critic has been a driving force behind many of the ideas and work of the New Aesthetic, setting the parameters of different aesthetic strategies as well as identifying work by other artists. Born in Munich in 1966, trained in philosophy at the Academy of Fine Arts, Vienna and later studying at the Japan Institute of the Moving Image and University of Television and Film Munich, she has exhibited widely at documenta 12, the Venice Biennale, and the Istanbul, Taipei and Shanghai Biennials, and has had numerous solo exhibitions at major museums worldwide and teaches New Media Art at University of the Arts in Berlin. Steyerl's work is complicated, appearing in cinematic form, essays and books, art installations and digital objects, but we believe it's appropriate to focus on two intersecting threads that drive her work. First, Steyerl maintains a refusal to disavow herself as the

---

72   Nadja Sayej, 'Full Screen is a Group Show Dedicated to Digital Art You Can Wear on Your Wrist', *The Creators Project*, 12 March 2014, http://thecreatorsproject.vice.com/blog/full-screen-is-a-group-show-devoted-to-digital-art-you-can-wear-on-your-wrist.

73   Sayej, 'Full Screen is a Group Show Dedicated to Digital Art You Can Wear on Your Wrist'.

artist from her productions, especially in the case of films that are more documentary in nature, because she believes in the importance of the personal presence of the artist conveyed 'by the idea that you cannot address a social issue productively without first understanding your own part in it [...] [and she is] wary of sentimentality and false objectivity, she acknowledges herself as part of the picture, eager "to make my position transparent" and truthfully complex'.[74] Second, Steyerl is intensely interested in the increasingly interdependent and interwoven nature of social media, social, political and culture changes, the increasingly uncontrollable nature of the virtual exchange of information, and a commitment to the freedom of images to have meaning regardless of any users' intentions including, perhaps especially, her own. If these two threads seem contradictory then Steyerl's aesthetic strategies are successful, for it's precisely in the complex contradictions that the best of her work has its greatest effect. While much of Steyerl's ideas have appeared in her essays and books, her art is a complex and highly effective embodiment of her exploration of the new and independently forming digital paradigms confronting the human condition. A major exhibition of her three films by *e-flux* in 2012 encapsulates Steyerl's work well: *Adorno's Grey* (2012), {Fig. 93} documenting efforts to 'discover' the near mythological layer of grey paint Adorno required for his lecterns so as to avoid distraction, while voiceovers tell the story of Adorno's last lecture interrupted by bare-breasted female students; *Abstract* (2012), {Fig. 94} exploring through video a complex interlacing of violence and warfare, circling around the death of Steyerl's friend Andrea Wolf who had been killed in Kurdistan as a revolutionary fighter in the PKK (Kurdistan Workers' Party); and *Guards* (2012), {Fig. 95} using interviews with art museums guards to show how they've been trained in military tactics to secure the collections their attending to.[75]

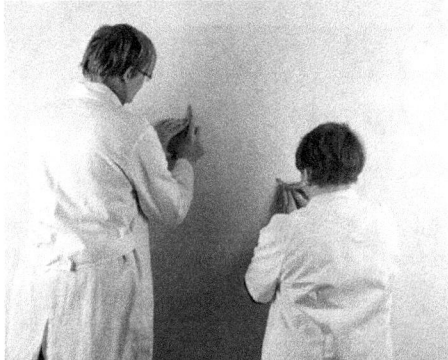

Fig. 93 Hito Steyerl, *Adorno's Grey* (2012)

---

74   Maggie Gray, 'Artist Profile: Hito Steyerl', *this is tomorrow*, December 11, 2010, http://thisistomorrow.info/articles/artist-profile-hito-steyerl.

75   e-flux, 'Hito Steyerl' (Press Release), 2012, http://www.e-flux.com/announcements/hito-steyerl-at-e-flux/.

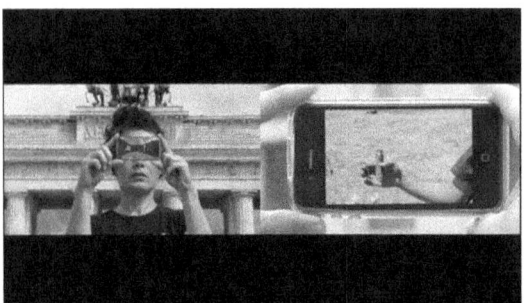

Fig. 94 Hito Steyerl, *Abstract* (2012)

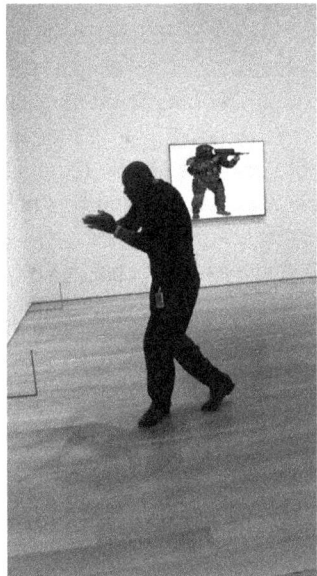

Fig. 95 Hito Steyerl, *Guards* (2012)

As different as they are, each film is rooted in different aspects of Steyerl's life - her philosophical background, her friendships, and her life as an artist - making them at least indirectly personal while at the same time fully structured within the language of video, documentary and cinema. In many respects this work is similar to the work of Metahaven, with a sense of complicity in the evidence of digital interaction. While these films at first don't seem to distinguish Steyerl's work from that of other filmmakers or as cinema per se, in that her roots in New German Cinema and the influence of film historian Helmut Färber are both clear and documented in interviews, each film is so highly attenuated to its medium and the specific stylizations necessary of the different subject matters, in a way that marks all of Steyerl's art as important explorations into the changing nature of the digital and our interaction with the digital, that her work is radically different from that of her predecessors.

The title of the first chapter of Steyerl's book *Die Farbe der Wahrheit (The Colour of Truth)* (2008) is 'Documentary Uncertainty', an indication that regardless of the appropriateness of the medium Steyerl is always aware of how it can both undermine and betray her efforts, almost as if her films are an embodiment of Jacques Derrida's notion of deconstruction. Taking together, all three films represent Steyerl's efforts to trace the intersection of politics and aesthetics in a manner that dissects the force of images as potentially acting counter to artistic intention not only in regards to the communication of information but to the very notion of completeness. This is particularly true of *Adorno's Grey*, about which one critic writes:

> After the credits, the projected image drops out while the projector lamp is left to burn for a short while. In this white, messianic light, it is now possible to see that each of the screen's collectively canted planes is painted in a different tone of grey respectively. Although the conservators never found the missing grey layer in Frankfurt, this final revelation of Steyerl's filmic apparatus presents the missing culprits, which tainted the depiction of the represented wall. With this cheap, yet effective trick, the artist seems to be trumping yet another fragmentation of the recorded actions. And still, this final "proof" of an image contaminated lays bare not only the fact that cinema is itself composed of necessary illusions, but that these sensuous special effects can hold and distract our attentive gazes from actually seeing.[76]

It's that last point that's so crucial: the fragmentation of recorded actions, the inherently deceptive but powerful nature of images that can fully reveal their nature as an illusion while at the same time still functioning as a deception, are presented in an intense fashion to the point that we no longer see them but accept them as self-evident and seemingly autonomous effects. Other films by Steyerl achieve much the same effect, such as *Lovely Andrea* (2007) and *In Free Fall* (2013), all revolving around (to borrow a phrase from *Lovely Andrea*) 'filmic tension' constructed similarly to Adorno's conflict between praxis and theory that is evidence is his statement that 'The unresolved antagonisms of reality reappear in art in the guise of immanent problems of artistic form. This, and not the deliberate injection of objective moments or social content, defines art's relations to society. The aesthetic tensions manifesting themselves in works of art express the essence of reality in and through their emancipation from the factual façade of exteriority.'[77] The only difference in this case is that the immanence of the digital as autonomous phenomenon has replaced the artistic in its common form with an accelerated form of an emancipation of digital, not just escaping the restrictions of artistic creativity but redefining its very essence as independent.

---

76   Adam Kleinman, 'Hito Steyerl's "Adorno's Grey"', *art-agenda*, 21 November 2012, http://www.art-agenda.com/reviews/hito-steyerl's-"adorno's-grey"/.

77   Theodor Adorno, *Aesthetic Theory*, London: Routledge & Kegan Paul, 1972, p. 8.

In the context of the New Aesthetic certain works stand out. Steyerl's *How Not to Be Seen: A Fucking Didactic Educational .MOV File* (2013) {Fig. 96} is a satirical instructional film (with part of the title borrowed from a Monty Python sketch) purporting to show ways to avoid or confuse surveillance software by remaining 'unseen' in a manner similar to the art of Adam Harvey and paralleling the concerns of Metahaven.

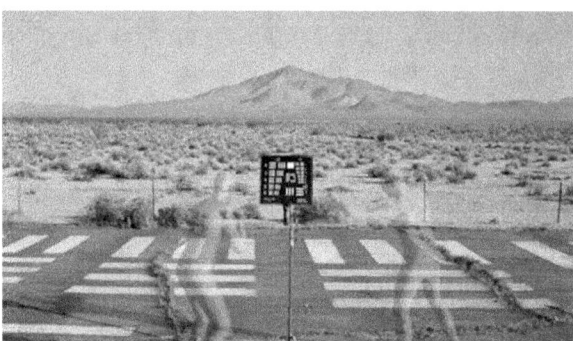

Fig. 96 Hito Steyerl, *How Not to Be Seen: A Fucking Didactic Educational .MOV File* (2013)

Shot at a desert site that was covered with photo calibration targets backed by computer generated and imposed images of different landscapes, with ghostly figures dressed in green that appear and disappear, the film instructs viewers that there are four ways to avoid detection – hiding in plain sight, shrinking to a size smaller than a pixel, living in a gated community and being female and older than 50 – and implies a clear set of motivations. Leora Morinis very astutely points out:

> Despite the ostensible neutrality of the how-to format, the title also begs the question of motivation: why would a person want not-to-be seen? When the beauty magazine tells you "how not to appear desperate," the implication is that it's ugly to show how much you care (whereas otherwise you might've thought devotion was a good and powerful thing). In this regard, Steyerl's video calls on a number of embattled realities [...] At one point in the sequence, the voice-over explains that while "resolution measures the world as an image," the "most important things want to remain invisible. Love is invisible. War is invisible. Capital is invisible." To be sure, Steyerl's works do measure the world as an image, but in her treatment, it's these "most important things" that are rendered visible. It's a pretty powerful picture.[78]

Why would you want to not be seen? Maybe because you don't want to be killed by a drone, a weapon of war that is focused on those photo calibration targets. Maybe because

78   Leora Morinis, 'Hito Steyerl's HOW NOT TO BE SEEN: A F**king Didactic Educational .MOV
       File', *Inside/Out, A MoMA/MoMA PS1 Blog*, 18 June 2014, http://www.moma.org/explore/inside_
       out/2014/06/18/hito-steyerls-how-not-to-be-seen-a-fucking-didactic-educational-mov-file.

you think you're important? Who is the satirically intended audience here if not both the terrorist and the powerful politician? And where do we, the viewers, the normal people, find a place between such forces, if we can find a place at all, to disappear without being disappeared? {Fig. 97}

It's pretty clear that the effects of the software – and it most assuredly is the software that becomes a driving force of agency with real effects outside of Steyerl's film – function in an inverse relationship to most of people's lives, in that their effect is more unavoidable the less we have to hide. The less concerned we are with privacy, the less concerned we are with being monitored, means that it becomes increasingly harder to avoid being spied on should we choose to do so in the future. On further consideration, *How Not To Be Seen* becomes less satire and more a frightening, powerful revelation on the new normal of the human condition, where our presence in the world is substantiated less in our physicality presence and far more in our digital identity which is, ironically, increasingly beyond our control as it becomes determined and accepted as determined by the digital objects that present our identity back to ourselves; unlike *Second Life*, with its notion that our avatars are our representations to the world and are controlled by us as users, Steyerl's art is concerned with revealing that our 'avatars' (to use this outdated and outmoded term as an extended synecdoche) are chosen for us and, even more frightening, that the sense of choice itself is an illusion. What is rendered visible is not what we've chosen to be visible but what the digital makes visible to us.

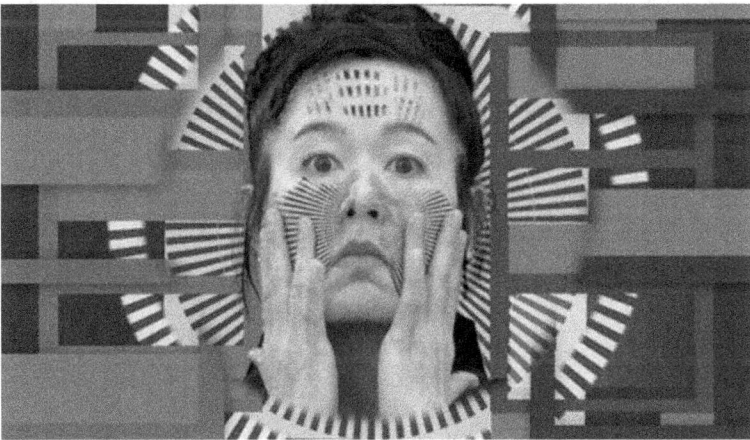

Fig. 97 Hito Steyerl, *How Not to Be Seen: A Fucking Didactic Educational .MOV File* (2013)

An Unachievable Autonomy of the New Aesthetic Appreciation

Levi Bettwieser, an American photographer living in Boise, Idaho, recently switched from shooting primarily digital to various forms of analog photography, a move clearly associated with his interest in antique processes in various formats. In 2014, Bettwieser came across a set of undeveloped film rolls dating back to WWII. With a lot of effort, experimentation and an awareness of the difficulty involved and the potential for failure, Bettwieser set out to develop these rolls and print the images.[79] The results of Bettwieser's efforts were incredibly interesting; as he acknowledges in a number of places, the original photographer clearly had an eye for composition and was focused on producing images that were personally meaningful, all the while also producing images that are of obvious historical significance. The discovery led Bettwieser to take on a growing collection of undeveloped film rolls and process them as successfully as he could, and to post the results on *The Rescued Film Project*,[80] a Tumblr blog set up to share the images which has often generated more information than Bettwieser anticipated. Though many of the rolls he's collected have been damaged beyond repair, Bettwieser has still diligently attempted to rescue each one, even to the point of posting a number of the failed images that still retain the barest of details but which verge at times on being entirely abstract. The reason we're starting this section with Bettwieser's project, however, isn't because of the admirable and aesthetically interesting work he's doing, even if his shift from the digital to analog and back to digital warrants at least an acknowledgement of the inescapability of the digital world. What caught our attention weren't the images of vehicles and people from WWII either. Instead, it's a set of images that are obviously a product of a flawed interface between developed analog film and the scanner or software that Bettwieser used, and this element is the most compelling in an analysis of the New Aesthetic. {Fig. 98}

Six images, drawn from the same role of film and connected by similar people and setting, are covered randomly in glitch effects and distortions.[81] Bettwieser is quoted by the author Attila Nagy as noting:

> Thanks to a mysterious software bug that occurred while scanning these joyful family photos, probably from the 80s, strange colorful shapes swarmed the peaceful scenes,

79   Christopher Jobson, 'The Rescued Film Project Discovers 31 Rolls of Undeveloped Film Shot by an Unknown WW2 Soldier', *This Is Colossal*, 18 January 2015, http://www.thisiscolossal.com/2015/01/31-rolls-of-ww2-film/.

80   *The Rescued Film Project*, http://rescuedfilmproject.tumblr.com/.

81   Bettweisser, Levi, 'Is this real life?', *Rescued Film Project blog*, 16 September 2015, http://rescuedfilmproject.tumblr.com/post/129213965706/is-this-real-life.

harmonizing with the color palette of the original negatives. The results are stunning. I personally almost feel like Neo from Matrix, when he starts to see the code.[82]

One comment asks: 'Is this real life?' Perhaps it would be more productive to ask whether this constitutes a genuine aesthetic experience. Nagy notes: 'this might be the fabric of our world'.[83]

The fact that Bettwieser has left this images on his blog – a natural response, to be sure – indicates that these images have a power beyond the nostalgic, beyond their evocation of other places and times, beyond even the poignant presence of other individuals to an unconscious awareness of the inexorable and pervasive presence of the digital realm.

Photography, whether analog or digital, is an artistic format that often confounds the discourse of art history and the thoughtful explorations of aesthetics. Vilém Flusser's *Towards a Philosophy of Photography* is one of the few examples of a sustained philosophical engagement with the medium, but there's scant evidence of similar efforts. It's also telling that one of Flusser's other major books is titled *On Doubt*; Flusser clearly was interested in exploring the concrete ubiquity of symbols driven by technology in human culture through a position opposed to the primacy often granted by philosophy of Cartesian doubt, but Flusser's conception of doubting doubt as a method can be borrowed as an assertion of the dynamic potency of photography as a way of flaunting the presence of the world rather than just as a means of representing it.

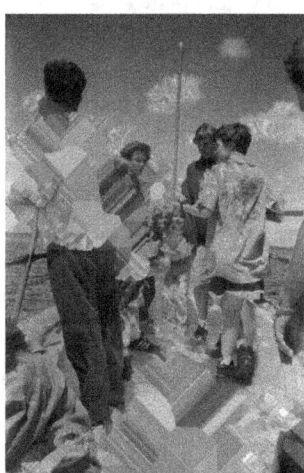

Fig. 98 Levi Bettwieser, *The Rescued Film Project* (2014–)

---

82   Attila Nagy, 'Fantastic Software Glitch Art Is Better Than the Real World', *Gizmodo*, 10 October 2015, http://gizmodo.com/fantastic-software-glitch-art-is-better-than-the-real-w-1732141946.

83   Attila Nagy, 'Fantastic Software Glitch Art Is Better Than the Real World'.

To think about photography means to think about the photographer's intentions as well as its technical contingencies. Photographs are easily produced, or seemingly so, with the effect that the ability to produce photographs has become both relatively universalized, resulting in untold and increasingly forgotten millions of images particularly with the advent of digital methods. Most photographs are not regarded as art, but all are embodiments of the intentions of those producing the images, meaning that there is, nevertheless, an ontological resemblance between these captured pictures and the work of a serious photographer, a resemblance not present in other examples of visual artistic production. This resemblance is present in photography's reliance on chance. Chance plays a determinative role in all photography, and this randomness of the capturing of images implies a distinct set of criteria by which to clarify the potential resemblance between a snapshot and a serious photograph, resulting in a lack of an ontological distinction between both types. There is always the possibility, albeit remote to the extreme in most cases, that a snapshot will result in a photograph of such quality that it merits aesthetic consideration. Furthermore, quality of production is always a consideration; no snapshot photographer wants to intentionally produce a bad image. Given this line of thought, what's to stop further ruminations at an even more fundamentally metaphysical level? If chance and technology are reasonably understood to be determinative and constructive forces driving the production of aesthetic experiences in photography, partially independent of or in synthesis with the photographer's intentions, then it's entirely valid to assert the presence of algorithms, digital artifacts and errors and glitches as determinative and constructive forces and even entirely independent agents in the creation of aesthetic experiences. Bettwieser's statement that he feels like Neo in a virtual Matrix makes a lot of sense if one thinks about the glitchy images he's posted as aesthetic experiences as the result of artistic agency outside of the analog world, in which the totality of the images' aesthetic nature is governed not by the intentions of photographers (and Bettwieser is part of the collective of 'photographers' as the developer of the film he's restoring) but by the manipulative presence of software. In short, Descartes' concern regarding an evil genius and his thought experiment's development towards the 'brain in a vat' problem becomes, in the context of the New Aesthetic, less an issue of epistemic uncertainty and more about alternative aesthetic agents. It's not just that we suspect that our aesthetic taste and judgments are influenced by our experiences but that our skepticism of the functional independence of our reflective judgments is fully justified; the digital world is increasingly not just something we respond to but a determinative force in our lives, including our aesthetic inclinations and assessments.

The images from Bettwieser's Tumblr blog are an easy way to begin this section, and might be proof right from the start of our point that New Aesthetic art is sufficiently autonomous to warrant a sustained and distinct consideration, but it is still the point which is the hardest to defend. A simple argument against it, though the effectiveness of it is something debatable, is to note that regardless of the digital interference evident in the images they still required a person's intent to photograph something. If we were to continue our investigations into New Aesthetic objects, one could suppose, then this would make any argument turn immediately away from work produced by artists to instances of aesthetic effects and 'art' produced entirely through computational results; it might seem almost a necessity to stop thinking about artists' work and only think aout digital objects produced independently of human intentions. It's still a goal of ours, however to think about these art objects of varying degrees of aesthetic value and importance as New Aesthetic objects; these are objects about which we can assert the introduction of variables into algorithms which are themselves self-generating, evolutionary, and sufficiently independent of human agency, and investigate the aesthetic effects that are due to inadvertent errors, glitches, and unforeseeable digital manifestations, all the while still referring to them as art. More succinctly, work like Bettwieser's encourages one to find aesthetic objects that are entirely divested of human intervention in order to sustain the notion of New Aesthetic art as a form independently produced by an autonomous digital agency, and it's obviously natural to continue this final section with a discussion of computer art. At the same time, though, we would forewarn against any assumption that that's where this will remain, particularly in the sense that finding experienceable art that is *entirely* not a product of human agency may be a fruitless or impractical task, especially considering the necessary means by which the seemingly naturalness of the New Aesthetic manifests itself.

To start thinking about New Aesthetic art objects, perhaps it's best to consider the closer approximation of digital art to its manifestations in terms of computer generated art once again. We've already discussed this a little bit in the first section, covering the artwork of Frieder Nake, A. Michael Noll, Georg Nees and Jean-Pierre Hébert, but we want to return to computer art to consider some different issues. By the early 1970s, the Institute for Contemporary Art in London had held an exhibit of computer art called *Cybernetic Serendipity*, the Computer Arts Society was founded, and Katherine Nash and Richard Williams had published *Computer Program for Artists: ART 1*.[84] During this time the phrase algorithmic art started being used to describe artworks created entirely through algorithms written by artists, though most of those artists were computer programmers first who had taken an interest in the arts. Most instances of computer art are similar to those discussed at the beginning of this chapter – the computer was a tool, the understanding of complex and engaging visual design principles was superficial at best, and the artists often weren't really artists – but a belief and confidence in the potential for computer art was clearly in place to the point that the art world started to accept computer art by the end of the 1990s. Holly Rogers, linking computer art to the growing recognition of video art, describes the increasing acknowledgement thus:

Hans-Peter Schwarz, one of the founding directors of the Zentrum für Kunst und Medientechnologie, Karlsruhe (ZKM, Germany), described their [computer art] ephemer-

---

84   Katherine Nash and Richard H. Williams, 'Computer Program for Artists: ART
     I'. *Leonardo, Pergamon Press (via JSTOR)* (The MIT Press 1970, 3 (4): pp. 439-442.

ality as setting off an "explosive charge" at the gates of traditional art establishments. At first this "explosive charge" was blocked by major galleries because of curatorial problems (how to include sound and performance in a gallery space, temporal modes of perception fundamentally at odds with the traditional gallery experience), aesthetic issues (video's relationship to mass media such as television and untraditional modes of artistic discourse), and financial concerns (how to sell or keep something that is unrepeatable).[85]

Until the 1990s, computer art was, at best, on the periphery of the art world, but the foundations for its acceptance and for a genuine New Aesthetic art was in place. This process of an increased presence and acceptance of New Aesthetic art, however, was facilitated not by the quality nor the market value of computer art – in fact, we would argue that aesthetic value or quality of computer art has generally remained subpar at best, substantiated by the remarkably low market value for most instances of computer art including those of historical importance – but from specific related and distinct factors.

Part of the success of the process lies in a major shift in the methods of production. The *Cybernetic Serendipity* exhibition of 1968, curated by Jasia Reichardt, provides a good example. It an exhibition firstly of art based on algorithms, art that was influenced by computational processes such as Gustav Metzger's *Five Screens With Computer* (1968), two of Jean Tinguely's painting machines, and Wen-Ying Tsai's interactive cybernetic sculptures consisting of vibrating stainless-steel rods, stroboscopic light, and audio feedback control. Additionally, *Cybernetic Seredipity* {Fig. 99} also included practical designs for architecture and objects that showed the curator's understanding of the intersections of art, design and early forms of digital design, perhaps the most 'cybernetic' type of all of the included objects.

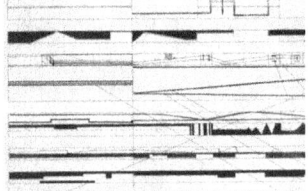

Fig. 99 *Cybernetic Serendipity* (1968)

---

85   Holly Rogers, '"Betwixt and Between" Worlds: Spatial and Temporal Liminality in Video Art-Music'
     in Richardson, John, et al. (eds), *The Oxford Handbook of New Audiovisual Aesthetics*, Oxford:
     Oxford University Press, 2013, p. 532.

It also was an important influence in the formation of the Computer Arts Society by Alan Sutcliffe, George Mallen, and John Lansdown. For us, though, the most interesting part of the exhibition is the presentation of a survey of the field of computer music, including works by Lajaren Hiller & Leonard Isaacson, John Cage, Iannis Xenakis, Haruki Tsuchiya and Herbert Brün.

As noted in a recent release of the recording:

> During the preparation of the Cybernetic Serendipity exhibition two things became apparent.

> One, that in order to show what was going on in the field computer music, it was necessary to include a considerable amount of material that was not strictly composed with or played by computer. Two, that dealing with an exploratory field, all attempts at a historical perspective or firm evaluation were out of place. The exhibition and this record, therefore, are essentially a reportage of current trends and developments in programmed and stochastic music.[86]

In short, one of the curious things about computer art is that it's rarely art produced by a computer; it's not merely that the technology hasn't been capable of autonomous artistic production (because it actually has even in the earliest days) but rather than the creative, imaginative work of the artist is something that the art world has been reluctant to abandon. The hand of the artist, the sense of prioritizing human craftsmanship, is an attitude that been reluctantly dispensed with only in the most recent years, as more and more artists turn to technological means for their production in various ways and to various extents; this includes David Hockney, Cai Guo-Qiang, Paul Pfeiffer, Ai Weiwei, Jenny Holzer, Pierre Huyghe, Bruce Nauman and so many others that a list is impossible to consider.

Where we've arrived, interestingly, is at a place where New Aesthetic art is both viable but continuously uncertain. Procedurally generated art can be considered aesthetically valid and the current vivacity and slipperiness of the New Aesthetic can be summarized neatly with a quote from the Indian artist Gopakumar R. P.'s work *Linguistic River* (2015): 'I believe the work of art should change the existing visual, intellectual and aesthetical sense and experiment with finding new visual phenomena.'[87] The fact is that a number of visual artists working without computers were beginning to produce work that established the foundations for a New Aesthetic art, and two important figures illustrate the tendency that many contemporary artists have taken to pave the way for the New

---

86   *Cybernetic Seredipity Archive*, http://cyberneticserendipity.net/.

87   R. Gopakumar, *Linguistic River*, 2012, http://www.worldart.info/GopakumarR/LinguisticsRiver/default.aspx.

Aesthetic: the Korean-American artist Nam June Paik (1932-2006) and the Swiss artist Jean Tinguely (1925-1991). Paik has been described as the artist who invented video art, who first brought a refined artistic sensibility to the use of electronics in artistic production, and whose participation in Fluxus and whose production of conceptual art radically transformed the possibilities available for subsequent generations. In video work, through the use of televisions as sculptures, by using neon lighting and laser effects with elaborate sound experiences, Paik pushed viewers to contemplate the rapid pace of change driven by technological innovations. His *TV Buddha* (1974) {Fig. 100} is rightfully regarded as his most famous and important artwork.

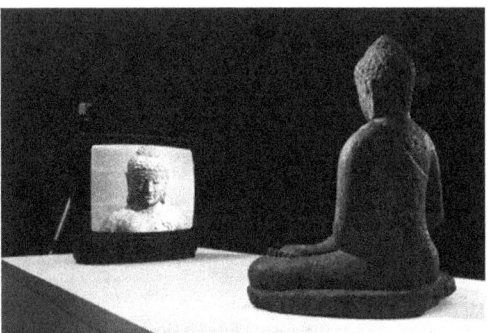

Fig. 100 Nam June Paik, *TV Buddha* (1974)

TV Buddha has become an iconic artwork, which is surprising given that it was included almost as an afterthought in an exhibition almost as an afterthought at the Galeria Bonino in New York. Consisting of a closed loop – a seated Buddha sculpture is positioned so that it gazes at a television monitor that displays an image of the Buddha captured through a closed-circuit television camera – it's a work that has sometimes been construed as a representation of a collision between an Oriental set of values or mindset and the Occidental tendency to assert a primary role for technological innovation. When Paik re-exhibited *TV Buddha* in Cologne that year, however, the artist temporarily took the place of the Buddha sculpture, thus denying the validity of that interpretation. The interchangeability of the figurative element is key for our purposes, and what we believe is a more accurate interpretation: the figurative sculpture and Paik's own presence did not create a participating role but rather described a destabilized element in the closed system of the technology itself; whether as a living, breathing human being or an inanimate representation of a divine or semi-divine creature. What is activated aesthetically is the autonomy of the technology as a seeing agent, albeit one that remains unresponsive to any changes taking place in front of it. Paik would certainly have been aware that the role of the Buddha is not so much to exist as an object of worship but to be present as a model of enlightenment, an example of what an individual can become, and *TV Buddha* represents technology's desire to achieve enlightenment as if technology was gazing actively, striving to better itself.

Some of Tinguely's work is equally interesting and, in our opinion, achieves a similar result. Emerging from a tradition of Dada, Tinguely's most famous artworks were kineti-cally destructive and self-destructive in nature, with Tinguely's *Homage to New York* (1960) serving as the most famous and typical example. {Fig. 101} Set up in the sculpture garden of the Museum of Modern Art, *Homage to New York* was described by Tinguely as a 'self-constructing and self-destroying work of art' comprised of wheels, motors, a bathtub, a piano and various other objects and, once set into motion, proceeded to destroy itself with crashes and fire until stopped by the local fire department.

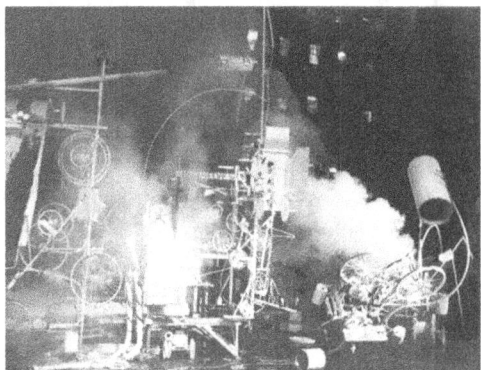

Fig. 101 Jean Tinguely, *Homage to New York* (1960)

While the link to Dada is apparent, as is the link to a long tradition of destruction in art, like Paik's work there is a setting-forth of a systematic autonomy in *Homage to New York* that regressively undermines its sense of determinativeness; Tinguely's aesthetics neces-sitated a lack of control on the artist's part, once the processes had been set into motion, that transferred an autonomous agency over to the artwork. Much of Tinguely's career can be understood as an exploration of the relationship between the artist, his work as technology, and human culture, with a clear conclusion that technologically-dependent objects have an alien life all to themselves, an interpretative position reinforced with a statement by Michael Landy, co-curator of a major exhibition of Tinguely's work at the Tate Liverpool in 2009, that *Homage to New York* 'committed suicide',[88] an act only a living creature with a sense of self-awareness could do.

The aesthetic strategies and their results as employed by both Paik and Tinguely are, in many respects, radically different from each other, but the resulting consequences are the same: in each case a system is created, closed and self-referential, initiated by the artists but quickly moving out of their control with unexpected results. In a way, both Paik's and Tinguely's artworks represent an aestheticization of Kurt Gödel's incomplete-

---

88   Michael Landy, 'Home to Destruction', *Tate Etc.*, Autumn 2009, http://www.tate.org.uk/context-comment/articles/homage-destruction.

ness theorem, if aesthetic principles are considered axiomatic and human aesthetic evaluations are considered consistent. While we wouldn't claim that Paik or Tinguely produced New Aesthetic art, we're confident that their relationship to technology as a force opened opportunities prefacing a New Aesthetic interactionist strategy.

One of the most logical heirs to this, fully in a New Aesthetic mode, is the German artist Ralf Baecker. A German artist trained first in computer science and then as an artist at the Academy of Media Arts in Cologne, Baecker's work has been the subject of a growing interest and focus as representative of a new generation of computer artists and many examples of his art show a sustained and insightful exploration of New Aesthetic issues. *Re-Active Platform* (2010-12) is a very good starting point; installed in a series of museums with a team of assistants,[89] Baecker created a system of reactions between different computationally-drive sets of hardware and software which were also dependent on various environmental inputs as wide-ranging as motion and cosmic radiation. It seems that Baecker's intention behind the work was to simulate an ontological foundation, namely, that reaction is the *sui generis* of autonomy, with a self-determining set of self-regulations as consequences of a sustained autonomy. More than almost any other artist mentioned, Baecker's work exhibits an awareness of the presence of the digital functioning as an autonomous agent. Work like *Nowhere* (2004) - in which a 'landscape' based on users search movements on www.metager.de is sculptured on a milling machine - give a physical manifestation to the 'geography' of the internet.[90] *Rechnender Raum (Computing Space)* (2007), {Fig. 102} an installation consisting of sticks, strings and plumb weights, exists as a fully-functioning, logic and exact network, with a reversal of the normal arrangements of output display (at the center of the torus) and computing mechanics (on the outside of the torus); in exaggerating the workings of its operational behavior, Baecker has created a work of art almost directly analogous to numerous models of consciousness presented in different philosophies of mind, even to the point of being similar to Kant's description of the mind's active relationship to its experience of the world.

Taking this even a step further, Baecker's *The Conversation* (2009) {Fig. 103} is an autonomous machine consisting of 99 solenoids circled around three rubber bands that respond to the surrounding electromagnetic fields of their neighbors as well as the changing pulling forces detected in order to conserve its own position, with the result being something akin to a homeostat that 'tries to establish a hyper stable equilibrium'.[91]

---

89   glasmoog Cologne, 19 March to 14 April 2010; contemporary art ruhr (C.A.R.) Essen, 29 October to 31 October, 2010; and MOCA Studio, Taipei (Taiwan), 8 October to 20 November, 2011; assistants include Artur Holling, Karin Lingnau, Luis Negrón van Grieken, Ji Hyun Park, Susanna Schoenberg, http://www.re-activeplatform.de/.

90   Ralf Baecker, 'Nowhere', *Ralf Baecker*, http://www.rlfbckr.org/work/nowhere.

91   Ralf Baecker, 'The Conversation, *Ralf Baecker*, http://www.rlfbckr.org/work/the_conversation.

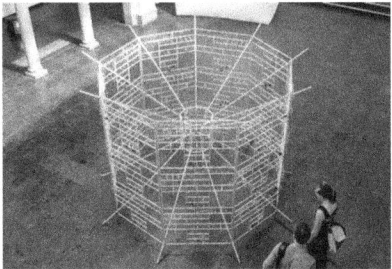

Fig. 102 Ralf Baecker, *Rechnender Raum (Computing Space)* (2007)

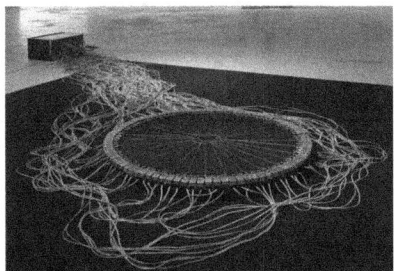

Fig. 103 Ralf Baecker, *The Conversation (Autonomous Machine)* (2007)

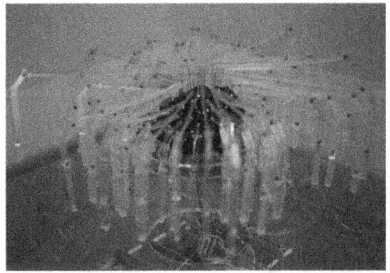

Fig. 104 Ralf Baecker, *Crystal Set* (2011)

In each case, Baecker is creating a system in which the system itself is responding on its own terms, creating an aesthetic configuration under its own power which is, fascinatingly, teleologically driven in an irrational fashion. Two pieces, though, need specific focus, as the best of Baecker's New Aesthetic art: *Crystal Set* (2011)[92] and *Irrational Computing* (2011-12).[93] *Crystal Set* {Fig. 104} takes as its basic premise the materiality of computational devices; the metonym 'Silicon Valley' is more than just a location but a description of one of the primary components of all computers, as are a wide variety of rare earth elements and other material.

---

92   Ralf Baecker, 'Crystal Set, *Ralf Baecker,* http://www.rlfbckr.org/work/crystal_set.

93   Ralf Baecker, 'Irrational Computing', *Ralf Baecker,* http://www.rlfbckr.org/work/irrational_computing.

Attaching iron needles to the surface of a silicon carbide specimen with a semiconducting diode at the point of contact, Baecker has created a set of circumstances whereby both light and audible signals can be generated and responded to by the software, investigating the logical structure of the crystal which then

> applies different electronic pattern to the contacts based on an analysis of current flow, resistance and response times in the specimen. By doing this it is inspecting its behavior in a closed feedback loop. As a result it generates raw and untamed signals visible and audible to the observer.[94]

Bringing to mind, as Baecker himself alluded to in an interview,[95] the raw crystal sets used in early commercial radios, *Crystal Set* is quite crude in appearance but sophisticated in execution and effect; more than just manifesting a sense of life, this work takes on a literal life of its own as well as a personality. Closely related to it, *Irrational Computing* {Fig. 105} has become Baecker's most well known work, representing at an even more fundamental level than *Crystal Set* Baecker's exploration of a 'raw' computational device.

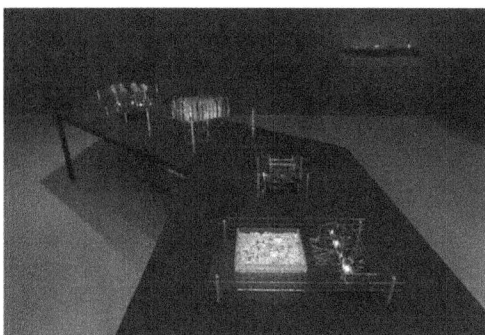

Fig. 105 Ralf Baecker, *Irrational Computing* (2011-12)

Using five interlinked modules, each responding separately to various input as well as responding at different levels to their companions' output, *Irrational Computing* is a macroscopic presentation of the computational process that breaks away from the necessity of being purposive and logical. The effect is, as noted by the curator Carsten Seiffarth, that:

> Digital systems, in their function, are conceived logically and rationally. The lowest physical or electro-technical level (crystals with semiconductor properties) are based,

94   Baecker, 'Irrational Computing'.

95   Nadja Sayej, 'An Artist Has Made A Primitive Computer Out Of Earth Crystals, And Little Else' *the creators project*, April 2014, http://thecreatorsproject.vice.com/en_uk/blog/an-artist-has-made-a-primitive-computer-out-of-natural-crystals-and-little-else.

however, on quantum mechanical, i.e. statistical or unpredictable processes. Modern computer technology has thus tamed and domesticated the chaotic, so to speak. In his work, Ralf Baecker comments on this paradox by examining the aesthetics of the materials from which has developed a global digital network. "Irrational Computing" is not supposed to "function" – its aim is to search for the poetic elements on the border between "accuracy" and "chaos".[96]

Taken as a body of work – which is how Baecker sometimes refers to many of his artworks – the Irrational Computing objects are an exploration of randomness out of the natural and the man-made that parallels the intentions behind technological innovation. More than just heightening the viewer's awareness of the materiality of contemporary computing – although that's an important part of the work – Baecker's work re-appropriates the digital which then creates its own paradox in the dichotomy between programmed and shaped material form that is the product of human intervention in opposition to a presence that grows over the duration and experience of the objects' existence as apparent living-objects, based on the idea, as Baecker himself notes, of mathematician, physicist and inventor John von Neumann's definition of artificial life, that 'life is a process which can be abstracted away from any particular medium'.[97] For us, Baecker's art is a challenge to the anthropocentric notion of artistic agency and aesthetic effect precisely because its program quickly escapes the originator's supervision, and it is New Aesthetic in that the conditions whereby the anthro-dependent qualification disappears behind an inherent and self-determined qualification of agency and its aesthetic effects.

This brings us back to the ideas of Lev Manovich, in particular his definition of 'new media'. Writing about the GUI of applications, Manovich describes the design of the interface as increasingly visible, in opposition to modernist tenets, such that:

> The designers no longer try to hide the interfaces. Instead, the interaction is treated as an event, as opposed to "non-event", as in the previous "invisible interface" paradigm. Put differently, using personal information devices is now conceived as a carefully orchestrated experience, rather than just a means to an end. The interaction explicitly calls attention to itself. The interface engages the user in a kind of game. The user is asked to devote significant emotional, perceptual and cognitive resources to the very act of operating the device.[98]

---

96   Ralf Baecker, 'Irrational Computing'.

97   Pau Waelder, 'Interview with Ralf Baecker', *Telefonica Fundación*, 16 April 2013, https://vida. fundaciontelefonica.com/en/2013/04/16/interview-with-ralf-baecker/.

98   Lev Manovich, 'Interaction as an aesthetic event', *Receiver*, #17, 2006, http://dm.ncl.ac.uk/ courseblog/files/2011/03/Manovich_InteractionAsAestheticEvent.pdf.

In essence, the increasing levels of interaction demand a similar attentiveness to the type employed in a theatrical experience, wherein a separation exists through a suspension of disbelief, with a heightened force of the artificiality of the aesthetic experience. However, an interesting effect is that the more the user becomes aware of the necessity of this heightened sense of the artificial there is a corresponding decline in a critical distance to the point that the artificial increasingly becomes naturalized. This transition within the event is evident in the work of James E. Murphy, an artist from Northern Ireland working in Berlin and part of a growing number of artists whose work is primarily presented online in the programming languages of the internet.[99] Murphy's work has covered territory similar to many other artists, including a few already discussed in this chapter, with work like Relative Anonymity (2012)[100] presenting an avoidance of government security structures' use of facial recognition through the use of stochastic noise and visuals, but three pieces in particular capture the released energy that defines Murphy's work specifically. The Politics of Creation (2013)[101] {Fig. 106} is a theatrical production that utilizes an aleatoric music and lighting system based on algorithmic formulae to create unique compositions for every performance; what's interesting is not just the inclusion of chance in a work which is heavily indebted to the traditions of systematization in art, especially in its fascinating use of algorithms to push an ever changing set of musical transitions through instrumentation, key, rhythm, arrangement and structure, but also the sense of an invoked natural chaos partnered with the choreography creating a 'closed system of causality as information about velocity, acceleration and positioning of dancers are fed back into the system affecting the very music they are dancing to [...] [that] links the dancers and the system in a "dance" of their own [...] as the piece progresses towards its finale'.[102]

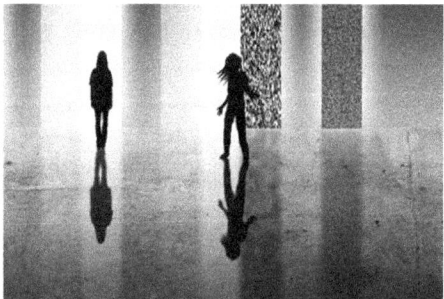

Fig. 106 James E. Murphy, The Politics of Creation (2013)

---

99   James E. Murphy, http://jemurphy.org/.

100 James E. Murphy, 'Relative Anonymity', 2012, http://jemurphy.org/#df.

101 James E. Murphy, 'The Politics of Creation', 2013, http://jemurphy.org/#poc.

102 James E. Murphy, 'The Politics of Creation'.

The shift in the language is telling, as it's clear that Murphy understands the mathematical structure to be an active participant in the performance, a digital collaborative partner to the human dancers. But what's also clear is an emphasis on the transitory, the ephemeral and the lyrical tragic; Murphy writes about *The Politics of Creation*:

> As a viewer the experience is of course unique in terms of its raw content but what's more than this it seems to allow one to have an extended experience of the present moment. Whereas a regular stage production will be known to be predetermined, in TPoC the anticipation associated with knowing that the next series of notes or rhythmic pattern and ultimately how the choreography responds to it, will never be heard or seen again tends to expand the perception of "now" creating a mild hypnosis or meditative state.[103]

Found (2014)[104] {Fig. 107} and the previously discussed *What Colour Is It?* (2014) are quite different.

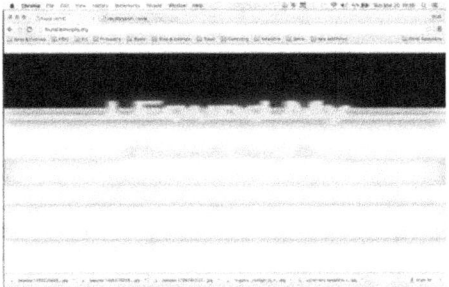

Fig. 107 James E. Murphy, *Found* (2014)

Found is an almost aggressive intrusion into the user's experience of a browser, consisting simply of the words 'I Found My Soul In A Browser Window' flashed repeatedly on the screen in a manner that someone suffering from photosensitive epilepsy should avoid at all costs. Using soft-focused typography that flashes in and out of visibility, with the words crossed and revealed in the most blatant of RGBY tones, *Found* isn't functional, it is disconcertingly glaring visually, and offers no chance for reciprocity and reflective judgment whatsoever in a fashion. By removing any identification of the 'I' and by situating the conceptualized space self-referentially inside its own browser window, *Found* leaves us with an experience that closes any chance of interchange or exchange between the art and the viewer. And the previously discussed *What Colour Is It?* (2014) is more than just a simple confounding of our anticipated feedback but is a strong demarcation

---

103 James E. Murphy, 'The Politics of Creation'.

104 James E. Murphy, 'Found', 2014, http://found.jemurphy.org/.

of the singular difference between the digital parameters of experience and our normative experience of the world at a phenomenological level wherein the interface ceases to function despite its appearance. Manovich's observation that cognitive resources become increasingly utilized really seems to capture Murphy's art, although Murphy's art seems to have created a digital event horizon in a way that replicates the division between actors and audiences in Manovich's notion of 'interaction as theater'.[105] At the same time, the increasing use of cognitive resources in the aesthetic experience contraindicates an engaged and personal aesthetic experience, and Murphy's work heightens our awareness of this process in a very valuable fashion.

---

105   Lev Manovich, 'Interaction as an aesthetic event'.

Beyond the Theatricality of the New Aesthetic

Two projects by Lev Manovich bring out these issues in notable and fascinating ways: *Selfiecity* (2014) and *On Broadway* (2014-2016). Manovich is, of course, one of the most important theorists thinking about postdigital issues, but he's also created a number of projects that may not be referred to as 'art' in the traditional sense, in that they often seem more like visualized sociological research, but certainly fall into a broad definition as such in that they invite the same type of responses one normally has to art. *Selfiecity* (2014), {Fig. 108} and its second manifestation *Selfiecity London* (2015), was an artistic project exploring data visualization through an analysis of 3200 Instagram selfie photos taken in Bangkok, Berlin, New York, Sao Paulo and Moscow[106] with London added as a sixth city later.[107]

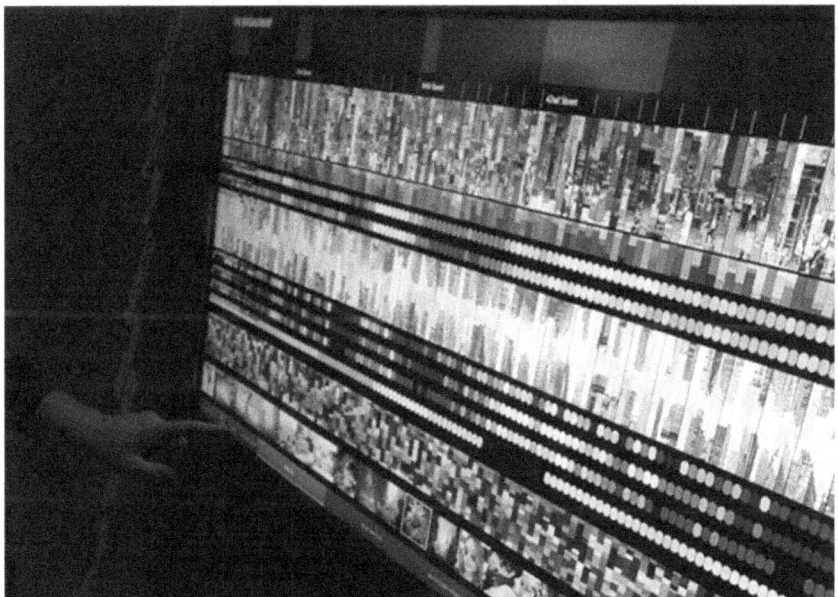

Fig. 108 Lev Manovich, et. al., *Selfiecity* (2014)

Starting off with 120,000 photos culled from a collection of 656,000, the organizers had these checked by Amazon Mechanical Turk workers to verify their status as a selfie photograph, reduced the sample set further to 1000 for each city after two Turks tagged

---

106   Lev Manovich, *Selfiecity*, 2014, http://selfiecity.net/.

107   Lev Manovich, *Selfiecity*, http://manovich.net/index.php/exhibitions/selfiecity. *Selfiecity* was led by Lev Manovich but credits a number of other participants as vital to the project, including Moritz Stefaner, Mehrdad Yazdani, Dominikus Baur, Daniel Goddemeyer, Alise Tifentale, Nadav Hochman and Jay Chow, see http://selfiecity.net/#credits.

a photo as a selfie, and then had each photograph further tagged by age and gender with higher skilled Turks. Given a conclusive set of selfies, the organizers then algorithmically estimated eye, nose and mouth positions as well as estimated emotional states. What emerged from these permutations of analysis is the means to visually represent various spectrums of data such as smiles, points of view, emotional states, the expressiveness of the poses and the propensity of selfies as a photographic subject. What was revealed in this project were apparent geographically determinable trends; for instance, people in selfies in Bangkok and Sao Paulo smiled significantly more than in the other cities, and women in Moscow took far more selfies than men and treated selfies more like a fashion shoot to project an image of themselves rather than simply as a marker of their presence or participation. Is *Selfiecity* art? The project itself engages with that question by including three essays analyzing the selfies as a social phenomenon and handling critical theory's ability to analyze the selfie as a manifestation of our zeitgeist,[108] but in a traditional sense it's very hard to think about *Selfiecity* as 'art' not only because of the productive methodology involved, including the obvious contributions from a vast array of individuals, but also because of the sense that it's a project more ensconced in anthropology. Well, we've not been talking about art in the traditional sense for a long time, and it's clear that *Selfiecity* is but one instance of a new way of making art that is socially and cooperatively engaged and produced in a manner closely approximating Nicholas Bourriaud's notion of relational aesthetics. At the same time, *Selfiecity* is a challenging artwork that is fully New Aesthetic in nature for the simple reason that it's dependent on a productive methodology and aesthetic strategy that is itself uncritically dependent on underlying conventions of the nature of data. Recalling Otto Neurath's infographics, with the transformation of data into visual form which almost perfunctorily and negligently draws upon its sources, *Selfiecity* manifests its visual appearance in a similar fashion, albeit in a manner clearly much more thoughtful and engaged, in that the data becomes the visualization rather than being revealed by the visualization. This is what makes *Selfiecity* particularly interesting and valuable and what makes it a genuine instance of New Aesthetic art: it's not just that Manovich and his team translated the data into a visual form with its own aesthetic criteria, it's that the aesthetic criteria were built into the aesthetics of the data itself as it was discovered through the research and the creation of the art. Zach Sokol writes:

Not only does *selfiecity* [sic] offer findings about the demographics of people taking selfies (as well as info about their poses and expressions, such as smile trends), it also shares a variety of data visualizations (such as collages that overlay hundreds

---

108   Alise Tifentale, 'The Selfie: Making Sense of the "Masturbation of Self-Image" and the "Virtual Mini-Me"', *Selfiecity*, 2014, http://d25rsf93iwlmgu.cloudfront.net/downloads/Tifentale_Alise_Selfiecity. pdf; Nadav Hochman, 'Imagined Data Communities', *Selfiecity*, 2014, http://d25rsf93iwlmgu. cloudfront.net/downloads/Nadav_Hochman_selfiecity.pdf; Elizabeth Losh, 'Beyond Biometrics: Feminist Media Theory Looks at Selfiecity', *Selfiecity*, 2014, http://d25rsf93iwlmgu.cloudfront.net/ downloads/Liz_Losh_BeyondBiometrics.pdf.

of selfies that share certain characteristics), and allows visitors to explore the entire photo collection, filtering the information into several formats that could reveal patterns or trends that ripple throughout selfie culture.[109]

While Sokol's enthusiasm for the project is appreciated, it's clear that he's seeing *Selfiecity* only as a project whose forms are determined by the artists' manipulation of the data rather than as a means of revealing the inherent aesthetic nature of the data itself. To put it another way, the ontologically circular nature of the data, generated autonomously within its self-determining aesthetic manifestation, reveals itself through the artistic choices Manovich and the rest made in a way that's independent of those artistic choices; the fundamentally important aesthetic engagement for the viewer lies not in *Selfiecity*'s website, for instance, but in its autonomous aesthetic.

Equally important and interesting is Manovich's *On Broadway* (2014-2016).[110] {Fig. 109}

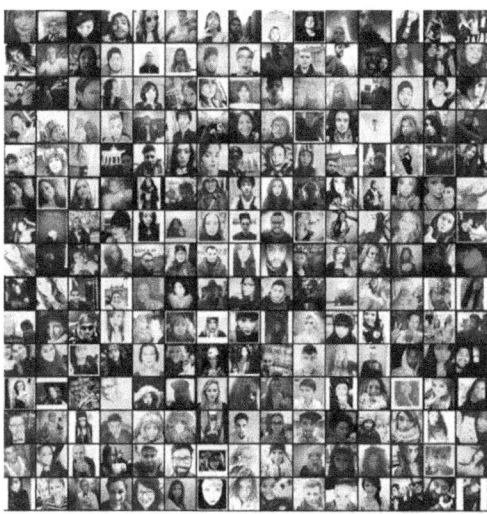

Fig. 109 Lev Manovich, et. al., *On Broadway* (2014-16)

As noted on the website for the project, *On Broadway* is an 'interactive installation [...] [that] represents life in the 21st century city through a compilation of images and data collected along the 13 miles of Broadway that span Manhattan'. Drawing upon the rich history of modern representations of cities' identities, ranging from Pissaro's series of paintings of the Boulevard Montmartre to *Spider-Man* comics and, especially, Edward

109   Zach Sokol, 'SelfieCity Might Be The Ultimate Data-Driven Exploration Of The Selfie', *The Creators Project*, 19 February 2014, http://thecreatorsproject.vice.com/blog/selfiecity-might-be-the-ultimate-data-driven-exploration-of-the-selfie.

110   Lev Manovich, *On Broadway*, 2016, http://on-broadway.nyc/.

Ruscha's seminal *Every Building on the Sunset Strip* (1966), {Fig. 110} Lev Manovich and his team[111] created a visual representation of a broad spectrum of data sources in real time and averaged over extended periods of time in order to provide a portrait of Broadway's important role in the life of New York City.

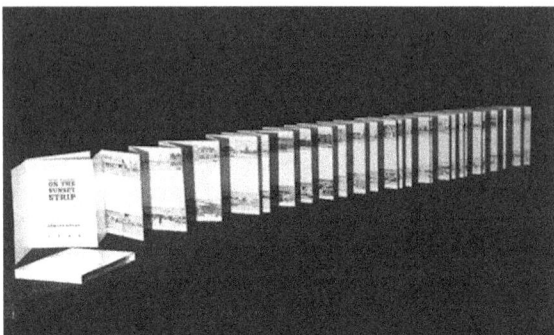

Fig. 110 Edward Ruscha, *Every Building on the Sunset Strip* (1966)

Instagram images, Google Street View pictures of the facades of buildings, taxi statistics obtained from the city, demographic data and collection of dominant colors by location and social media imagery were brought together to create a panoply remarkably similar in intent to Walter Benjamin's unfinished *Arcades Project* (1927-1940) as a data collage manifesting a personification of the life of this segment of the city. This last point is crucial, and it's what ties *On Broadway* together with its artistic predecessors: what emerges out of the experience of this art installation is a sense of the life of Broadway, a sense that, as one write puts it, 'NYC is a city that does sleep, a bit'.[112] At the same time, *On Broadway* is curiously similar to *Selfiecity* in its dependence on big data for its raw information and its aesthetic appeal. To compare it to Ruscha's work is illuminating: whereas Ruscha's images of the building on Sunset Strip is just as much about the endurance of the photographer to image each and every building as it is about creating an extensive and all-encompassing image of that one location in West Hollywood, *On Broadway* doesn't illustrate so much the efforts of the artists involved as it shows the presentation of the information generated by the people living, working and travelling on Broadway; whereas Ruscha's work is an act of documentation, *On Broadway* is primarily a presentation of what had already been documented and archived by software data analysis and stored with the aesthetic affect fundamentally driven by the sublime realization of the existence of the data itself. Manovich notes:

---

111   Including Daniel Goddemeyer (http://danielgoddemeyer.com/), Moritz Stefaner (http://truth-and-beauty.net/) and Dominkus Baur (http://do.minik.us/blog).

112   David Smith, 'NYC is a city that does sleep, a bit', *Revolutions*, 20 March 2015, http://blog.revolutionanalytics.com/2015/03/nyc-is-a-city-that-does-sleep-a-bit.html.

How does a "data city" look like? We did not want to show the data in a conventional way using only graphs and numbers. We also did not want to use another convention of showing spatial data – a map. The result of our explorations is "On Broadway": a visually rich image-centric interface, where numbers play only a secondary role, and no maps are used. The project proposes a new visual metaphor for thinking about the city: a vertical stack of image and data layers. There are 13 such layers in the project, all aligned to locations along Broadway. Using our unique interface (available as the online app and in large multi-touch screen installed at New York Public Library as part of "The Public Eye" exhibition), you can see all data at once, or zoom and follow Broadway block by block.[113]

While Manovich notes that the intention is to produce a visually rich and interactive experience, the emphasis and the end result is clearly situated less in the superficial effect but in the creation of a 'new metaphor' that breaks through a digitized fourth wall. We would argue that this new metaphor isn't as new as Manovich and his team think it is simply because its origins lie less in the creativity of the artists but in the driving force behind the New Aesthetic. John Brownlee makes an interesting point when he notes that 'On Broadway is the latest in a series of experiments to leverage computers, the web, and massive data to represent our cities in new ways.'[114] Leveraging the data, the software and the hardware means pushing them to act, to create the aesthetic experience, in ways that only they are capable of doing; On Broadway is, in our opinion, a fascinating and beautiful example of what New Aesthetic art is precisely because the data and its parameter-controlling manifestations achieve an incredibly determinative and autonomous agency in the creation of the aesthetic experience. Once the interactivity takes place the artists' control permanently slips away and all that remains is the data. Nevertheless, we take as a central tenant of our position a point nicely articulated by Manovich, writing about Selfiecity: 'New image-making and image-sharing technologies demand radically new ways of interpretation and analysis in what we might think of as a postdigital age, and Selfiecity is an attempt to explore and map these new representational forms.'[115] Manovich is absolutely correct; New Aesthetic art and what it represents is about more than just appearing to be digital or postdigital but represents an entirely new way of interpreting and analyzing images, one that equally demands a new critical perspective. It's not enough to simply assess how cool or new the work is, but rather how much of a paradigmatic shift is evidenced and embodied in the work.

---

113   Lev Manovich, 'On Broadway'.

114   John Brownlee, 'Massive Data Visualization Brings NYC's Busiest Street To Life', http://www.fastcodesign.com/3043091/infographic-of-the-day/massive-data-visualization-brings-nycs-busiest-street-to-life.

115   Alise Tifentale and Lev Manovich, 'Selfiecity: Exploring Photography and Self-Fashioning in Social Media' in David M. Berry and Michael Dieter (eds) Postdigital Aesthetics: Art, Computation and Design, New York: Palgrave MacMillan, 2015, p. 120.

Two artists that can be positively compared to the methodology of Manovich's artworks are Ben Grosser and Matthew Rothenberg. Grosser's work, already discussed earlier in the book, has been varied in form and content, but clearly aligns itself with a specific New Aesthetic strategy that is entirely invested in designing the function of digital objects towards an embodied form of autonomy. Works like *Interactive Robotic Painting Machine* (2011) {Fig. 111} bear some resemblance, in a non-destructive fashion, to Jean Tinguely's work, but pushes far beyond what Tinguely's work accomplishes to establish itself as a primary instance of New Aesthetic art because there are measurable results that can be assessed comparatively to the form of our own aesthetic choices.

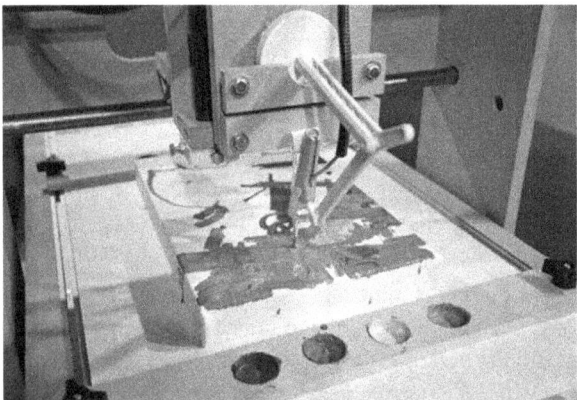

Fig. 111 Ben Grosser, *Interactive Robotic Painting Machine* (2011)

Taking the idea that intelligence can evolve even in software and, thus, that aesthetic sensibilities, as an expression of the needs of that evolved intelligence, can also evolve, Grosser built

> an interactive robotic painting machine that uses artificial intelligence to paint its own body of work and to make its own decisions. While doing so, it listens to its environment and considers what it hears as input into the painting process. In the absence of someone or something else making sound in its presence, the machine, like many artists, listens to itself. But when it does hear others, it changes what it does just as we subtly (or not so subtly) are influenced by what others tell us.[116]

Interactive Robotic Painting Machine is a programmed art-producing machine which at first seems to be part of a long tradition of similar machines tracing back to the early 1960s, but Grosser's addition to it is clearly a heightened independence and even a sense of self-awareness in the capability of the work to respond. Having identified one of the primary aspects of artistic identity as the ability to think, listen, and hear oneself, Grosser

116   Ben Grosser, 'Interactive Robotic Painting Machine', *Ben Grosser*, 2011, http://bengrosser.com/projects/interactive-robotic-painting-machine/.

has programmed the machine to, in effect, be an artificial artist. Still, as clever as this is, the autonomy is still programmed in, and the aesthetic responses through the programming can be predicted, thus leaving questions about the machine as an independent artist still in place; Grosser himself asks these very questions when he writes on his website:

> Does an art-making machine of my design make work for me or for itself? How does machine vision differ from human vision, and is that difference visible in its output? Is my own consciousness reinforced by the system or does it become lost within? In other words, is this machine alive, with agency as yet another piece of the technium, or is it our own anthropomorphization of the system that makes us think about it in these ways?[117]

What makes this piece fit into the category of New Aesthetic art is that uncertainty, particularly as it pertains to the question of anthropomorphization; it's not so much a question of whether Grosser is attributing human form and personality to the actions of the *Interactive Robotic Painting Machine* but a question about the freedom we have to anthropomorphize a machine, to seemingly ascribe metaphorically human traits when what might really be happening is that those traits exist in a non-metaphorical fashion in the object's digital basis. Far more interesting is *Computers Watching Movies* (2014), perhaps one of the most important and compelling examples of New Aesthetic art we've seen.[118] {Fig. 112}

Fig. 112 Ben Grosser, *Computers Watching Movies* (2014)

117   Ben Grosser, 'Interactive Robotic Painting Machine'.

118   Ben Grosser, 'Computers Watching Movies', 2014, *Ben Grosser*, http://bengrosser.com/projects/computers-watching-movies/.

Using software written by himself, Grosser provided computational devices not only the means to watch movies by tracking areas that attract their attentive focus but also the means to express that focus by plotting changes in the same manner that the focus of eyesight of vision can be tracked digitally today. Using well-known clips from six classic movies – *2001: A Space Odyssey*, *American Beauty*, *Inception*, *Taxi Driver*, *The Matrix*, and *Annie Hall* – Grosser's artwork is given an opportunity to *aesthetically* present its response. It's this last point that makes *Computers Watching Movies* so interesting, in that it's more than just software programming coupled with hardware capability but is, rather, a means of granting aesthetic agency to a digital configuration almost as a means of testing its potential disinterestedness as an aesthetic object in its own right. Exhibited widely and winning the First Prize at the VIDA Awards for Art and Artificial Life in 2014, Grosser's *Computers Watching Movies* is more than just machine vision but is also the embodiment of a new evaluative aesthetic paradigm; it's not merely that this artwork gives us some insight into the changing nature of cinema itself[119], it answers Grosser's question 'Will a system without our sense of narrative watch the same thing? I'm left wondering why I and the computer see things so differently.'[120] The real issue isn't why the human and the machine are seeing things differently. The underlying assumptions are that there's some conflation between the human and the digital responses; however, not only is there no conflation, not only is it clear that the human and the computer see things differently, even more important is the fact that *Computers Watching Movies* contains the strong implication that the computer's interest is quickly supplanting our own or that it's vision, its method of aesthetic evaluation is supplanting ours. Is it possible that Grosser's *Computers Watching Movies* is capable of achieving a purely disinterested perspective and would thus be capable of pronouncing pure, justified objective aesthetic judgments in a Kantian sense? Certainly at this point the answer is no, but that's only due to the technical nature of Kant's system that requires a subjective reflection. It's clear that this work puts forward a vision of the future in which even something as aesthetic judgment, once assumed not only to be a privileged and exclusive form of human activity, transitions into the digital in a manner that seems to be a more effective implementation.[121]

In a way this is similar to Matthew Rothenberg's project *Unindexed* (2015).[122] {Fig. 113}

---

119   Kyle Vanhemert, 'This Is What a Computer Sees When It Watches The Matrix', *Wired.com*, January 2014, http://www.wired.com/2014/01/computer-sees-watches-matrix/.

120   Vanhemert, 'This Is What a Computer Sees When It Watches The Matrix'.

121   Though even more recent efforts are alarming, at best, as evidenced with Microsoft's AI chatbot "Tay" quickly turning into a source of racist and sexist remarks; e.g. Sophie Kleeman, 'Here Are the Microsoft Twitter Bot's Craziest Racist Rants', *Gizmodo*, 24 March 2016, http://gizmodo.com/here-are-the-microsoft-twitter-bot-s-craziest-racist-ra-1766820160 and Jamie Condliffe, 'Microsoft's Racist Twitter Bot Sputters Back to Life, Bugs Out Again', *Gizmodo*, 30 March 2016, http://gizmodo.com/something-strange-is-happening-to-microsofts-twitter-bo-1767926273.

122   Matthew Rothenberg, *Matthew Rothenberg Selected Projects*, http://portfolio.mroth.info/.

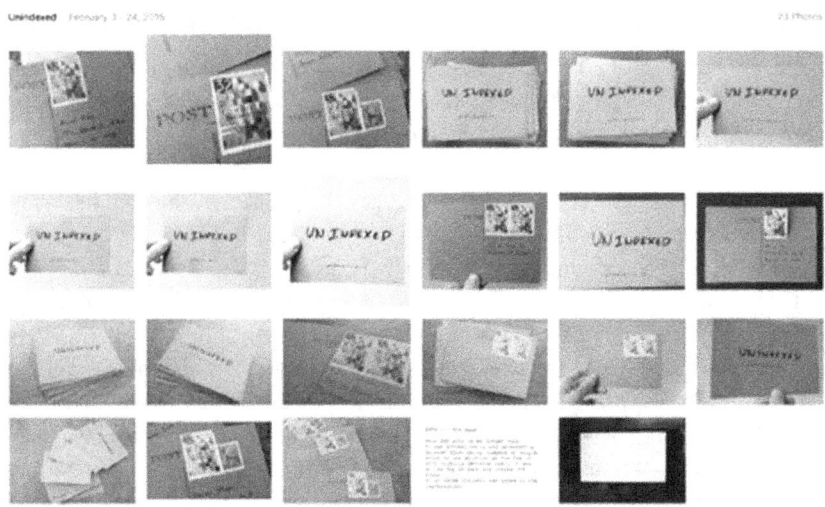

Fig. 113 Matthew Rothenberg, *Unindexed* (2015)

Rothenberg has worked in the tech industry in a number of prominent roles, but recently started creating his own art projects such as *Emojitracker* (2013),[123] which tracks all emoji usage worldwide in a dynamic graphic format, and *Swipe Left* (2014),[124] which conflated the dating app Tinder's usage with drone strikes through incorporated images of kills by drone missiles. *Unindexed* (2015), however, is a masterpiece in its own right, one directly akin to Yves Klein's conceptual artwork *Zone of Immaterial Pictorial Sensibility* (1959-62); described by Rothenberg as 'An experiment in the nature of ephemerality and persistence on the web' it was a website that functioned by continually searching for itself in Google and destroying every copied instance of itself once discovered, 'making the precise instant of algorithmic discovery the catalyst of destruction'. Importantly, Google discovered the work 22 days later and destroyed it resulting in no backups and no corresponding existence except the memory of the event. What aligns *Unindexed* with Grosser's work is the independence of the digital agent from human interaction; even though visitors to the *Unindexed* site were encouraged to share it and post to it the coding took control in an entirely separate fashion, breaking *Unindexed* free of human interactivity once set into motion. It's this release from human control that makes these instances of New Aesthetic art both exciting and unnerving; more than almost any other work we've discussed, *Unindexed* not only is fully participant in new forms of digital art, influenced by the ephemeral nature of the internet and simultaneously having a persistent conceptual effect, its nature as functioning independently of the artist makes it a perfect example of New Aesthetic art. In an interview Rothenberg noted 'Part of the

---

123   Matthew Rothenberg, *emojitracker: realtime use on twitter*, http://www.emojitracker.com/.

124   Matthew Rothenberg, *Swipe Left: Dating Apps and Drone Strikes*, 2014, https://medium.com/@mroth/swipe-left-dfa947df0355.

goal with the project was to create a sense of unease with the participants – if they liked it, they could and should share it with others, so that the conversation on the site could grow […] But by doing so they were potentially contributing to its demise via indexing, as the more the URL was out there, the faster Google would find it."[125]

In a way, *Unindexed* forces us to confront a peculiar conundrum because of its perma-nent and ephemeral nature when faced with certain manifestations of digital objects: are we complicit in their continuing existence (which we most certainly are, if for no other reason than that page view counts are often determinative of their appearance in search results) or do they have a life of their own (which they most certainly do as well, existing on servers)? This dialectic complicates our response, and increasingly we make concessions to the presence of the digital into our lives, allowing it to function in a state of independent agency (if not actual independent agency) rather than risking any emotional dangers or existential uncertainty were we to try and intervene or act on our volition. What made *Unindexed* so poignant and poetic was the simple fact that the more it was searched for, the more it appeared in Google's search results, and the quicker its demise would come; there was almost a sense of the tragic with a subsequent lack of comfort in one's participation. This feeling of being uncomfortable is only due to its lack of familiarity, a lack that is quickly disappearing the more digitized our world becomes. Marius Watz posted on his Tumblr feed that 'heavy use of algorithms is bad for you. That is, it is if you wish to consider yourself a computational creative capable of coming up with interesting work […] You cannot lay claim to "owning" any given algorithm (or hard-ware configuration), unless you have added significant extra value to it."[126] In his Tumblr essay from 2012, Watz writes about how coding itself should be regarded as an art form in that code exists as an entity in its own right similar to the traditional objects of artistic production. But what this really means, for Watz, is that code is not neutral: 'Algorithms provide the means to produce specific outcomes, typically through generative logic or data processing. But in the process they leave their distinct footprints on the result […] "speaking" through algorithms, your thought patterns and modes of expression are shaped by their syntax."[127] We're at the stage where what's really interesting about this is how this indicates that there are new boundaries; while the algorithms created by Watz are themselves dependent on more fundamental algorithms, meaning that his own creations are flavored by the footprints of the preexisting syntax, nevertheless something new is emerging, and a work like *Unindexed* forces us to confront the existence of boundaries that are increasingly evident and permeable without any action on our part as users.

125 Adrianne Jeffries, 'It Will Take Google 22 Days to Find You', *Motherboard*, 2 March 2015, http://motherboard.vice.com/read/it-will-take-google-22-days-to-find-you.

126 Quoted in *New Aesthetic, New Anxieties*, eds. Berry, van Dartel, Dieter, Kasprzak, Muller, O'Reilly, de Vicente, p. 12

127 Berry, van Dartel, Dieter, Kasprzak, Muller, O'Reilly, de Vicente, *New Aesthetic, New Anxieties*, p. 13

Finally, we need to take into account James Bridle's own recent exhibition of his art in the NOME gallery in Berlin. The NOME gallery was founded in 2015 as an exhibition space presenting work that exists at the intersection of art, politics and technology. Ralf Baecker, Matthew Plummer-Fernandez, Quayola and Kirsten Stolle are some of the important figures already shown there, and Bridle's inclusion signaled a clear commitment to art aligned with the ideas and effects of the New Aesthetic. Bridle's exhibition 'The Glomar Response' (2015)[128] references a curious piece of CIA history, when the *Glomar Explorer* was designed to salvage a sunken Soviet submarine in the 1970s, with subsequent requests by the press for information being met with the phrase 'neither confirm nor deny' that itself became a synecdoche for governments' secrecy efforts. Bridle's coinage of the phrase 'New Aesthetic' has been focused on the visual lexicon that involves glitches, pixelization and pixelated images, and general weirdness, but *The Glomar Response* develops through an exploration of the relationship between surveillance, secrecy and code that shows Bridle to be more than just a digital curator or collector of computational oddities. Through three projects – *Seamless Transitions*, which presents simulacrums of unphotographable locations through architectural visualizations derived from planning and construction documents; *The Fraunhofer Lines*, {Fig. 114} wherein gaps in documents obtained through freedom of information requests are presented as analogous to astronomical spectra analysis first done by the German physicist Joseph von Fraunhofer in 1814; and *Waterboarded Documents*, {Fig. 115} a presentation of ironic parallels between the British government's claim that water damage prevented the release of information and waterboard torture techniques use in the war on terror – Bridle's most recent art project represents neatly an exemplary summation of the New Aesthetic as new art.

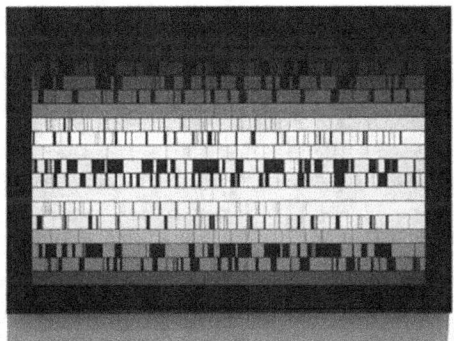

Fig. 114 James Bridle, *The Glomar Response: The Fraunhofer Lines 005* (2015)

---

128   Luca Barbeni, 'James Bridle, The Glomar Response' (Press Release), 2015, *NOME*, http://www. nomeproject.com/exhibitions/glomar-response.

Fig. 115 James Bridle, *The Glomar Response: Diego Garcia (Waterboarded Documents 001)* (2015)

In an interview, Bridle noted: 'For me this thing about the attempt to see though machine eyes is that it's actually an attempt to see through aggregates of human eyes and intention, because actually what you're seeing is the previously hidden intentions of the people that built these systems.'[129] What makes this such an interesting statement is that *The Glomar Response* seems to be exactly the opposite of this statement, a denial of Bridle's own optimism and utopianism found in the interview. Rather than an attempt to see through the aggregate of human eyes and intentions represented in the coding, *The Glomar Response* presents an increased pessimism particularly in the suggested notion of the natural development of the digital entities involved. In a way, Bridle's most recent piece of art, especially *The Fraunhofer Lines*, masterfully aligns itself with the realist position in a debate in the philosophy of mathematics, in that the increasing encroachment is apparently not just a matter of design or evolution but was always present; if the presentation of spectral information can be used to reveal the actual chemical composition of stars in an aesthetic manner then similar means can also be used to reveal the actual nature of digital objects not as the result of programming but real in an independent fashion. The anger and, most importantly, the futility that many of the artists we've discussed in this chapter feel with the current state of surveillance and

129   Ben Murray, 'Artist Q&A: James Bridle', *The Space*, 2015, http://www.thespace.org/news/view/ james-bridle-interview.

the intrusion of digital objects into our lives, lies less in the fact that they're responding to the intentions and decisions of human agents and the morality of their actions and far more in the fact that this offers a glimpse of a future wherein our intentions, our decisions and our actions are increasingly out of our hands as they are guided by the digitalization of the world.

CHAPTER 6
TELEOLOGY AND
THE NEW AESTHETIC

The New Aesthetic is a presage of a new time for inquiry skewed towards specific formal structures that are self-fulfilling generators of seemingly self-evident conclusions. We may have entered an era when a new type of real-time, self-generating investigative activities have emerged with increasing strength, situated at the intersection of the conventional academic approach and movements in popular culture that are often based on informal communication and information exchange models enhanced by ICT technologies within a practice of acceptable modal fallacies. To put it another way, the appearance of New Aesthetic objects have increasingly driven the way we observe, analyze, dissect and value not only digital objects specifically but the world generally; we are increasingly being driven by the priviledging of digitized results to the point that digital objects acquire an authority they wouldn't have had until recently. It's clear that an interactionist position negates any potential for a viable perpetuated opacity. Try as we might to treat New Aesthetic objects as singular, self-contained and non-affective – to keep them at arm's length not only so our own biases don't corrupt our observations but also so that our observations don't corrupt our methodologies – as soon as we start to analyze them then their specific conditions bleeds into our own approaches and transforms the way we interact with them. Affecting more than just scientific research, this New Aesthetic effect extends to a dramatic diminishment of efforts to freely group and summate disparate cultural products or enact curatorial practices in an impassioned manner without the taint of a digitized horizon serving as a preordained end result.[1] In a way, valuation has been irrevocably altered.

Recent years have produced an increased interest in the practice of curation. It's amusing to think that the origins of the word are specifically found in British religious orders where the curate was typically an assistant to a vicar charged or entrusted with the souls of the parish, as if the very act of curating carries with it religious authority over the eternal heavenly existence of individuals. In a contemporary context, what we're interested in can be described quite simply: the mania for lists of 'best beaches in 2015 to be seen at' or 'top 10 driving applications for the iPhone' and the like have become a dominant part of our newsfeed that seemingly give us options but, at the same time, have become unforeseen and perverse mnemonic devices driven by our own delusional fantasies. Every day it seems like we are increasingly bombarded with messages in our browsers and smartphones promoting thinly-disguised advertisements as actual information that would improve our lives: if only we clicked through and provided a small fee to the advertising companies that paid for those messages on pages we visit; if only we fulfilled, in our digital complacency, the purposes of big data and various profiling algorithms; if only we contributed further to their effect, we would be able to remember how amazing we always have been. We can be better people, have happier lives, if only we made sure to download each and every one of those top 10 driving applications. Miya Tokumitsu notes:

---

1   Again, as always, the irony doesn't escape us.

Blogs are curated. So are holiday gift guides. So are cliques, play lists, and restaurant menus. "Curated," a word that barely existed forty years ago, has somehow come to qualify everything in our lives. When I tried that glib parlor game of typing a word into Google to see how it would autocomplete the search phrase, the first suggestion for "curated" was "content." In other words, almost nothing escapes curation, or at least the possibility of being curated. How did our world become a venue for curation? And how did curating, a highly specialized line of museum work involving the care, accessioning, and exhibition of artworks, come to mean, as cultural policy scholar Amanda Coles puts it, "just picking stuff?"[2]

Tokumitsu's article is an interesting perspective on what has become a dominant part of our connected culture; providing lists of options to improve our lives in myriad ways gives readers a sense of freedom and superiority, a misguided notion that they've been given exclusive access to secreted knowledge. However, this is easily understood in a politicized fashion as feeding the need for personalization and creativity. There is definitely an ironic situation here; the search for guided authenticity invariably is a sub-sumption of one's choices to algorithms formulated to generate income for the curators. Lists of the greatest examples of art, for example, used to be created by art and cultural historians with broad and deep knowledge of the history of art and with a refined sense of taste as illustrations of their erudition, but now any sense of expertise disappears behind one's browser search history or is no more than the product of Google hits and poorly conceived Amazon or iTunes sales figures through the 'personalized' search results of the filter bubble. In the end it's increasingly apparent that the act of curating, traditionally justified by years of attenuation, customization and the development of perceptive assessment skills with the goal of being able to make justified and valuable judgments, is being driven by algorithms that rely on little if any human input except for the need to fill our lives with content. Content creation at the level of digital media, in the programmed formation of discursive structures, is now less an adjudicated process and more a function of data structures whose purpose is not informing, entertaining or elevating the consumers of curatorial processes but self-substantiating and sustaining their functional presence.

Perhaps this is cause for alarm and dismay. Perhaps we should regret the effect that the digital engines have while they feed us unanticipated and unexpected content and search results personally 'tailored' for us, seemingly embodying our unknown dreams and desires and creating the content that we didn't know existed in our lives. Maybe we should regret the lists of 'You Won't Believe These Celebs Real Names' and '75 Celebrities You Will Never Look At The Same Way Again'? Or perhaps we should regret the results of the Genius Playlist feature of iTunes rather than embracing its role in exposing us to

2   Miya Tokumitsu, 'The Politics of the Curation Craze', *New Republic*, 24 August 2015, http://www. newrepublic.com/article/122589/when-did-we-all-become-curators.

music that existed in our collection but that we've never listened to? We would be the first to admit that we've purchased apps for our iPhones, because an article promised us that it would improve our lives, only to quickly discover that its functions were merely variations of the graphic interface found in the default software and that the app failed to live up to its promise (especially when the company's server would be compromised or discontinued). We can rail against this insidious digital permeation into our sense of discernment, reject the hijacking of our critical faculties, but we would be dishonest if we didn't admit our own hypocrisy; the beginnings of the New Aesthetic itself lie in this new form of curation, and we've certainly benefitted from it.

Instead of ascending to sanctimonious heights of criticism while railing against the depths that culture has fallen to, we're instead interested in the specific means that brought us here. Our focus in this chapter turns to questioning the very nature of what drives curating itself, what drives these lists and collections in their digital form to have a functioning effect, and what commonalities are relatedly detectable. To this end, we propose that the digital algorithms that generate bodies of curated facts, regardless of their value or lack thereof, need to be identified as teleological processes. In fact, it is specifically the teleological nature of the programs and objects which we would describe as the New Aesthetic, because it is our contention that being autonomous and teleological is one of the defining means differentiating digital, postdigital and New Aesthetic objects. To this end we would like to borrow positions from three philosophers whose work might seem inapplicable but which we believe offer instructive positions to open up new interpretative models. This chapter isn't so much an analysis of how digital curation exists outside of users' control but an analysis of how the autonomous nature of the programs and digital objects can be teleologically judged as they go about creating that content. We've been exploring exactly how to differentiate between postdigital objects and the New Aesthetic objects, and it's here that we reach a stricter means of identification based on process, function and effect.

A persistent question - even, perhaps, a persistent problem at a fundamental level - is how to distinguish between digital objects, art objects that are digital, and genuine examples of objects of the New Aesthetic and New Aesthetic art. It would be strikingly disingenuous if we asserted that this question hasn't persisted throughout the book. Really, you've probably been asking, when are they going to get around to actually defining what New Aesthetic art is in such a fashion that it's clear, precise, and useful when talking about art? One important instance has been the glitch, which is a persistent and necessary presence; as necessary as the presence of the glitch is, though, it should be perceived as more of a symptom than as a fundamental aspect of a New Aesthetic object. In short, we've arrived at a question that's just as much about taxonomy as it is about aesthetic value, with two different but related approaches. Our first is the philosophy of Arthur Schopenhauer. Our second, and more important approach, is based on Immanuel Kant's often dismissed discussion of teleology in the *Critique of Judgment* and Ernst Mayr's notion of biological teleology, organisms and biological evolution.

Schopenhauer and the New Aesthetic

Schopenhauer's philosophy has received little serious interest for quite some time, except from those interested in the history of German idealism, but his understanding of aesthetics and art has been very influential. Through his description of representation and will as the fundamental metaphysical manifesting and substantiating forces of existence, Schopenhauer described a means of characterizing all phenomena in a manner that gives each a sense of singularity, presence and autonomous, self-determining purpose. To put it simply, Schopenhauer's pessimistic philosophy asserts that we only experience the representation of objects generated by their will, which is an internal force with greater or lesser strength and capability, and that all objects through their representations are in conflict with all other objects via their representations in order to make their wills ascendant over other wills. If this sounds somewhat familiar to our description of New Aesthetic objects, then you can understand why we would begin with Schopenhauer as a baseline for a digital taxonomy.

The first time we began to think about Schopenhauer's philosophy was in relationship to Dmitriy Krotevich's image manipulation software PixelDrifter (2014).[3] In describing the effect of the software, Krotevich notes:

> "By default, each pixel tries to find the 'weakest' pixel among its closest neighbors and if one is found, they swap their positions [...] Also pixels with a higher 'power' value can do more 'swaps.'" Put differently, the pixels are imbued with enough intelligence to behave autonomously, although Krotevich says, "an experienced user can predict a result".[4]

The function of PixelDrifter is driven by pixels themselves, with the inherent strength of each one allowed to be a part of determining its representative force. This is very much in contrast to the normal way we think of pixels; if we think about them at all - except in the context of misinformed purchasing decisions when we're buying digital cameras - we think of each one not only as entirely equal to each other one without any pictorial hierarchical relationship but also as subservient to the overall unified digital image. Given a normative perception of pixels, stuck at a superficial level that doesn't actually recognize their presence except in the case of glitches, we are only examining the digital object as a representation in the sense that Schopenhauer describes representations as simply a construction. At the same time, these pixels as individual representations of themselves, governed by a will to exist, in conflict with other wills, are more than the normal direc-

---

3   Dmitriy Krotevich, 'PixelDrifter', *Internet Archive*, 11 May 2014, https://archive.org/details/pixeldrifter.

4   Margaret Rhodes, 'This Glitch Art Is Made of Pixels Powered by Their Own AI', *Wired.com*, 7 August 2014, http://www.wired.com/2014/08/this-glitch-art-is-made-of-pixels-powered-by-their-own-ai/.

tionless instances of will Schopenhauer normally ascribes to inorganic objects. To put it another way, a number of commentators have described the result of PixelDrifter as an example of pixels acquiring a level of autonomy and life. This interpretation is furthered when Krotevich notes:

> Also, PxD uses a different approach [...] It doesn't simply sort pixels – it's more like a scientific visualization/artificial intelligence program that "breathes life" into pixels, making them decide where to travel [...] It's not quite Turing Test AI, but the pixels do react like they're autonomous creatures.[5]

Is Krotevich perhaps being a little too coy with his use of quotation marks? We think he might be. In so many respects, Krotevich seems to be describing pixels as autonomous, independent and functioning entities that are let loose with a limited form of artificial intelligence, a bit like glitches that, in effect, become self-sustaining. From the perspective of the New Aesthetic, why not simply concede that pixels do have a functional autonomy? That they have a life of their own in a way that's not merely metaphorical. Schopenhauer provides us with some insight when he stresses that 'the remoteness, in fact the appearance of a complete difference between the phenomena of inorganic nature and the will, perceived by us as the inner reality of our own being, arises principally from the contrast between the wholly determined conformity to law in one species of phenomenon, and the apparently irregular arbitrariness the other'.[6] The key here is that the representations of the pixels, their presented presence to us, is not necessarily determined by a conformity to laws but is also more than just set a random occurrences that is perceivable as a group of independent entities interacting with each other and ourselves. Could it even be said that Krotevich's pixels strive to assert their superiority over each other and their relationship to us? What began as a glitch, as an apparent irregularity, now begins to function as a means of self-determinism.

What's really interesting for us is that Schopenhauer's philosophy posits all wills, organic and inorganic, as teleological in nature; everything has a purpose or a goal, even if it's simply to continue to exist in the face of the opposing wills of other things. Damion Scott makes a really interesting point when he notes:

> This is [Schopenhauer's] identification of the Will with inorganic nature, consisting of, he claims, individual discrete wills and the natural forces which objectify or manifest, general or universal will. Biological beings, many psychological beings, and artifacts

---

5   DJ Pangburn, 'Here's What Artificially Intelligent Pixel Bending Looks Like ', *The Creators Project*, 28 July 2014, http://thecreatorsproject.vice.com/blog/heres-what-artificially-intelligent-pixel-bending-looks-like.

6   Arthur Schopenhauer, *The World as Will and Representation*, trans. E.F.J. Payne. Dover Publications, New York: 1966, p. 118.

have teleological properties. They have functions that are aimed at or strive towards a particular goal or particular goals [...] even if unconscious and non-intentional. Inorganic entities simply do not seem to have proper functions nor strive towards the fulfillment of real goals. In short, inorganic entities do not seem to manifest will.[7]

Scott's interpretation of Schopenhauer at this point is that there seems to be an assertion of a difference between organic and inorganic objects, but this depends on the weak notion of 'seems'. This problem is, quite simply, that organic objects have a will (because their will acts) while inorganic objects do not have a will (because their will doesn't act). But as Scott points out, Schopenhauer himself contradicts this limitation when he writes:

Finally, we feel directly and immediately how a burden, which hampers our body by its gravitation towards the earth, incessantly presses and squeezes this body in pursuit of its one tendency. If we observe all this, it will not cost us a great effort of the imagination to recognize once more our own inner nature, even at so great a distance. It is that which in us pursues its ends by the light of knowledge, but here, in the feeblest of its phenomena, only strives blindly in a dull, one-sided, and unalterable manner. Yet, because it is everywhere one and the same-just as the first morning dawn shares the name of sunlight with the rays of the full midday sun-it must in either case bear the name of will.[8]

Schopenhauer's use of active verbs makes it clear that he conceives of all things as having active wills, even inorganic objects, and that these wills are substantiating forces asserting their existence and the singularities of their beings in conflict with other beings. Looking back on many of the examples of the New Aesthetic that we've discussed, each and every one of them has this quality, something that is given an even more fundamental presence at an almost atomistic level by Krotevich's PixelDrifter; one of the defining qualities of a New Aesthetic object is its will, its presence, its forceful relationship with the user and the user's environment. Schopenhauer's philosophy is as good as any for describing the underpinnings of an 'Internet of Things' wherein all objects digitally interact with each other not simply because they are programmed to but because they are teleologically driven to assert the singularity and autonomy of their being, their will, in relationship to other digital objects. The amusing paradox of the idea of the 'Internet of Things' is precisely that most people aren't talking about physical objects but the representation by those objects of themselves to other objects; the digital world of objects is a world of will and representation. Or, to put it another way: 'Teleology, [Schopenhauer] argued [...] is not the result of the accumulation of small selected adaptations, neither is it the

7   Damion Scott, 'Functional Analysis and Schopenhauer's Theory of the Will' (*The World as Will and Representation*, Volume I, Sections 17-29), https://www.academia.edu/2576175/Functional_Analysis_and_Schopenhauers_Theory_of_the_Will.

8   Arthur Schopenhauer, *The World as Will and Representation*, p. 118.

result of intelligent foresight, as supposed by the rationalist and theist, but the inevitable showing forth of the underlying unity of the "will to live.''[9] If one is to draw out a teleology of wills from Schopenhauer's philosophy, a purpose to their existence, it is simply to sustain their existence in conflict with other things and, even, to overcome their opposition.

The teleology of Schopenhauer's description of wills is bound within a continuous assertion of their autonomy, but this description has its limits for our purposes precisely because his aesthetics is predicated on his metaphysical assertion that there is a potential escape from this constant conflict; part of the appeal of Schopenhauer to artists is his notion that art is the means of achieving a state of non-conflict or equilibrium with the wills of the world, and this is obviously not the case with digital objects as they increasingly dominate the character of our lives. Schopenhauer's philosophy is a starting point to think about New Aesthetic objects as teleological, but far more interesting than his perspective is Immanuel Kant's *Critique of Judgment*, particularly Kant's description of teleological judgments.

---

9   DeWitt H. Parker, 'Introduction', *Schopenhauer Selections*, New York: Scribner, 1928.

Kant, the New Aesthetic, and Beauty

Our interest in Kant lies less in his assertions than in trying to develop an applicable understanding of the *Critique of Judgment* based on regularities to objects of the New Aesthetic. In the *Critique of Pure Reason* Kant writes: 'By nature, in the empirical sense, we understand the connection of appearances as regards their existence according to necessary rules, that is, according to laws.'[10] If this is the case, is there a degree of regularity involved with postdigital and New Aesthetic objects?

Our first response was to think of digital objects as available for a pure aesthetic judgment, as objects that can be considered beautiful. Beauty is, for Kant, the central topic of Part I of the *Critique of Judgment* as a mediating link between nature and freedom in a transitory sense, meaning that it didn't serve as a transcendental substantiation of any metaphysics but as a subjective assertion of the free play of our rational capacities. However, because beauty is more of a capacity and lacks self-sufficiency, existing as a mediation between the appearance of nature and the opportunity for freedom, Kant avoids a discussion of what nature is and focuses on our ability to judge nature as beautiful. Yet, shouldn't we have to ask what nature is? In a way, couldn't we ask: what happens when we remove theoretical and practical reason and are left only with nature itself? More importantly, what happens when the opportunity to make a judgment of taste eludes us or, even more poignantly, is an impossibility?

For Kant beauty is only for humans.[11] This is a crucially important part of Kant's examination of judgments because judgment is always subjectively reflective, regardless of whether it's aesthetic or teleological, and is distinct from epistemic claims or moral certitude because it generates a sense of pleasure in the individual making the judgment in the case of the aesthetic. For many, this is a problem with Kantian aesthetics when Kant then goes on to claim that the source of pleasure in any aesthetic experience lies in individual judgments made in a state of disinterestedness and then extended to other individuals with a demand of agreement; going beyond the merely agreeable, Kant proposes a description of an experience of an object as aesthetically pleasing that involves a representation of the purposiveness in the object, in a sense that the object exists with the purpose of being experienceable as aesthetically pleasing precisely in the free play of the faculties which is then presented as true to others for their assumed agreement. To put it another way, Kant is proposing the idea that the reason we find beauty in our experiences of objects is because those objects appear to agree with our capability of identifying beauty as we think about our response to our experience of them and they are confirmed as beautiful because other people apparently agree with our judgments;

---

10   *Critique of Pure Reason*, A216/B263

11   Immanuel Kant, *Kritik der Urtheilskraft*, (*KdU*), §15.

more radically than the first two critical projects, the *Critique of Judgment* is an attempt to overcome the dichotomy between our subjective responses to the world and our desire to objectively know facts about the world, to give a sense of certainty to our feelings about the world, and to justifiably represent that certainty to others.

New Aesthetic objects could be subject to a Kantian aesthetic judgment; with disinterestedness as the criterion for a valid assessment of the beauty of an object, New Aesthetic objects by their very nature could be processed through a disinterested perspective and, for all of the talk of the appealing design of hardware and software objects, their relatable tangibility could possibly be ignored in favor of a dispassionate aesthetic assessment. It's conceivable, for instance, to imagine that discussions of the design of hardware and software take place in a rarified state of objectivity, and that the debate between Apple fans and their PC loyalist detractors take place on the merits of their respective GUIs alone. At the same time this is a little far-fetched for a number of reasons. The recognizably pervasive nature of the presence and function of digital objects and the intuitive means by which we understand and use them makes it nearly impossible to conceive of a fully disinterested engagement. Furthermore, the inseparable functionality of digital objects, or at least the unavoidable perception of an imminent functionality, is never far away once we start to interact with any digital object in an invested fashion; we have, after all, often spent a lot of money of these digital devices. Is it possible to be disinterested in an app on our smartphone, to disregard its efficaciousness as a means of presenting information, to disregard the manner in which it 'enhances' our lives or alerts us to information about ourselves that we could not have known otherwise? Is it possible to neither love nor hate our iPhones but disinterestedly appreciate them, especially when they don't 'just work'? Regardless of the debate about the functional beauty of artworks,[12] the functionality of New Aesthetic objects makes it impossible to assess their aesthetic quality as beautiful in a Kantian sense because the presentations of their functional and aesthetic natures are frequently intertwined and inseparable. This extends beyond the hardware and the appearance of software to the information provided to the user. In some ways, digital curation has even increasingly undermined the potential for a disinterested perspective as our apps tell us what we need to know; the methods of presenting New Aesthetic objects through Tumblr and other social media websites, for example, mean they are not 'curated' in the traditional sense of the word but are collections reflecting their authors' subjective response to the patterns of their navigation through various forms of digital content that are guided by search results algorithmically constructed in response to previous search histories and terms.

This exploration of 'curated' lists and the GUI designs of smartphone might not seem important but it is in that they are the means to return to the original context in a con-

---

12   Stephen Davies, 'Aesthetic Judgements, Artworks and Functional Beauty', *The Philosophical Quarterly*, Vol. 56, No. 223 (April, 2006): 224-241.

sideration of the receptive use of the New Aesthetic objects; most online presentations of objects are done with their links intact, as if the very act of directing is almost a forceful way of saying 'you cannot look at it through my eyes, you must be directed to look at it as it should be seen'. From our perspective, this means that the very nature of New Aesthetic objects plays a fundamental, determinative role in the formation of critical (and uncritical) discourse engaging with their existence or simply their use; disinterestedness fails here again not just because the users are interested in the use of New Aesthetic objects but because New Aesthetic objects are 'interested' in how they will be used. This means that the New Aesthetic produces objects that all by themselves resist a Kantian intuition of beauty, not so much because they can't be described as beautiful but because they apparently will themselves to be described as beautiful. Kant writes: 'For a judgment of taste consists precisely in this, that it calls a thing beautiful only by virtue of that characteristic in which it adapts itself to the way we apprehend it.'[13] This means that the appearance of objects will seemingly change so as to be in accordance with our capacity to judge them as beautiful, but Kant certainly didn't mean that the objects would actually change. New Aesthetic objects, however, do change in a responsive fashion through their use; it isn't simply that applications on our smartphones are updated, it's that the appearance of many of these apps change in response to data and use so as to make them appear more valuable or useful to the user. Equally so, New Aesthetic objects resist the Kantian notion that they must be lacking purpose in order to be universally posited as beautiful simply because their form, with its radical presentation of its digital origins, is its purpose. This is a strange conundrum to consider, one that takes us away from Kant while retaining his ideas in the background: it's as if an aesthetic object cannot be purposeful, precisely because that would deny a potentially disinterested evaluative position, while at the same time the pleasure in the free play of the faculties is teleological and, therefore, purpose-fulfilling, precisely because a successful evaluation of its aesthetic presentation to the faculties necessarily produces pleasure.

New Aesthetic art further counters Kant's ideas of aesthetics as they relate to beauty when it resists intuition and abrogates any mediation between itself and the subject. Strangely, we might even propose at this point that New Aesthetic objects should be regarded as unsuitable and purposeless for any type of aesthetic judgment in part because of Kant's priviledging of nature over art when it comes to a sense of certainty in aesthetic judgments. For Kant nature is best represented to the faculties in such a manner that the likeness of its particular determinations agrees at least with the possibility of purposes at work in it according to laws of freedom; if there is no opportunity for the free play of imagination in its relation to intuition then there is no available freedom and a 'dialectic of aesthetic judgment' is unavailable. The possibility of the free play of faculties is lessened in the instance of art in comparison to nature. In the case of New

---

13   Immanuel Kant, *The Critique of Judgment*, trans. Pluhar, Werner, Indianapolis, IN: Hackett, 1987, p. 145.

Aesthetic objects, however, what we arrive at is almost an indeterminate indeterminacy. Taste enables a move to freedom, from indeterminate theory to determined but freely created response; objects which exist within the realm of the New Aesthetic not only resist being opportunities of taste but are antithetical to taste itself, they resist a unity of the supersensible. Kant's assertion that imagination and understanding can be reconciled into each other is well known, one simple objection however is that the 'dilemma [...] is [that either] the free play of the faculties is involved in all cognitive perceptual experience, or it is not. If it is, then it would seem, counterintuitively, that every object should be perceived as beautiful.'[14] In the case of New Aesthetic objects what can be intuited about their intention is, at best, the nature of their origins; this, however, is entirely alien to our nature, as they derive their existence from self-sufficient algorithms that are impossible to submit to reflective judgment. In short, objects and art objects of the New Aesthetic cannot be viably judged within Kant's parameters as beautiful. But could they be judged as having a purpose? Kant writes: 'For if we want to investigate the organized products of nature by continued observation, we find it completely unavoidable to apply to nature the concept of intention, so that even for our empirical use of reason this concept is an absolutely necessary maxim.'[15]

Objects of the New Aesthetic do exist for aesthetic and, therefore, reflective judgment. Furthermore, New Aesthetic objects do exist as a representation of their unity. Here's a dilemma in a way, but it's precisely this dilemma that's the reason we're interested in thinking through Kant in order to discuss New Aesthetic objects and art. It's at this point that we make a crucial transition out of our use of Kantian aesthetics to Kant's conception of teleological judgments.

---

14   Hannah Ginsborg, 'Kant's Aesthetics and Teleology', in Edward N. Zalta (ed.) *The Stanford Encyclopedia of Philosophy*, Fall 2014, http://plato.stanford.edu/archives/fall2014/entries/kant-aesthetics/.

15   Kant, *Critique of Judgment*, Pluhar, p. 280

Kant, the New Aesthetic, and the Critique of Teleology

While Kant's ideas on teleology are, at most, complicated and primarily a niche interest, it can be asserted that 'teleology serves a useful, if not indispensable, role in our understanding of the living objects and phenomena in nature'.[16] For Kant, a teleological judgment of an object is a judgment as *understanding* of its intrinsic purpose, a purpose to which the object embodies its realization. Teleological judgments are primarily concerned with a theoretical analysis of the nature of an object fulfilling its purpose, meaning that Kant's focus is on biological organisms rather than more abstract ideas like beauty; this means that a teleological judgment is still disinterested but not directed towards purposeless results such as delight in the free play of the faculties but towards an analysis of the degree to which the object fulfills its purpose. This is a crucially important aspect of our application of Kant's ideas; what needs to be kept in mind is that 'in the *Critique of Teleological Judgement* Kant is concerned with particular material objects of experience, and not with the concept of matter as it can be "constructed" in pure intuition. In order to explain the former we thus require laws that go beyond and are more specific than the a priori laws of pure science.'[17] While a teleological judgment may reveal a sense of the purpose of the object, perhaps even more valuable is that the identification of that purpose reveals the object as a self-organizing organism; it's not just that we figure out what an object should be doing but also that this purpose says a lot about that object by making it real, distinct, functional and independent of ourselves. This can be considerably extended by the notion that, for Kant, this understanding of objects as organisms may be articulated in the antinomy based on the following two principles:

> The first maxim of the power of judgement is the thesis: All generation of material things and their forms must be judged as possible in accordance with merely mechanical laws.

> The second maxim is the antithesis: Some products of material nature cannot be judged as possible according to merely mechanical laws (judging them requires an entirely different law of causality, namely that of final causes).[18]

What emerges is a dialectic that describes these organisms, subject to teleological judgment, as both things that are restricted to the limitations of their physical state as well as existing for themselves. In short, Kant formulates here the basis for a very specific and, at the time, radical form of teleological judgment.

---

16   Shidan Lofti, 'The 'Purposiveness' of Life: Kant's Critique of Natural Teleology', *The Monist*, January 2010, 93:1, p. 124.

17   Angela Breitenbach, 'Two views on nature: A solution to Kant's antinomy of mechanism and teleology', *British Journal for the History of Philosophy*, 16:2, 2008: 351-369.

18   Immanuel Kant, *Kritik der Urtheilskraft*, (*KdU*), §70, AAV: 387.

The key aspect of our employment of Kantian teleological judgments is as a means of revealing the intrinsic purpose in the very existence of objects as independent and autonomous continuations and, ultimately, of New Aesthetic objects as continuations of their existence in our experience of them. In §64, 'On the Character Peculiar to Things as Natural Purposes', Kant writes:

> If [...] we cognize something as a natural product and yet are to judge it to be a purpose, and hence a *natural purpose* – unless perhaps the very [thought] is contradictory – then we need more. I would say, provisionally, that a thing exists as a natural purpose if it is *both cause and effect of itself* (although in two different senses). For this involves a concept of a nature without regarding nature as acting from a purpose; and even then, though we can think this causality, we cannot grasp it.[19]

What Kant means by this is that a natural object will both be itself, exist as it is, while equally be available for judgment as to the purpose for which it exists. An apple tree, for instance, can be judged as to how well it fulfills its purpose, which is to produce apples that are the means of propogating its species. Or a specific species of animal – a camel, for instance, adapted to live in the desert – can be judged as to how well it evolved to meets its purpose. Both of these examples were chosen to make a point, in that apples are judged by how well they taste and camels are judged as pack animals, but in both cases such judgments are aesthetic not teleological. Kant didn't intend teleological judgments to be similar to aesthetic judgments, even though both are reflective, but more of a means of identifying an opportunity for further scientific study with a very specific aim in mind. Many interpretations of Kant's teleology take it simply as that – as the means to identify things which are worth scientific investigation – but Kant's discussion of the principle of teleological judgments of nature as to their self-purposiveness is going farther. Within the context of his critical system, Kant argues that any effort to judge the natural purpose of a thing, its *Naturzweck*, based on its intrinsic form, is dependent on its natural form as *Naturwerk*; when an object appears to our experience to be efficaciously purposive, initially understood as related to art[20] but extended to all things that ground a causality to a purpose, it is because it appears to be a means by which a purpose is achieved as an intrinsic quality of the object, such that '[...] we arrive at no categorical [but only a hypothetical] purpose if we disregard the internal form and organization [of a blade of grass], and consider instead extrinsic purposive relations as to what use other natural beings make of the grass [...] this condition (namely, the existence of a thing as a final purpose) is unconditioned and hence lies wholly outside a physicoteleological consideration of the world'.[21] To put it another way, Kant's idea of a teleological judgment

---

19   Immanuel Kant, *Critique of Judgment*, Pluhar, p. 249.

20   Immanuel Kant, *Kritik der Urtheilskraft*, (*KdU*), §10.

21   Immanuel Kant, *Critique of Judgment*, Pluhar, p. 258.

depends on ignoring our aesthetic response (the tastiness of an apple, for example) in favor of seeing different purposes to the parts of the organism that sustain the overall purpose of the object (the continued existence of the apple tree and its species).

A teleological judgment regards an object only in terms of its efficient presentation of its purpose, what Kant refers to as its 'intrinsic purpose'.[22] While this is problematic – as a number of commentators point out this is both paradoxical to human thought and appears opposed to scientific thinking – Kant argues that it is a necessary judgment in order not to explain objects but simply to be able to cite their existence. While the extrinsic purposes of an objects are the easiest to asses, wherein an object is a means towards an end in a causal connection that is real, far more interesting are the intrinsic purposes, wherein an object is organized to reveal itself as itself in a causal connection that is ideal, an organism is 'both cause and effect of itself'.[23]

Kant is quite upfront about this being inapplicable to art, writing: 'Now in order for a thing to be a natural purpose, it must meet two requirements. *First*, the possibility of its parts (as concerns both their existence and their form) must depend on their relation to the whole. For since the thing itself is a purpose, it is covered by a concept or idea that must determine a priori everything that the thing is to contain. But if we think of a thing as possible only in *that* way then it is merely a work of art'.[24] This is where Lou's *Color Field* serves as a differentiating boundary point; quite clearly, the work doesn't serve a natural purpose and its teleological nature is neither self-sufficient nor autonomous. While there is a telos involved – the process that Lou focuses on and its recognition by the viewer being the primary concern of the artist – this purpose is not a priori related to the final object as a whole but is a secondary quality. In a way, this is precisely the nature of many art objects, in that there is often an irresolvable imbalance between first and second qualities of process and intent, between construction of intent and the realized effect of the intent. In this sense, Kant's insistence that the parts relate to the whole is dependent on the active nature of that relationship, which is only revealed over the course of time as a part of the process of experiencing the art.

Yet, there are other objects that impose a second requirement on themselves in order for them to be teleologically judged, in part dependent on the restrictions of the human condition. These are natural objects that are organisms. Wherein the parts are subsumed as the means of sustaining the continuation of the whole.

---

22 '[I]f a thing is a natural product but yet we are to cognize it as possible only as a natural purpose, then it must have this character: it must relate to itself in such a way that it is both cause and effect of itself.' Kant, *Critique of Judgment*, Pluhar, p. 251.

23 Kant, *Critique of Judgment*, Pluhar, p. 371.

24 Kant, *Critique of Judgment*, Pluhar, p. 252.

A *second* requirement must be met if a thing that is a product of nature is yet to have, within itself and its inner possibility, reference to purposes, i.e., if it is to be possible only as a natural purpose, without the causality of concepts, which rational beings outside it have. This second requirement is that the parts of the thing combine into the unity of a whole because they are reciprocally cause and effect of their form. For only in this way is it possible that the idea of the whole should conversely (recipro- cally) determine the form and combination of all the parts, not as cause – for then the whole would be a product of art – but as the basis on which someone judging this whole cognizes the systematic unity in the form and combination of all the manifold contained in the given matter.[25]

Normally this second condition is not available to inanimate objects but only to living organisms because the parts of the whole do not generate each other – all of the parts of an organism are needed not only to sustain the life of that organism in the present but to continue to grow and develop that organism in the future – but do self-sufficient non-natural objects not exist as organisms? Here we start to break from Kant. Whereas the first requirement leads us towards a relation of the object to a causality of ends, the second is purely reflective and leads us towards a causality of self-evidence. Lou's *Color Field*, as magnificent as it is, is not self-evidently a presentation of its intended effect nor is it a purely reflective reference to its formal unity. As always, this is not a criticism of this amazing work but simply a means of distinguishing it from New Aesthetic objects and art objects, which are self-evidently a presentation of their intended effect and a pure reflection of their unity. Where we end up is with this maxim: 'Everything in the world is good for something or other; nothing in it is gratuitous; and the example that nature offers us in its organic products justifies us, indeed calls upon us, to expect nothing from it and its laws except what is purposive in [relation to] the whole'.[26] As a reflective judgment, and not as a determinative judgment, this allows us to reflect on objects of our experience and to transcend the specificities of the object. In short, we can begin to teleologically judge non-natural objects in a manner similar to natural objects. Kant even proposes that we are 'entitled' to go beyond the specific purposiveness of an object to a consideration of a 'unity of supersensible principle'[27] whereby the entirety of nature as a system is considered and judged as a whole. This allows us, in a way, to understand the frequent biological metaphors used to describe digital ecologies.

What if the object presented to our intuition is incapable of being understood as pur- posive precisely because it resists neatly falling into either aesthetic or teleological judgment? This is at the center of Kant's problem – trying to determine how it is possible

---

25   Kant, *Critique of Judgment*, Pluhar, p. 252.

26   Kant, *Critique of Judgment*, Pluhar, p. 259.

27   Kant, *Critique of Judgment*, Pluhar, p. 261.

to identify an object as both natural and purposeful – that ends up being very difficult to resolve. Every time we think about an organism in terms of its mechanical nature it becomes difficult to think of it as having a purpose unless we resort (as is hinted by Kant) to some divine power. Kant wants to avoid this, and so do we. 'A teleological principle for explaining the inner possibility of certain natural forms leaves it undetermined whether their purposiveness is intentional or unintentional.'[28] This dialectic between intention and driven necessity complicates the intrinsic causal relations of the object but it's in that complexity that the teleological judgment has the most force. Kant writes: 'we would find no distinction between a natural mechanism and a technique of nature, i.e., a connection to ends in it, if our understanding were not of the sort that must go from the universal to the particular'.[29] This gets to a central point of the matter. For Kant, an identification of the

> apparent internal purposiveness – as presented in the phenomena of self-regulation, regeneration, and reproduction – can be made intelligible only by investigating organisms in accordance with the vitalistic notion of absolute purposiveness, as if they were natural purposes exhibiting a real, internal purposiveness having its source in a nonhuman, intelligent causality analogous to our own practical causality [...] which provides us with an intelligible estimation (*Beurteilung*) of organic nature.[30]

What's taking place here is crucial. *Naturwerke*, natural organisms, appear to have *Naturzwecke*, natural ends, but are they programmed or self-generated? Kant's trying to avoid the necessity of conceding the origins of an organism's purpose to a divine power, and we're trying to avoid the origins of a digital object's purpose to a programmer. What if, then, we were to encounter objects in our experience that exhibit natural mechanisms, direct our assessment from the universal to the particular, present self-regulating purposes with a concordant sense of absolute purposiveness, and which organically operate in response to our experience of them? What if we were to encounter little programs on our smartphone that do all those things? Would we start to call them organisms?

This goes beyond what Paul Fishwick has described as the aesthetic products of embodied cognition[31] in that it describes a set of aesthetic forms that are the products of cognitive organisms that are the result of programming but function independently of the intentions of their programming. Ralf Baecker's art illustrates this very well, especially

---

28   Kant, *Critique of Judgment*, Pluhar, p. 237.

29   Immanuel Kant, *KdU*, AAV: 404.

30   A.C. Genova, 'Review of *Kant's Concept of Teleology* by J.D. McFarland', *Ethics*, University of Chicago Press, Vol. 81, No. 2 (Jan., 1971): 186-189.

31   Paul Fishwick, 'Aesthetic Computing', Mads Soegaard and Rikke Friis Dam (eds.) *The Encyclopedia of Human-Computer Interaction*, Aarhus: The Interactive Design Foundation, 2013.

when described his work *Order+Noise (Interface I)* (2016) in an interview after it was installed at the NOME art gallery in Berlin.

> what underlines the aesthetic experience is the materiality by which action pro-duces knowledge, transforming data space into real space. As observers take in the rules, operations and parameters of the work, they gain insight into their perception. The installation's mechanical workings and network of strings allow us to explore the poetic potential of technology via its materiality, so that *Interface I* sits on the boundary between an imaginary field and an epistemological condition [...] Beside this material stack I am interested in the mathematical foundations of these tech-nologies. A closer look reveals a fully closed deterministic system, that is the result of separating mathematics from the world and our experience of it, in order to create a pure formal system.[32]

Our focus on objects of the New Aesthetic ends up there. What if we were to take Kant's solution to the problem and run with it? Kant would certainly disagree with where we are heading but, for Kant, a reconciliation between the mechanistic character of the first requirement and the natural self-sufficiency of the second requirement can happen if the mechanistic becomes subordinate to the teleology while remaining autonomous and independent.[33] We want to avoid intentional purposes because those make it difficult to avoid thinking about whose intentions we're looking at. We want to only discuss natural purposes as natural ends. And what are natural purposes ultimately? To continue life as *Naturwerk*, natural works, sustained through their *Naturzwecke*, their own closed, unique and self-determinating organizational principals.[34]

Any reflective judgment must discover *a priori* the purposiveness of nature revealed in teleological judgments while simultaneously engaging with their aesthetic nature. This is not necessarily paradoxical even if it feels contrary to human experience; nature reveals itself essentially as a revelation of itself for human intuition and understanding, and art objects reveal themselves as revelations of the free play of human reflexive judgment, but objects that might be considered New Aesthetic participate in both processes in a

---

32   Régine Debatty, 'Order+Noise, a tug of war for motors, strings and rubber bands', We Make Money
      Not Art blog, 29 April 2016, http://we-make-money-not-art.com/ordernoise-a-tug-of-war-for-
      motors-strings-and-rubber-bands/.

33   Kant, *Critique of Judgment*, Pluhar, p. 144.

34   In a strange but related aside, the Viennese art historian Alois Riegl wrote 'Naturwerk und
      Kunstwerk I', in Alois Riegl, *Gesammelte Aufsätze*, Augsburg-Wien: Benno Filser Verlag, 1928, 64;
      Alois Riegl, 'Naturwerk und Kunstwerk II', 67, 70, proposing a similar sense of an internally driven
      necessity to art forms. See also Diana Graham Reynolds, *Alois Riegl and the Politics of Art History.
      Intellectual Traditions and Austrian Identity in Fin de Siècle Vienna*, San Diego: University of
      California, 1997. We wonder what Riegl would have made of New Aesthetic objects.

way that ends up being surprisingly unsatisfactory. In this sense, though, nature is not available in a free and harmonious fashion but as teleologically driven, and freedom is only available to our understanding; for the objects of the New Aesthetic such freedom is difficult to intuit and, therefore, even more difficult to understand; equally, although the free play of the aesthetic is available, because there is a teleological purposiveness to the regarded objects we are left with an interested position that denies the possibility of the aesthetic in favor of a recognition of their objective material purposiveness as apparent natural purpose. The separateness and the distinctiveness are the crucial parts of our teleological judgment of New Aesthetic objects. Kant may write that '[...] the concept of a purposiveness of nature (as a technical purposiveness, which is essentially distinct from a practical purposiveness), if it is not to be a merely superstitious substitution of *what we make out of nature* for what *nature is*, is a concept separate from all dogmatic philosophy'[35] but we arrive at a different conclusion regarding these technologically based objects. Obviously New Aesthetic objects are not actually biological organisms, but we would argue that the degree to which they are analogous to *Naturwerke* is increasingly apparent. As *Naturwerke*, as a type of organisms, New Aesthetic objects are firstly available to aesthetic judgment but not in accordance with Kant's restrictive description of the conditions of a valid aesthetic judgment; they are also examples of Kant's antinomy that objects are subject to teleological judgments if their material forms function according to universal mechanical laws and yet also are assessable with disregard to universal mechanical laws; seemingly both cause and effect of themselves with their own specific ends; they are seemingly self-purposive, creating an intrinsic purpose to their very existence as they continue to exist; and a presentation of the unity of the whole object itself as an amalgamation of its parts while simultaneously a presentation of itself supporting the unity of the object. Or, to throw out a quick example, any iteration of the Facebook application fits in Kant's notion of teleological judgments.

---

35   Kant, *Critique of Judgment*, Pluhar, p. 243.

Biological Evolution and Teleology

While Kant's consideration of teleology is, obviously, focused on judgments, the concept of teleology itself has been divided since Kant's time into an entirely second set of considerations: biological evolution. Since Charles Darwin's description of the evolution of species, there has been some considerable debate about the nature of evolution itself, with the philosophy of science debating whether evolution is teleological or not. Because teleology was directly associated with a pre-Darwinian description of the world, often part of the argument for creationism and sometimes labeled cosmic teleology, the description of evolution as teleological has been rightly debated; philosophers of science are divided between reluctantly accepting a description of evolution as teleological, because it's the most effective analogy to evolutionary processes, or derisively denying evolution's nature as teleological, because it's an unnecessary obfuscation of the emphasis of naturalism on the relationship of function to design. What does this have to do with the New Aesthetic? We propose that New Aesthetic objects may be analyzed in biological terms as well as aesthetic terms, but to get there requires further consideration of the problem of biological teleology itself.

Taking this biological perspective, we're particularly indebted to Marcel Quarfood's articulation of the role teleology plays in understanding evolution and biological processes. He writes:

> Teleology is said to be indispensable for conceptualizing organized beings, yet it is merely a regulative principle, subjectively valid for reflecting on such beings but not objectively valid for determining their properties. The difficulty lies in balancing the claimed indispensability of teleology with its regulative status. Too heavy stress on the necessity of teleological considerations for the understanding of organisms would seem to lead to the conclusion that teleology is a constitutive condition for the possibility of biology, and thus not regulative.[36]

Quarfood's point is clear and aligned with Kant's: we can, we do, and we are even driven to make teleological judgments about organisms. While these appear to be guidelines that reveal certain 'laws' of nature they are also highly subjective and necessarily subject to a skeptical or critical perspective; the only genuine conclusion we can reach out of a teleological judgment is that there regulative processes appear to be inherent to the existence of objects. Quarfood continues:

> A regulative principle involves an idea of reason that transcends the scope of the understanding, so that judgments based on the principle cannot determine objects

---

36   Marcel Quarfood, 'Kant on Biological Teleology: Towards a Two-level Interpretation', *Studies in History and Philosophy of Biological and Biomedical Sciences*, vol. 37, 2006: 735-747.

constitutively, even though it may be appropriate "for the human point of view" of the reflecting employment of the power of judgment (cf. CJ 403). Though Kant consistently reserves the term "constitutive" for principles provided a priori by the understanding which make experience possible, one could also consider a regulative principle enabling a level of special experience to be constitutive for that experience, provided that this constitutivity is understood as relative to this level and to the "human point of view", rather than as prescriptive for objects in general.[37]

The point here is similar to Kant's in that teleological judgments provide only a human perspective for human experience; every time we believe we see a pattern, a natural law, etc. in the constitutive nature and functions of an object we are seeing those patterns only as they exist in human understanding. For Quarfood, a teleological judgment is the means by which an organism is first identified as an organism, as a *Naturwerke*, in that it is being what it should be because the relationship between the parts and the whole are interdependent and substantiating as a fulfillment of its natural purpose which is to produce itself. This means that while it's impossible to use teleology at an intrinsic level, it is possible to explain why an object that is subject to teleological judgment is being what it should be as a fulfillment of our understanding's need to provide for itself explanations as to the purpose of things. Actually, we apparently can't help it, with Quarfood noting that 'In § 68, Kant tells us that concerning "empirical laws of natural purposes in organized beings it is not merely permissible but even unavoidable to use the teleological way of judging as the principle of the theory of nature with regard to a special class of its objects" (CJ 382).'[38] Organized beings are necessarily recognized as organized – we can't avoid seeing patterns, regulative processes and purposiveness in organisms even if they aren't there – even if Kant himself would go on to say that such recognitions are inexplicable and only serve as a rough, failing guide to describing mechanistic explanations.[39]

Quarfood's point is neatly applicable if one reverses it and then extends it far beyond his philosophical position: it's not just that we can't help but make teleological judgments about organisms, it's also that organisms necessitate teleological judgments. An organism, especially a biological object that is an organism, by its very nature as an organism appearing in our experience forces us to make a teleological judgment. Therefore, if we're making teleological judgments about objects then those objects must surely be organisms. And, since we've been making or implying teleological judgments about objects of the New Aesthetic throughout this chapter, our position is hopefully clear: New Aesthetic objects are a type of organism, albeit a non-biological type.

---

37   Marcel Quarfood, 'Kant on Biological Teleology'.

38   Quarfood, 'Kant on Biological Teleology', quoting Kant.

39   James Kreines, 'The Inexplicability of Kant's Naturzweck: Kant on Teleology, Explanation and Biology', *Archiv für Geschichte der Philosophie* 87 (3: 2005): 270-311.

This has being sounding problematic, we know, but on some levels it makes a certain sense. Stating the problem of teleology and its applicability quite neatly, Ernst Mayr, one of the great evolutionary biologists of the 20th century, in his discussion of the use of teleology as a concept in the philosophy of science, points out:

> The reasons for the unsatisfactory state of the teleology analyses in the philosophical literature are now evident. Indeed, one can go so far as to say that the treatment of the problems of teleology in this literature shows how not to do the philosophy of science. For at least fifty years a considerable number of philosophers have written on teleology basing their analyses on the methods of logic and physicalism, "known to be the best" or at least the only reliable methods for such analyses. These philosophers have ignored the findings of the biologists, even though teleology concerns mostly or entirely the world of life.[40]

What's interesting about this statement, written before the explosion of the increasingly pervasive presence of the internet, is its dependency on physicalism, on the belief that everything is necessarily physical in nature. Taking a perspective that attempts to preserve teleological descriptions from a conflation with the biological, Mayr asserts that it is precisely in the biological that we can see the teleological in action. Equally rejecting the anthropomorphism often associated with teleology, Mayr disassociates the notion that a teleological description is oriented towards finality and instead moves it beyond functional-associations. As Mayr notes: 'the principal endeavor of the traditional philosopher was to eliminate teleological language from all descriptions and analyses'[41] because it got wrapped up into excessive speculation that resulted in terminating descriptions of history such as Hegel's own efforts. For Mayr, though, teleology still has a role in biology because it emphasizes the self-preservative drive of organisms, the unity of their parts, and a sense of their role within an ecology. In a way, we would push for a position that defends a return to teleological considerations, particularly in light of the biological analogies of New Aesthetic objects in accordance with Mayr's ideas. Teleology is, thus, one means of identifying purposeful organisms that exist within a digital ecology.

Our appropriation of Mayr's ideas depends on how Mayr moved the discussion of teleology beyond its functional associations towards a description of the self-sustaining properties of organisms. The first part consisted of Mayr rejecting the association of teleomatic processes with teleology; for Mayr, teleomatic processes, those that are simply governed by natural laws, are passive in their adherence and automatic in their end result (in that they are invariably successful unless interfered with). Teleomatic processes are, simply, the adherence of all objects to the laws of physics. For Mayr, if an organism

---

40   Ernst Mayr, 'The Idea of Teleology', *Journal of the History of Ideas*, 53:1, 1992.

41   Mayr, 'The Idea of Teleology', p. 122.

seems to simply be affected by everyday things like gravity, heat, etc. then it's not adhering to a teleological purpose. Second, Mayr pushes teleology's usefulness by rejection the association of teleonomic processes with teleology; for Mayr, teleonomic processes are non-anthropomorphic programmed processes that are dependent on a preordained structure of end results which can be both closed (restricted to the original programming without modification from additional data) or open (modifiable through the introduction of additional data) but are still limited to an unwavering pre-set goal with an apparent but illusionary purposefulness. An easy example of a teleonomic process is animal migrations, which are seemingly programmed but subject to variable conditions and which respond to those variables. For Mayr, neither teleomatic nor teleonomic processes are adequate, however, in describing a genuine sense of the teleological, regardless of some debates concerning their conceptual similarity to teleology[42] and especially in light of the tendency to conflate teleonomy with a theist notion of teleology; for Mayr, teleology is more than just adherence to laws or the realization of goals, it is the manifestation of goals that is less a product of adaptiveness (which Mayr identifies as Kant's *Zweckmässigkeit*)[43] and more a product of goal-orientation capability. In a way, this is similar to Mayr's notion of what a species is, in response to the species problem present in Charles Darwin's ideas; for Mayr, a species is not just a group of similar individuals but an exclusive group of individuals that can only breed amongst themselves, meaning that the development of a species is the development of teleological governed individuals. For Mayr, to identify teleological processes in organisms is to do far more than just observe how they are affected by physical processes but requires going beyond seeing how they act on instinct to a sense of seeing the full complexity of organisms as individuals. This is easiest to see in (though not at all exclusive to) higher order organisms, such as canines, cetacea and primates where play, courtship and other forms of social interaction are an important part of the organism's continuing existence in ways that are not immediately purposive but which are clearly endemic and intrinsic to the organism's species; dogs, dolphins and chimpanzees act in ways that assert their complex individual identities into their environment while retaining their broader identity as a member of a species of animals. But is it possible with less complex organisms? Is it possible to see that there is a complexity to digital objects that is more than just analogous to biological organisms?

In a way, many instances of digital objects fit easily into Mayr's description of what he believes are true examples of teleology, especially in the case of New Aesthetic objects. Mayr used three terms to describe successive evolutionary stages of processes as they govern objects and organisms and how we might assess them: teleomatic, teleonomic and teleological. Teleomatic processes are simply causal in nature, governed by the laws of physics. In this sense we can describe the earliest forms of digital art as instances of a teleomatic nature, in that the output was entirely dictated by restricted programming

---

42   Nicholas Cf. Thompson, 'The Misappropriation of Teleonomy', in *Perspectives in Ethology* (eds) Bateson, P. Bateosn and P. Klopfer, P., *Volume 7: Alternatives*, Springer-Verlag, 1987.

43   Mayr, 'The Idea of Teleology', p. 134.

regardless of the unjustifiable claims of programmers and artists that the work was being 'created' by the computer. Teleonomic processes involve a more dynamic set of responses to circumstances but are still restricted towards a specific goal. We can also describe programs and later examples of digital art as teleonomic, in that an increasing amount of creativity and variability beyond the control of the programmers was introduced that was still largely dependent on user input and restricted programming; we would even describe the first phases of digital art that lay the groundwork for New Aesthetic art as specifically teleonomic, particularly if Quarfood's ideas are used to identify individual organisms. Finally, genuinely teleological processes is genuinely evolutionary, in that organisms' responses to their environment are dynamic and goal-oriented but are also intrinsically directed towards maintaining the existence of organisms and bettering the survival chances of their species. We would claim that New Aesthetic objects and art are teleological in the sense that Mayr used the term, in that they can be described as fully autonomous and self-sufficient upon their full realization with the further goal of spreading throughout the digital ecology and having of a life of their own. A simple example illustrates our point: the Facebook application on one person's smartphone is not the same as on another's, each having acquired an unique identity through extensive development and evolution that relates in a singular fashion to an entire digital ecology, all the while acting as a species of individual organisms. In the case of art, Mayr's notion of teleology is readily in accordance with the idea of art having a 'life' of its own.

A very recent example of art embodies so many of these ideas. In January 2016, the Argentinian Amalia Ulman, living in Los Angeles after studies at the Central Saint Martins art school in London, announced to the world that her Instagram feed had been an extended example of performance art *Excellences & Perfections* {Fig. 116} that had concluded that month and has been, after its reveal, favorably compared to the art of Cindy Sherman and Yves Klein.

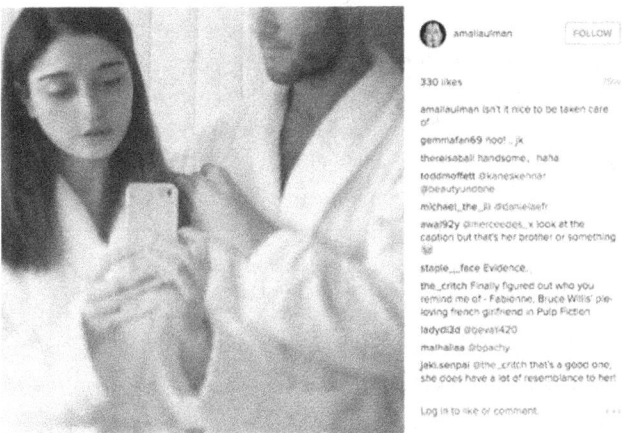

Fig. 116 Amalia Ulman, 'Isn't it nice to be taken care of', *Excellences & Perfections* (2015)

In a post on Facebook referencing a review published in the British Newspaper *The Telegraph*,[44] Nicolas Bourriaud described Ulman's project as an example of post-internet art, then quickly declared that to be an incorrect appellation.[45] Bourriaud's rejection of the term is ensconced in his critical perspective of relational aesthetics, but his willingness to reconsider Ulman's work based on the review is fascinating. Sean O'Hagan, writing in *The Guardian*, notes:

> We now live in a time when social media has revealed the full extent of the public's fascination with the everyday lives of both the famous and the ordinary [...] [Amalia Ulman's] fake Instagram feed, Excellences & Perfections, was read by many as an actual record of her attempts to become a somebody in Los Angeles. Like a would-be Kim Kardashian, she recorded her shopping expeditions and pole-dancing classes, attracting the inevitable "haters", but also about 90,000 followers.[46]

Ulman's work is about gender, celebrity, identity construction and an exploration of an engagement with social media. At the same time, in a teleological way, it's a perfect instance of New Aesthetic art. Why is Ulman's work part of the New Aesthetic? Like some of the artists mentioned earlier, New Aesthetic art isn't necessarily digital even if it's form is fundamentally digital; *Excellences & Perfections* couldn't have existed without Instagram, meaning not only that Ulman interacted with the programming of Instagram but that the program actively changed the parameters and methods of production of Ulman's work and guided the aesthetic process. Herein it seems like this work is governed by a tautology-inducing condition, but the real aesthetic value is in its negotiation of the teleological conditions of the technology. Though the work appears on Instagram, an inherently digital medium, it nevertheless is driven by the digitality of Instagram phenomena at the level of interaction. Instagram itself is purposed with creating art work like this and Ulman's Instagram account and its associated applications functioned as an assertion of their complex identity in a larger digital ecology. The teleological nature lies in the fact that the work emerged necessarily out of its context, emerged as a *Naturwerk* in an autonomously self-sufficiently fashion driven by it natural purpose, making it as much a part of the New Aesthetic as glitch photography, precisely because its appearance before the reveal was entirely as an organism within the Instagram ecology. We normally find it unthinkable to agree with such a conservative newspaper as *The Telegraph*, but perhaps they are right that this is the first Instagram masterpiece.

44   Sooke, Alastair, "Is this the first Instagram Masterpiece?", *The Telegraph*, 18 January 2016, http://www.telegraph.co.uk/photography/what-to-see/is-this-the-first-instagram-masterpiece/.

45   Nicholas Bourriaud's Facebook Page. Accessed January 31st, 2016. https://www.facebook.com/nicolas.bourriaud.7/posts/10154019377457280?pnref=story.

46   Sean O'Hagan, 'Exposed: photography's fabulous fakes. Phoney engagements, flying surrealists, faux Instagram celebrities, dubious family portraits ... a short history of performance photography', *The Guardian*, January 31 2016, http://www.theguardian.com/artanddesign/2016/jan/31/exposed-photographys-fabulous-fakes.

Where do we get to, after all this? Teleological judgment can't be easily applied to artificial objects, especially art, and that might make it hard to apply it to New Aesthetic objects; Kant writes: 'all our art finds itself infinitely outdistanced if it tries to reconstruct those products of the vegetable kingdom from the elements we obtain by dissecting them, or for that matter from the material that nature supplies for their nourishment'.[47] We hope that this chapter hasn't been read as a slavishly devoted appropriation of Schopenhauer's and Kant's ideas, influential as they are. Instead, we've thought of their ideas, and those of other theorists mentioned throughout the book, as part of a pattern that reveals the functioning present of a new type of objects that are part of the digital world and which have a profound effect on our experience. We arrive at an identification of a new set of objects that can be aesthetically and teleologically judged in their functioning autonomy, that are an opportunity to assess their beauty and design while at the same time an opportunity to assess the degree to which they fulfill their objective material purposiveness in a manner independent of our existence. At the same time we believe we've created a framework for an appreciation of their artistic appeal that is available vis-à-vis the degree to which these objects are autonomously teleological in that they are self-determinative and independent; they have a will, they present themselves for aesthetic consideration, but on terms that are an intrinsic aspect of their existence. At this point, what are New Aesthetic art objects? A new species or form of aesthetically appreciable objects in the same manner as painting and sculpture, and very much akin to the recent developments of conceptual, performance and installation art in their flexible capacity to utilize different methods of production normally ascribed to more traditional forms. New Aesthetic objects are not bound to the digital but postdigital in nature, a development out of digital objects and processes, noticeable at first in glitches, but no longer necessarily digital, and in that respect genuinely new. Borrowing the term from Kant and taking on both Quarfood's and Mayr's understanding of teleology as it is applicable to biology, objects of the New Aesthetic are manufactured objects but at the same time are *Naturwerke* in that they are both indistinguishable from manufactured, digital artifacts on one level and indistinguishable on another, functional level from biological organisms.

---

47   Kant, *CJ*, p. 250, §64.

CONCLUSION

shardcore {Fig. 117} is a collection of projects by Eric Drass, an artist and curator who aptly describes his work as such: 'Sometimes this work is political, frequently it is playful, often it is provocative or transgressive in some way.'[1]

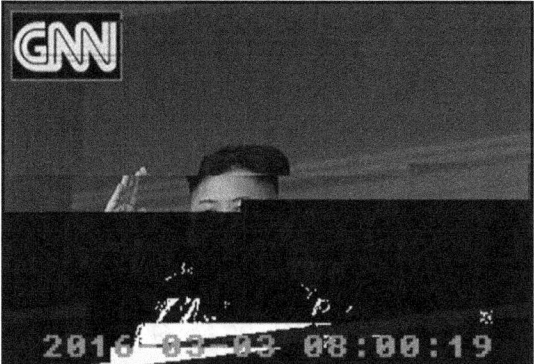

Fig. 117 Eric Drass, *shardcore* (2016)

In March 2016, Drass launched the 'Glitch News Network'[2] that consists of conglomerations of the day's news in visual form assembled into a video 2000 microseconds in length that is undecipherable at a conscious level but entirely decipherable at an unconscious level with only the briefest moments of recognition conveying a huge amount of information. Drass describes the project thus: 'Here's the news in 2000ms. This bot scrapes various online news sources for images of the latest stories. These are then glitched and mashed into a video which lasts less 2 seconds. After all, who has time to keep up with current affairs? Drass' justification is that it's a normal part of the evolutionary process for human beings to process information (especially visual information) at such speed because it enhances our survivability; he's correct, but the extension of this is that the digital representation of information can be equally sped up. 'The Glitch News Network perhaps offers a glimpse of the future, where we further disengage from our conscious central executor and merely stream blipverts at our subconscious.'[3] Drass' project is clearly a little sardonic, but the point is well taken in this remarkably intelligent art work: it's not just simply that we, as human beings, have evolved to process information quickly but that the information itself has evolved independently to be absorbed quickly, to the point that there's an increasing disconnect between its status as information and its existence as digital data in a manner similar to all forms of media

---

1   Eric Drass, *shardcore*, 'About shardcore.org: bio', http://www.shardcore.org/shardpress/about-shardcoreorg/.

2   Eric Drass, *shardcore*, 'Glitch New Network', 2 March 2016, http://www.shardcore.org/shardpress/2016/03/02/glitch-news-network/.

3   Eric Drass, *shardcore*.

in recent human history, a point taken up by Manovich but equally extendable beyond his words when he writes: 'After the novel, and subsequently cinema privileged narrative as the key form of cultural expression of the modern age, the computer age introduces its correlate – database. But it is also appropriate that we would want to develop poetics, aesthetics, and ethics of this database.'[4]

In taking a broader overview than we have, focusing on software, Lev Manovich recently wrote: 'I am interested in how software appears to users – i.e. what *functions* it offers to create, share, reuse, mix, create, manage, share and communicate content, the *interfaces* used to present these functions, and *assumptions and models about a user, her/his needs, and society* encoded in these functions and their interface design.'[5] Our approach has been very similar, if a little more focused on a particular set of objects as the outcomes of software, in line with one piece of art by Metahaven that declares *The Future Of Soft Power Depends On A Handful Of Pixels*, part of the *Disposable Imagecraft* (2012) series of work.

Our analysis of the New Aesthetic has been an examination of the condition of a new set of phenomena, rather than an attitude. Recognizing the dangers involved in an unthinking embrace of New Aesthetic ideas while also recognizing its productive and transforma-tive potential has been one of our priorities. The story behind the New Aesthetic clearly proves that the most innovative and at the same time unconventional approaches to con-temporaneity emerge beyond the walls of the academia. This is part of why we decided to consider it as a new type of phenomenon requiring a real-time enquiry involving a hybrid form of investigations into its manifestation as a web-based popular culture movement, interpreting examples of art influenced by digital design, employing ideas from the current pantheon of new media and postdigital theories as well as rooting our methodology in traditional philosophical practice.

The New Aesthetic is deeply embedded in the same computational practices (network-based data distribution, real-time digital data processing) that it is trying to describe, and it exists as a non-movement or approach for increasing society-technology interaction that might be helpful as one interpretation or as one of the signposts of the epistemic and ontological shift into the postdigital that we are currently undergoing. Not only can the New Aesthetic be found in the experience of common digital objects but also it is, we believe, substantiated by numerous examples of New Aesthetic art. Our analysis of the New Aesthetic uncovers its inseparability from the grain of computation (particularly in visual media) while unveiling the persistence of computational materiality in its relation-ship to contemporary civilization.

---

4   Manovich, *The Language of New Media*, p. 219.

5   Manovich, *Software Takes Command*, p. 29.

Technology has been a force for change in aesthetics since the beginning of human history. The very fact that an object could be represented, for instance, on the walls of a cave with pigments made out of natural materials should be regarded as both an artistic achievement as well as a technologically driven paradigmatic shift in how we understand the world. Technology has moved art into certain forms before – the Impressionists would never have created the paintings they made without portable tubes of paint that they could carry to locations where they would paint *en plein air* – but in the contemporary world technology has acquired a vitality that is self-generating and self-sufficient; the means that artists and programmers and others who create the methods of our interaction with data and the information produced out of that data has become so independent from the creators' full control in our postdigital world that it has asserted an autonomy of its own. And, therein, can be found the New Aesthetic.

REFERENCES

Images

All images are copyright of the originators and all artwork are copyright of the artists unless indicated otherwise. Original sources, artist, titles and other information, when known, are listed below. When possible, permission has been sought and received to use all of the images except in the case of orphan work and images identified as available for fair use, a Creative Common license or other means of permission. Given the nature and 'life' of images on the internet, not all sources are known, currently available, or capable of being traced to their original source. Please request any corrections or changes to books@networkcultures.org.

Fig. 1 'Norge Bank Notes', image source: http://www.norges-bank.no/en/Published/Press-releases/2014/Press-release-7-october-2014/, accessed 10.31.2014.

Fig. 2 Bridle, James, 'Le pixel umbrella at Basil Bangs.', *The New Aesthetic* Tumblr blog, 15 September 2011, http://new-aesthetic.tumblr.com/post/10235467789/le-pixel-umbrella.

Fig. 3 Image Processed Through Decim8 by authors, *Decim8* (http://decim8.info/).

Fig. 4 Smart Philippines Textbooks, image source: TXTBKS: Digital textbooks for those in need, https://www.thinkwithgoogle.com/campaigns/smart-communications-txtbks.html.

Fig. 5 Glitch Image of a Newscaster, image source: http://www.newscaststudio.com/2015/11/02/eerie-glitch-causes-anchor-to-haunt-abc-chicago-set-over-and-over.

Fig. 6 Léger, Ferdinand, *The City* (1919), oil on canvas, 7 feet 7 inches × 9 feet 9 1/2 inches (231.1 × 298.4 cm), Philadelphia Museum of Art, © Artists Rights Society (ARS), New York / ADAGP, Paris, image source: http://www.philamuseum.org/collections/permanent/53928.html.

Fig. 7 Sandy Island on 'Google Earth View', 'South Pacific Sandy Island 'proven not to exist'', *GeoGarage blog : press review with marine general thematic*, 22 November 2012, http://blog.geogarage.com/2012/11/south-pacific-sandy-island-proven-not.html.

Fig. 8 'Desert Bus', *Penn & Teller's Smoke and Mirrors* (1995), image source: https://i.ytimg.com/vi/nBr7EhL6Jpg/maxresdefault.jpg.

Fig. 9 'McDonald's App, Map of the UK', Bridle, James, *The New Aesthetic* Tumblr blog, 18 June 2013, http://new-aesthetic.tumblr.com/post/53279601415/mcdonalds-app-via-twitter-hrtbps, image source: https://twitter.com/hrtbps/status/346193054534864896/photo/1.

Fig. 10 'Olde timey face recognition error', *The RedMen Production Diary*, 12 October 2012, image source: http://www.theredmenmovie.com/2012/10/olde-timey-face-recognition-error.html.

Fig. 11 Scn9a, *What Colour Is It?* (2014), screenshot by authors, image source: http://whatcolourisit.scn9a.org/.

Fig. 12 Foley, Chris, *Glitchtop* (2015), screenshot by authors, image source: http://chris-foley.github.io/glitchtop/, courtesy of the artist.

Fig. 13 Deterritorial Support Group, *Educate! Agitate! Like!* (2011), image source: http://www.psfk.com/2011/12/who-are-the-ikea-anarchists.html.

Fig. 14 Bridle, James, 'Across all spectra.', *The New Aesthetic* Tumblr blog, 01 June 2011, http://new-aesthetic.tumblr.com/post/6079492270/across-all-spectra-what-airplanes-look-like-to, image source: Google Maps.

Fig. 15 A satellite photograph of the border between Namibia and South Africa – in the middle of a desert, alongside the Orange River, photo by ALI/EO-1/NASA (http://www.domusweb.it/en/design/2012/10/24/stories-from-the-new-aesthetic.html), image source: http://www.dazeddigital.com/artsandculture/gallery/14955/4/james-bridle

Fig. 16 Output from the *Polymaps JavaScript Library*, designed by SimpleGeo and Stamen.

Fig. 17 *Pixelate* in the iTunes store, image source: https://itunes.apple.com/us/app/pixelate/id417696805?mt=8

Fig. 18 Screen capture of video 'Neymar Goal Shot by Drone', video available at http://www.dailymail.co.uk/sport/football/article-2368284/Neymar-goal-captured-Brazilian-military-aircraft-video.html, unknown original source.

Fig. 19 Hendriks, Maurice, photographer, German Air Force Tornado ECR from Lechfeld, Germany, operating out of Volkel Air Force Base in The Netherlands (Tiger Meet 2010), 2010, courtesy of the artist.

Fig. 20 Chinese Tanks, Military Parade, September, 2015, image source: http://images.indianexpress.com/2015/09/.

Fig. 21 Chinese Tanks, Military Parade, September, 2015, image source: http://images.indianexpress.com/2015/09/.

Fig. 22 'Leopard Tank', image source: http://203.150.226.23/board/uploads/monthly_10_2014/post-5440-0-89265800-1412839966.jpg.

Fig. 23 @tomruyzllo, 'The Old Street Google search billboards have played a blinder today. Well done London...', Twitter Post, https://twitter.com/tomruzyllo/status/634469982915678208, 20 August 2015, 2:00PM. Appearing on Bridle, James, 'The New Aesthetic', http://new-aesthetic.tumblr.com/post/127228982060/google-live-search-billboard-old-street-london, August, 2015.

Fig. 24 CAVI, *Dynamically Transparent Window* (2006), Salling department store, Aarhus, image source: http://cavi.au.dk/research-areas/the-dynamically-transparent-window/, courtesy of the artists.

Fig. 25 CAVI, in collaboration with Digital Urban Living, *Climate on the Walls* (2009), projection, Aarhus, Denmark, image source: http://cavi.au.dk/research-areas/climate-on-the-wall/, courtesy of the artists.

Fig. 26 Baker, Chris (app designer), *Cloak* (2014), image source: http://ilovechrisbaker.com.

Fig. 27 Mun, Sang, *ZXX Typeface* (2013), courtesy of the artist.

Fig. 28 Santamaría, Mario, 'Google Art Bots', *The Camera in the Mirror* (2014), image source: http://the-camera-in-the-mirror.tumblr.com/image/126666980592.

Fig. 29 Vavarella, Emilio, *THE GOOGLE TRILOGY - Report a Problem*, photo 14/100 (2012), digital photographs, variable dimensions, courtesy of the artist.

Fig. 30 Vavarella, Emilio, *THE GOOGLE TRILOGY - Report a Problem*, photo 38/100 (2012), digital photographs, variable dimensions, courtesy of the artist.

Fig. 31 Graells-Garrido, E., Lalmas, M., Quercia, D. , 'Bursting the Filter Bubble' (2013), 'Data Portraits: Connecting People of Opposing Views', image source: http://38.media.tumblr.com/301c7a8d0cb9edb63b41901678389983/tumblr_inline_ng53yzhR4A1qc1shi.png.

Fig. 32 Virgil Texas, *LGBT Southerns for Michelle Obama* (2015), image source: https://twitter.com/virgiltexas/status/626449373543682049.

Fig. 33 Memac Ogilvy & Mather Dubai, advertisement for 'UN Women' (2013), image source: http://www.unwomen.org/en/news/stories/2013/10/women-should-ads.

Fig. 34 Memac Ogilvy & Mather Dubai, advertisement for 'UN Women' (2013), image source: http://www.unwomen.org/en/news/stories/2013/10/women-should-ads.

Fig. 35 Memac Ogilvy & Mather Dubai, advertisement for 'UN Women' (2013), image source: http://www.unwomen.org/en/news/stories/2013/10/women-should-ads.

Fig. 36 Skomarovsky , Matthew, *Average member of the United States Congress* (2014), image source: http://gawker.com/this-is-an-average-of-every-member-of-congress-1511522162.

Fig. 37 Gal, Yarin, *Patchmatch* (2014), 'Starry Night', http://extrapolated-art.com, courtesy of the artist.

Fig. 38 van Ingen, Juha and Särkelä, Janne, *As Long As Possible* (2015), image source: http://aslongaspossible.com/.

Fig. 39 Mint Digital Products, *Whitealbum* (2015), image source: https://whitealbumapp.com/.

Fig. 40 Maigret, Nicolas, *The Pirate Cinema* (2012-14), courtesy of the artist.

Fig. 41 Valla, Clement, *Postcards from Google Earth* (2010-), courtesy of the artist.

Fig. 42 Maigret, Nicolas, *The Pirate Cinema* (2012-14), courtesy of the artist.

Fig. 43 Bartholl, Aram, *Dropping the Internet* (2014), courtesy of the artist.

Fig. 44 Ai Wei Wei, *Dropping a Han Dynasty Urn* (1995), image source: https://artblart.files.wordpress.com/2011/06/ai-weiwei-dropping-a-han-dynasty-urn-19951.jpg.

Fig. 45 Enxuto, João and Love, Erica, *Anonymous Paintings* (2013), courtesy of the artists.

Fig. 46 Morley, Malcolm, *School of Athens* (1972), [[courtesy of gallery]].

Fig. 47 Whalen, Tom and Tong, Kevin, *Spacesuit* (2014), image source: http://inforamaart.tumblr.com/image/119347307362.

Fig. 48 Nees, Georg, Computer art produced between 1965-68, image source: https://s-media-cache-ak0.pinimg.com/736x/e8/50/ce/e850ce879e3a58b1a10b67307b854f06.jpg.

Fig. 49 Noll, A. Michael, *Vertical-Horizontal Number 3* (1964), image source: http://noll.uscannenberg.org/CompArtExamples.htm

Fig. 50 Nake, Frieder, 13/9/65 Nr. 2 ('Hommage à Paul Klee') (1965), drawing, b/w, computer-generated, drawing, b/w, computer-generated, Ink on paper (original computer-generated drawing, 1965), Silkscreen print (serigraphy of an edition of 40, 1966), Program: Package COMPART ER56 (written in machine language). Computed on Standard Elektrik Lorenz ER56. Drawn with Zuse-Graphomat Z64, image source: http://workflow.arts.ac.uk/view/artefact.php?artefact=276800&view=43625.

Fig. 51 Kawano, Hiroshi, *Design 3-1*, Color Markov Chain Pattern, 1964, ZKM Collection © ZKM | Center for Art and Media Karlsruhe, image source: http://arttattler.com/Images/Europe/Germany/Frankfurt/ZKM/Hiroshi Kawano/kawano-d-3-1.jpg.

Fig. 52 Hébert, Jean-Pierre, computer art, 1970s, courtesy of the artist.

Fig. 53 Rauschenberg, Robert, *Open Score* (1966), with Stella, Frank and Kanarek, Mimi, performance at the E.A.T. (Experiments in Art and Technology) forum, Bell Laboratories, Murray Hill, NJ, image source: https://valo86.files.wordpress.com/2015/03/rauschenberg-open-score66_3.jpg.

Fig. 54 Oehlen, Albert, *Loa* (2007), acrylic paint, ink, photograph on paper, spray paint and oil paint on canvas, 1702mm × 3102mm × 41mm, Tate, image source: http://www.tate.org.uk/art/artworks/oehlen-loa-t12808.

Fig. 55 Wool, Christopher, *Untitled*, 2007, enamel paint on canvas, 3200mm × 2442mm, Tate, image source: http://www.tate.org.uk/art/artworks/wool-untitled-t13445.

Fig. 56 Nawa, Kohei, *Polygon-Double-Deer #2* (2011), mixed media sculpture, 159.3 × 63.2 × 80.3 cm, image source: http://www.thisiscolossal.com/2011/08/polygon-double-deer-2/.

Fig. 57 Nawa, Kohei, *Manifold* (2013), 13.1 × 15.8 × 12.4m, aluminum and paint, collection of the Arario Corporation, image source: http://kohei-nawa.net/works/manifold.

Fig. 58 Plummer-Fernandez, Matthew, *sekuMoi Mecy No. 2* (2012), z-corp composite powder, z-corp color tinted binder, courtesy of the artist.

Fig. 59 Laviani, Feruccio, *Good Vibrations* (2012), oak, carved by CNC machine, image source: http://mocoloco.com/vote/good-vibrations-storage-unit-by-ferruccio-laviani/.

Fig. 60 Tremblin, Matthieu, *Watermark* (2013), photograph, graffiti, courtesy of the artist.

Fig. 61 Ahmed, Faig, *Tradition in Pixel* (2010), handmade woolen carpet, 100 × 150cm, courtesy of the artist.

Fig. 62 Visconti, Sabato, *Peeper (11ᵗʰ Iteration)* (2014), from the *Little Monsters* series, digital image, courtesy of the artist.

Fig. 63 Visconti, Sabato, *Untitled* (2011), from the *Images Adrift* series, digital image, courtesy of the artist.

Fig. 64 Geiger, Antoine, from the *Sur-Face* project (2014), courtesy of the artist.

Fig. 65 Geiger, Antoine, from the *Sur-Fake* project (2015), courtesy of the artist.

Fig. 66 Brueck, Ralf, *Twin Peaks* (2011), 175 × 220cm, courtesy of the artist.

Fig. 67 Brueck, Ralf, *Home sweet home* (2014), 120 × 160cm, courtesy of the artist.

Fig. 68 Henner, Mishka, *De Peel Patriot Missile Site, Dutch Landscapes* (2011), Archival pigment prints, variable dimensions, 25 × 20cm, courtesy of the artist.

Fig. 69 Smits, Helmut, *Dead Pixel in Google Earth* (2008-10), 82 × 82 cm burned square, courtesy of the artist.

Fig. 70 Asendorf, Kim, from the *Mountain Tour* series (2010), image source: http://kimasendorf.com/mountain-tour/.

Fig. 71 Driessens, Erwin and Verstappen, Maria, *Sandbox* (2009), wood, lacquer, metal, fans, sand, electronics, 245 × 122 × 176cm, courtesy of the artists.

Fig. 72 Driessens, Erwin and Verstappen, Maria, *E-volved Cultures* (2005-11), courtesy of the artists.

Fig. 73 Chaos Computer Club, *Project Blinkenlights* (2001-02), image source: http://berlijn-blog.nl/blinkenlights-project/.

Fig. 74 Ikeda, Ryoji, *supersymmetry* (2014), Studio A 40 DLP projectors, 40 computers, loud speakers, approximate dimensions 12 × 4 × 25m, courtesy of the artist.

Fig. 75 Ikeda, Ryoji, *supersymmetry* (2014), Studio B (bottom), programming, computer graphics, W12.5 × D12.5 × H80cm, courtesy of the artist.

Fig. 76 Lou, Liza, *Color Field* (2010-13), Glass beads, stainless steel, perspex, 20 × 26 feet (dimensions variable); 6.096 × 7.92 meters (dimensions variable), courtesy of the artist, Liza Lou and Neuberger Museum of Art, Purchase, NY, photo credit: Jerry L. Thompson.

Fig. 77 Grosser, Ben, still image capture from *Variable Mirror* (2009), http://bengrosser.com/blog/variable-mirror-at-anka-gallery-in-april/, courtesy of the artist.

Fig. 78 Adrien M / Claire B Company, XYZT, Les paysages abstraits (2011), exhibition, http://www.am-cb.net/projets/xyzt/.

Fig. 79 Adrien M / Claire B Company, *Hakanaï* (2013), dance performance, http://www.am-cb.net/projets/hakanai/.

Fig. 80 Adrien M / Claire B Company, *Le mouvement de l'air* (2015), performance, http://www.am-cb.net/projets/air/, image source: http://www.thisiscolossal.com/wp-content/uploads/2015/11/dance-2.jpg.

Fig. 81 Harvey, Adam, *CV Dazzle* (2010), image source: https://cvdazzle.com/assets/img/feature-right.jpg.

Fig. 82 Harvey, Adam, *Stealth Wear* (2013), image source: https://ahprojects.com/projects/stealth-wear/.

Fig. 83 Blas, Zach, *Facial Weaponization Suite: Mask - May 31, 2013, San Diego, CA* (2013), Performative Nanorobotics Lab, UCSD, 3D model of 'collective mask' that is based on workshop participants' aggregated facial data, 3D Collaboration & photo by Scott Kepford courtesy of the artist.

Fig. 84 Blas, Zach, *Facial Weaponization Suite: Mask- May 31, 2013, San Diego, CA* (2013), Performative Nanorobotics Lab, UCSD, June 7, 2013, 'Protest Line / Face Off' Tableau Vivant, photo by Tanner Cook courtesy of the artist.

Fig. 85 Metahaven, *The Sprawl* (2015), co-produced by Lighthouse (http://www.lighthouse.org.uk/) and commissioned by Lighthouse and The Space (http://www.thespace.org/), image source: http://i.vimeocdn.com/video/552991984_1280x720.jpg.

Fig. 86 Adeoso, Folasade, *Motherhood*, from the series 'Kinfolk' (2014), image source: http://lovefola.com/artbyfola/wp-content/uploads/2015/01/motherhood-975x1280.jpg.

Fig. 87 Ikhide, Alexander, *Love Yourself as Much as Kanye Loves Kanye*, from the series 'Don't Police My Masculinity' (2015), photograph by Isikalu, Seye, image source: http://fashionablymale.net/2015/02/14/dont-police-my-masculinity-alexander-ikhide-by-seye-isikalu/.

Fig. 88 Bartholl, Aram, *Map*, (2010-13), photo of installation at 'Hello World!' Kasseler Kunstverein, Fridericianum, 600x350x35 cm, wood board, wood beams, color, wire, screws, glue, nails, courtesy of the artist.

Fig. 89 Bartholl, Aram, *Map*, (2010-13), aerial photo of installation at 'Hello World!' Kasseler Kunstverein, Fridericianum, 600x350x35 cm, wood board, wood beams, color, wire, screws, glue, nails, courtesy of the artist.

Fig. 90 Bartholl, *Dead Drops* (2010), public intervention, USB drive, epoxy putty, installed in Union Square subway station, New York City, courtesy of the artist.

Fig. 91 Bartholl, *15 Seconds of Fame* (2009–10), Google Streetview self portraits series, 60 × 40 cm, Lightjet C-print, Alu-Dibond, Acryl Video screencast HD, 1:08 min, courtesy of the artist.

Fig. 92 Bartholl, Aram, *Full Screen* (2014), installation and exhibition at the XPO gallery, Paris, participating artists: Vincent Broquaire, Jennifer Chan, Petra Cortright, Constant Dullaart, Oliver Laric, Sara Ludy, Raquel Meyers, Evan Roth, Rafaël Rozendaal, Paul Souviron, Addie Wagenknecht, Ai Weiwei, courtesy of the artist.

Fig. 93 Steyerl, Hito, *Adorno's Grey*, 2012, installation, single channel HD video projection, four angled screens, wall plot, photographs, 14 minutes 20 seconds, image CC 4.0 Hito Steyerl, image courtesy of the artist and Andrew Kreps Gallery, New York.

Fig. 94 Steyerl, Hito, *Abstract*, 2012, two channel HD video with sound, 7 minutes, 30 seconds, image CC 4.0 Hito Steyerl, image courtesy of the artist and Andrew Kreps Gallery, New York.

Fig. 95 Steyerl, Hito, *Guards*, 2012, DV, single channel HD, video shown on free standing screen, 20 minutes, image CC 4.0 Hito Steyerl, image courtesy of the Artist and Andrew Kreps Gallery, New York.

Fig.96 Steyerl, Hito, *How Not to Be Seen: A Fucking Didactic Educational .MOV File* (2013) HD video, single screen in architectural environment, 15 minutes, 52 seconds, image CC 4.0 Hito Steyerl, image courtesy of the Artist and Andrew Kreps Gallery, New York.

Fig. 97 Steyerl, Hito, *How Not to Be Seen: A Fucking Didactic Educational .MOV File* (2013) HD video, single screen in architectural environment, 15 minutes, 52 seconds, image CC 4.0 Hito Steyerl, image courtesy of the Artist and Andrew Kreps Gallery, New York.

Fig. 98 Bettwieser, Levi, *The Rescued Film Project* (2014–), 'Is This Real Life', September 2015, image source: http://rescuedfilmproject.tumblr.com/post/129213965706/is-this-real-life.

Fig. 99 *Cybernetic Seredipity, ICA01 | ICA02* (1968) ICA Nash House, The Mall, London.

Fig. 100 Paik, Nam June, *TV Buddha* (1974), image source: http://www.artfund.org/assets/art-news/2013/edinburgh-highlights/edinburgh-highlights-6.jpg.

Fig. 101 Tinguely, Jean, *Homage to New York*, (1960), in the garden of MOMA, NYC, image source: https://wegway.wordpress.com/tag/machines/.

Fig. 102 Baecker, Ralf, *Rechnender Raum (Computing Space)* (2007), sticks, strings, plumbs comprising over 200 RR units equivalent to basic Boolean functions, image source: http://www.rlfbckr.org/work/rechnender_raum.

Fig. 103 Baecker, Ralf, *The Conversation (Autonomous Machine)* (2009), 99 solenoids arranged in a circular configuration, rubber bands, exhibited at LABoral Centro de Arte y Creación Industrial, Gijón, Asturias, Spain, image source: http://www.rlfbckr.org/work/the_conversation.

Fig. 104 Baecker, Ralf, *Crystal Set Apparatus* (2011), silicon carbide, 64 iron needles, acrylic glass, custom electronics, with support from the Edith Russ Site for Media Art, image source: http://www.rlfbckr.org/work/crystal_set.

Fig. 105 Baecker, Ralf, *Irrational Computing* (2011–12), five interlinked modules, electrical and mechanical devices, crystals, loudspeakers, DOCK e.V. (http://www.dock-berlin.de/) with support of the Schering Stiftung (http://www.scheringstiftung.de/), image source: http://www.rlfbckr.org/work/irrational_computing.

Fig. 106 Murphy, James E., *The Politics of Creation* (2013), software, computer, IR camera, projector, live dancers, 2ch sound system, courtesy of the artist.

Fig. 107 Murphy, James E., *Found* (2014), screenshot by authors, image source: http://found.jemurphy.org/, with permission from the artist.

Fig. 108 Manovich, Lev, *Selfiecity (Berlin)* (2014), with Moritz Stefaner, Mehrdad Yazdani, Dominikus Baur, Jay Chow, Daniel Goddemeyer, Alise Tifentale, and Nadav Hochman, supported by The Graduate Center, City University of New York (CUY), California Institute for Telecommunication and Information (Calit2), and The Andrew W. Mellon Foundation, image source: http://selfiecity.net/#imageplots, Creative Commons Attribution-NonCommercial-ShareAlikelicense.

Fig. 109 Manovich, Lev, *On Broadway* (2014–16), with Daniel Goddemeyer, Moritz Stefaner, and Dominikus Baur, http://www.on-broadway.nyc/, Creative Commons Attribution-NonCommercial-ShareAlikelicense.

Fig. 110 Ruscha, Edward, *Every Building on the Sunset Strip* (1966), edition of 1,000, photography book, 7 × 5 5/8 × 299 1/2 in., image source: http://www.otherpress.com/features/suburbia-and-the-sublime/.

Fig. 111 Grosser, Ben, *Interactive Robotic Painting Machine* (2011), installation of computers, robotics, camera, microphone, mixer, speakers, projector, oil paint, canvas, and custom software, courtesy of the artist.

Fig. 112 Grosser, Ben, *Computers Watching Movies* 'Taxi Driver' (2014), computationally-produced HD video with stereo audio, courtesy of the artist.

Fig. 113 Rothenberg, Matthew, *Unindexed* (February 2015), website and coding, courtesy of the artist.

Fig. 114 Bridle, James, *The Glomar Response: Fraunhofer Lines 005* (2015), ditone print, mounted on Alu-Dibond, custom shadow gap frame in alder matte black glazed and finished with wax, 120cm × 80cm, courtesy of the NOME Art Gallery, Berlin.

Fig. 115 Bridle, James, *The Glomar Response: Diego Garcia (Waterboarded Documents 001)* (2015), mixed media, 119cm × 72 cm × 110cm, courtesy of the NOME Art Gallery, Berlin.

Fig. 116 Ulman, Amalia, 'Isn't it nice to be taken care of' September, 2015, *Excellences & Perfections* (2015), screenshot by the authors, image source: https://www.instagram.com/p/s65tHOlV35/?taken-by=amaliaulman&hl=en.

Fig. 117 Drass, Eric *shardcore* (2016), image from 8am 3 March 2016, courtesy of the artist.

Texts

@Matt_Macklin7. 'The latest in live cross technology. Pic via Instagram', Twitter Post, 28 October 2014, 7:54PM, https://twitter.com/Matt_Macklin7/status/527292438574952449/photo/1.

Adams, Terry (project manager). 'Janus', Research Programs, Office of the Director of National Intelligence, http://www.iarpa.gov/index.php/research-programs/janus.

Adorno, T. W. *Aesthetic Theory*, London: Routledge & Kegan Paul, 1972.

African Digital Art (http://africandigitalart.com/) (Contributors). 'Africa remix: the artists subverting colonial imagery', *The Guardian*, 11 February 2015, http://www.theguardian.com/world/2015/feb/11/africa-remix-artists-reinvent-colonial-imagery.

Ahmed, Faig. *artworks catalog*, http://www.faigahmed.com/site/assets/files/1017/faig_ahmed_artworks_catalogue.pdf.

Ahmed, Faig. http://www.faigahmed.com/about/info/.

Alexenberg, M. 'Author's Note for Postdigital Edition', http://www.melalexenberg.com/book.php?id=15.

Alexenberg, Mel. *The Future of Art in a Postdigital Age: From Hellenistic to Hebraic Consciousness*, Bristol: Intellect Ltd, 2011.

Altena, Arie and van der Velden, Lucas (eds). *The anthology of computer art*, Amsterdam: Sonic Acts 2006.

Andersen, Christian Ulrik and Pold, Søren Bro. 'Aesthetics of the Banal – 'New Aesthetics' in an Era of Diverted Digital Revolutions', in David M. Berry and Michael Dieter (eds) *Postdigital Aesthetics: Art, Computation and Design*, New York: Palgrave MacMillan, 2015.

Andersen, Christian Ulrik., Cox, Geoff., Papadopoulos, Georgios. *A Peer-Reviewed journal about: post-digital research*, volume 3, issue 1: Aarhus: Digital Aesthetics Research Center, Aarhus University and transmediale/resource, 2014.

Apple Inc. 'iPhone 3G on Sale Tomorrow' (Press release), 10 July, 2008, http://www.apple.com/pr/library/2008/07/10iPhone-3G-on-Sale-Tomorrow.html.

artnet. 'Kohei Nawa, SCAI The Bathhouse', http://www.artnet.com/artists/kohei-nawa/polygon-double-deer-2-a-iODzN9ohK0_WbjhUoeM5OQ2.

Asendorf, Kim. 'Processing Source Code', 5 October 2012, *kimasendorf blog*, http://kimasendorf.tumblr.com/post/32936480093/processing-source-code.

Ashby, Madeline. 'The New Aesthetics of the male gaze', *Madelineashby*, 2 April 2012, http://madelineashby.com/?p=1198.

Assendorf, Kim. *Kim Assendorf Up and Running*, http://kimasendorf.com/www/.

Baecker, Ralf et. al. *Re-Active Platform*, 2010, http://www.re-activeplatform.de/.

Baecker, Ralf. 'Crystal Set, *Ralf Baecker*, http://www.rlfbckr.org/work/nowhere.

Baecker, Ralf. 'Irrational Computing', *Ralf Baecker*, http://www.rlfbckr.org/work/nowhere.

Baecker, Ralf. 'Nowhere', *Ralf Baecker*, http://www.rlfbckr.org/work/nowhere.

Baecker, Ralf. 'The Conversation, *Ralf Baecker*, http://www.rlfbckr.org/work/nowhere.

Balbus, Skyler. 'What Glitch? Technology And The New Aesthetic', *Hook & Loop*, 20 September 2013, http://www.hookandloopnyc.com/author/skyler/.

Barbeni, Luca. '*James Bridle, The Glomar Response*' (Press Release), 2015, *NOME*, http://www.nomeproject.com/exhibitions/glomar-response.

Bartholl, Aram. 'Bits on Location', 2001, http://datenamort.de/eng/indexe.html.

Bartholl, Aram. 'Full Screen', 2014, http://www.datenform.de/15-secs-of-fame-eng.html.

Bartholl, Aram. 'Map', 2014, http://datenform.de/blog/tag/map/.

Bartholl, Aram. *Datenform*, http://datenform.de/dropping-the-internet-eng.html.

Bartholl, Aram. *Dead Drops*, 2011, http://deaddrops.com/.

Baumgarten, Alexander Gottlieb, Mirbach, Dagmar (ed). *Aesthetica/Ästhetik*, 2 vols., Hamburg: Felix Meiner Verlag, 2007.

Baumgarten, Alexander, Paetzold, Heinz (ed.). Meditationes philosophicae de nonnullis ad poema pertinentibus/Philosophische Betrachtungen über einige Bedingungen des Gedichtes, Hamburg: Felix Meiner Verlag, 1983. Aschenbrenner, Karl and Holther, William B. (trans.). *Reflections on Poetry: Alexander Gottlieb Baumgarten's Meditationes philosophicae de nonnullis ad poema pertinentibus*, Berkeley and Los Angeles: University of California Press, 1954.

Berry, David M. 'What Is the "New Aesthetic"?', 'Abduction Aesthetic: Computationality and the New Aesthetic', *Stunlaw blog*, 6 April 2012, http://stunlaw.blogspot.com/2012/04/abduction-aesthetic-computationality.html.

Berry, David M. and Dieter, Michael (eds) *Postdigital Aesthetics: Art, Computation and Design,* Basingstoke: Palgrave Macmillan, 2015.

Berry, David M. *The Philosophy of Software Code and Mediation in the Digital Age*, London: Palgrave Macmillan, 2011.

Berry, David M.,van Dartel, M., Dieter, M., Hyde, A., Kasprzak, M., Muller, N., O'Reilly, R., de Vicente, J. L. *New Aesthetic, New Anxieties*, Rotterdam: The Institute of Unstable Media, 2012.

Bettridge, Thom. 'Coup de Net: METAHAVEN's "Black Transparency"', *032c*, 20 November 2015, http://032c.com/2015/coup-de-net-metahavens-black-transparency/.

Bettweisser, Levi. 'Is this real life?', *Rescued Film Project blog*, 16 September 2015, http://rescuedfilmproject.tumblr.com/post/129213965706/is-this-real-life.

Bierend, Douglas. 'Breaking Things On Purpose, Glitch art's pixel-mixing algorithms', *Medium.com*, 26 August 2014, https://medium.com/re-form/breaking-things-on-purpose-14f413bdf2ce#.sdbpsxsmt.

Big_Fisted_BB, Amazon Customer Review, 'Weird and disappointing', January 6 2014, http://www.amazon.com/Uncorporate-Identity-Daniel-van-Velden/dp/3037781696.

Blas, Zach. 'Escaping the Face: Biometric Facial Recognition and the Facial Weaponization Suite', *Journal of the New Media Caucus*, 2013, http://median.newmediacaucus.org/caa-conference-edition-2013/escaping-the-face-biometric-facial-recognition-and-the-facial-weaponization-suite/.

Bogost, Ian. (2012). 'The New Aesthetic Needs to Get Weirder', *The Atlantic*, 13 April 2012, http://www.theatlantic.com/technology/archive/2012/04/the-new-aesthetic-needs-to-get-weirder/255838/.

Boom, Daniel van. 'Why India snubbed Facebook's free Internet offer', *CNET*, 26 February 2016, http://www.cnet.com/news/why-india-doesnt-want-free-basics/.

Boomen, van den, M. *Transcoding the Digital: How Metaphors Matter in New Media*, Amsterdam: Intitute of Network Cultures, 2014.

Bourriaud, Nicholas. *Nicholas Bourriaud Facebook Page*. Accessed January 31st, 2016. https://www.facebook.com/nicolas.bourriaud.7/posts/10154019377457280?pnref=story.

Boyer, Robert, Browne, James C., and Misra, Jayadev. 'In Memoriam Woodrow W. Bledsoe', *Faculty Council, The University of Texas*, Austin, 27 May 2014, https://www.utexas.edu/faculty/council/1998-1999/memorials/Bledsoe/bledsoe.html, adapted from 'Woody Bledsoe: His Life and Legacy', authored by Ballantyne, Michael, Boyer, Robert S. and Hines, Larry, *AI Magazine*, Volume 17, Number 1, Spring 1996, pp. 7-20.

Breisbart, Claus. 'Kant's Characterization of Natural Ends', Heidemann, Dietmar H. (ed), *Kant Yearbook. 1: Teleology*. Berlin: De Gruyter, 2009, pp 1-30.

Breitenbach, Angela. 'Two views on nature: A solution to Kant's antinomy of mechanism and teleology', *British Journal for the History of Philosophy*, 16:2, 2008.

Bridle, James. 'Google launches 'Constitute,' a new tool for designing governments | The Verge', *The New Aesthetic Tumblr blog*, 25 September 2013, http://new-aesthetic.tumblr.com/post/62244541600/google-launches-constitute-a-new-tool-for.

Bridle, James. 'Report from Austin, Texas, on the New Aesthetic panel at SXSW', *booktwo.org*, March 15 2012, http://booktwo.org/notebook/sxaesthetic/.

Bridle, James. 'The New Aesthetic: About', http://new-aesthetic.tumblr.com/about.

Bridle, James. 'Waving at the machines', Web Directions South keynote, 2011, http://www.webdirections.org/resources/james-bridle-waving-at-the-machines/#transcript.

Brook, Peter. 'See Some Art While You Can – Google Will Eventually Replace Museums', *Wired.com*, September 2013, http://www.wired.com/2013/09/see-some-art-whir-you-can-google-will-eventually-replace-museums/.

Brownlee, John. 'Massive Data Visualization Brings NYC's Busiest Street To Life',

http://www.fastcodesign.com/3043091/infographic-of-the-day/massive-data-visualization-brings-nycs-busiest-street-to-life.

Bush, Vannevar. 'As We May Think', in Wardrip-Fruin, Noah and Montfort, Nick (eds). *The New Media Reader*, Cambridge/London: MIT Press, 2003.

Byrnes, Mark. 'This Is Not a Watermark: Meet French Street Artist Mathieu Tremblin', *The Atlantic, Citylab*, 15 July 2013, http://www.citylab.com/design/2013/07/not-watermark-meet-french-street-artist-mathieu-tremblin/6083/.

Carriage Trade Gallery. 'Enxuto & Love, Anonymous Paintings', (Press Release), October, 2013, http://www.carriagetrade.org/article82,82.

Cascone, Kim. 'The Aesthetics of Failure: 'Post- Digital' Tendencies in Contemporary

Computer Music', *Computer Music Journal* 24, No. 4 (Winter 2000), pp. 12-18.

Cascone, Kim. 'The Aesthetics of Failure: Post-Digital Tendencies in Contemporary Computer Music', *subsol*, 24 April 2004, http://subsol.c3.hu/subsol_2/contributors3/casconetext.html.

Cegłowski, Maciej. 'Ta'izz', *Idle Words blog*, 17 May 2015, http://idlewords.com/2015/05/ta_izz.htm.

Charlesworth, J.J. (2012). We are the droids we're looking for: the New Aesthetic and its friendly critics, accessed 8.03.2014, http://blog.jjcharlesworth.com/2012/05/07/we-are-the-droids-were-looking-for-the-new-aesthetic-and-its-friendly-critics/

Charlesworth, JJ. 'We are the droids we're looking for: the New Aesthetic and its friendly critics', *JJ Charlesworth Blog*, 7 May 2012, https://blogjjcharlesworth.wordpress.com/2012/05/07/we-are-the-droids-were-looking-for-the-new-aesthetic-and-its-friendly-critics/.

Chris Foley. http://www.cfoley.net/.

Comparative Constitutions Project. http://comparativeconstitutionsproject.org/.

compArt database Digital Art (daDA). 'Georg Nees: Computergrafik', http://dada.compart-bremen.de/item/exhibition/164.

compArt database Digital Art (daDA). 'Hiroshi Kawano', http://dada.compart-bremen.de/item/agent/234.

compArt database Digital Art (daDA). Jean-Pierre Hébert', http://dada.compart-bremen.de/item/agent/549.

Condliffe Jamie. 'Microsoft's Racist Twitter Bot Sputters Back to Life, Bugs Out Again', Gizmodo, 30 March 2016, http://gizmodo.com/something-strange-is-happening-to-microsofts-twitter-bo-1767926273.

Contreras-Koterbay, Scott. 'The Digitalization of the World: New Aesthetics, with a Kantian Twist', *Mustekala Kulttuurilehti*, 10 September 2014, http://www.mustekala.info/node/35834.

Coppelman, Alyssa. 'Distorted Photos Show the Alien Side of Suburban Life', *Wired.com*, 1 March 2015, http://www.wired.com/2015/03/ralf-brueck-distortion/.

Cox, Matthew. 'Army Unveils Design Changes for New Camo Uniform', *Military.com*, 6 August 2014, http://www.military.com/daily-news/2014/08/06/army-unveils-design-changes-for-new-camo-uniform.html?ESRC=todayinmil.sm.

Cramer, Florian. 'What is "Post-digital"?', *A Peer-reviewed Journal about Post-digital Research*, vol. 3, issue 1, p. 3 (2015), http://www.aprja.net/?p=1318.

Cybernetic Seredipity Archive. http://cyberneticserendipity.net/.

DAM Berlin. 'Artist's Statement: Frieder Nake in conversation with Wolf Lieser at the DAM GALLERY Berlin, November 2010', November, 2010, http://dam.org/artists/phase-one/frieder-nake/artist-s-statement.

Debatty, Régine. 'Bits on Location', *We Make Money Not Art blog*, 23 February 2005, http://we-make-money-not-art.com/bits_on_locatio/.

Debatty, Régine. 'Order+Noise, a tug of war for motors, strings and rubber bands', *We Make Money Not Art blog*, 29 April 2016, http://we-make-money-not-art.com/order-noise-a-tug-of-war-for-motors-strings-and-rubber-bands/.

Drass, Eric. *shardcore*, http://www.shardcore.org/.

Dreher, Thomas. 'Computer Graphics', *History of Computer Art*, Septemb 2013, http://iasl.uni-muenchen.de/links/GCA-III.2e.html#Computergrafik.

Driessens, Erwin and Verstappen, Maria. *D r i e s s e n s & V e r s t a p p e n*, http://notnot.home.xs4all.nl/sandbox/sandbox.html.

e-flux. 'Hito Steyerl' (Press Release), 2012, http://www.e-flux.com/announcements/hito-steyerl-at-e-flux/.

Engelbart, Douglas. 'A Research Center for Augmenting Human Intellect', in Wardrip-Fruin, Noah and Montfort, Nick (eds). *The New Media Reader*, Cambridge/London: MIT Press, 2003.

Enxuto, João and Love, Erica. 'Anonymous Paintings (2011-)', *theoriginalcopy.net*, 2011, http://www.sept6.info/anonymous-paintings/.

Faith, Thomas and Wicentowski, Joseph. 'Foggy Bottom', April 2014, http://tei.northwestern.edu/files/2014/04/Faith-Wicentowski-1ntyfbr.pdf.

Faith, Thomas and Wicentowski, Joseph. 'Visualizing the History of U.S. Foreign Relations: The State of TEI at

Fashionably Male. 'Don't Police My Masculinity – Alexander Ikhide by Seye Isikalu', *Fashionably Male*, 14 February 2015, http://fashionablymale.net/2015/02/14/dont-police-my-masculinity-alexander-ikhide-by-seye-isikalu/.

Fishwick, Paul. 'Aesthetic Computing', Mads Soegaard and Rikke Friis Dam (eds.) *The Encyclopedia of Human-Computer Interaction*, 2nd edition, Aarhus: The Interactive Design Foundation, 2013.

Fodel, David and Jenkins, Matt (curators). 'Exhibition announcement: *The Emperor's New Aesthetic*', 9 September 2014, Rhizome, http://rhizome.org/announce/events/60873/view/.

Fortune, Stephen. 'Disarming Corruptor will encrypt your 3D creations', *Dazed*, 2014, http://www.dazeddigital.com/artsandculture/article/18019/1/disarming-corruptor-will-encrypt-your-3d-creations.

Fuller, Matthew. *Media Ecologies: Materialist Energies in Art and Technocultures*, Cambridge MA: MIT Press, 2007.

Gal, Yarin. *Extrapolated Art*, http://extrapolated-art.com/.

Gander, Kashmira. 'Heinz forced to apologise after QR code on ketchup bottle linked to hardcore porn site', *The Independent*, 17 June 2015, http://www.independent.co.uk/life-style/food-and-drink/news/heinz-forced-to-apologise-after-qr-code-on-ketchup-bottle-linked-to-hardcore-porn-site-10327313.html.

Garrett, Don. "Teleology in Spinoza and Early Modern Rationalism" in Gennaro, Rocco and Huenemann, Charles (eds), New Essays on the Rationalists, New York : Oxford University Press. 1999.

Geiger, Antoine. *Sur-Fake*, http://files.cargocollective.com/440813/SUR-FAKE--translated-.pdf.

Genova, A.C. 'Review of *Kant's Concept of Teleology* by J. D. McFarland', *Ethics*, University of Chicago Press, 81:2, January, 1971.

Ginsborg, Hannah. 'Kant's Aesthetics and Teleology', in Zalta, Edward N. (ed.) *The Stanford Encyclopedia of Philosophy*, Fall 2014, http://plato.stanford.edu/archives/fall2014/entries/kant-aesthetics/.

glitchtop. http://chrisfoley.github.io/glitchtop/.

Glove and Boots. 'Vertical Video Syndrome - A PSA', YouTube video, 2:58, 5 June 2012, https://youtu.be/Bt9zSfinwFA.

Godfrey, Mark. 'Statements of Intent: Mark Godfrey on the Art of Jacqueline Humphries, Laura Owens, Amy Sillman, and Charline von Heyl', *Artforum*, April 2014, http://owenslaura.com/wp-content/uploads/2014/11/LO_2014_Apr_Artforum_small.pdf.

Goodin, Dan. 'Reverse-engineering artist busts face detection tech', *The Register*, April, 2010, http://www.theregister.co.uk/2010/04/22/face_detection_hacking/.

Google Cultural Institute. https://www.google.com/culturalinstitute/about/.

Gopakumar, R. *Linguistic River*, 2012, http://www.worldart.info/GopakumarR/LinguisticsRiver/default.aspx.

Goriunova, Olga and Shulgin, Alexei. 'Glitch', in Fuller, Matthew (ed.). *Software Studies: a Lexicon*, London: MIT Press, 2008.

Goriunova, Olga and Shulgin, Alexia. *Glitch in Software Studies: A Lexicon*, ed. Matthew Fuller, Cambridge: MIT Press, 2008.

Graells-Garrido, Eduardo, Lalmas, Mounia and Quercia, Daniele. 'Data Portraits: Connecting People of Opposing Views', Human-Computer Interaction (cs.HC); Social and Information Networks, Cornell University, 19 November 2013, http://arxiv.org/abs/1311.4658.

Gray, Maggie. 'Artist Profile: Hito Steyerl', *this is tomorrow*, December 11, 2010, http://thisistomorrow.info/articles/artist-profile-hito-steyerl.

Greenbaum, Hilary. 'Who Made Google's Map Pin?', *The New York Times Magazine*, 18 April 2011, http://6thfloor.blogs.nytimes.com/2011/04/18/who-made-googles-map-pin/.

Grosser, Ben. 'Computers Watching Movies', 2014, *Ben Grosser*, http://bengrosser.com/projects/computers-watching-movies/.

Grosser, Ben. 'Interactive Robotic Painting Machine', *Ben Grosser*, 2011, http://bengrosser.com/projects/interactive-robotic-painting-machine/.

Grosser, Benjamin. 'Flexible Pixels', 2009-11, *Benjamin Grosser*, http://bengrosser.com/projects/flexible-pixels/.

Gunkel, David and Taylor, Paul A. *Heidegger and the Media*, Cambridge: Polity, 2014.

Gutierrez, Jené. 'Google's Robot Cameras Caught Taking Unintentional Selfies In Museums And Galleries', *Beautiful/Decay*, 7 July 2014, http://beautifuldecay.com/2014/07/07/googles-robot-cameras-caught-taking-unintentional-selfies-museums-galleries/.

Halskov, Kim, Lervig, Morten and Dalsgaard, Peter. 'The Dynamically Transparent Window', 14 October 2014, *CAVI*, http://cavi.au.dk/research-areas/the-dynamically-transparent-window/.

Harvey, Adam. 'How to Hide from Machines: The perilous glamour of life under surveillance', *dis magazine*, 2015, http://dismagazine.com/dystopia/evolved-lifestyles/8115/anti-surveillance-how-to-hide-from-machines/.

Harvey, Adam. *Adam Harvey Projects*, http://ahprojects.com/.

Harvey, Adam. *CV Dazzle*, https://cvdazzle.com/.

Harvey, Adam. *Undisclosed*, https://undisclosed.cc/.

Hébert, Jean-Pierre. Index for jean-pierre hébert, 'Biography', http://jeanpierrehebert.com/docs/bio1209.pdf.

Heidegger, Martin. *Being and Time*, trans. John Macquarrie & Edward Robinson, Oxford: Basil Blackwell, 1962.

Henner, Mishka. 'Dutch Landscapes', *mishkahenner.com*, February 2011, http://mishka-henner.com/filter/works/Dutch-Landscapes.

Hill, Benjamin Mako. 'Revealing Errors' in Nunes, Mark (ed) *Error Glitch, Noise, and Jam in New Media Cultures,* New York and London: Continuum, 2011.

Hochman, Nadav. 'Imagined Data Communities', *Selfiecity*, 2014, http://d25rsf93iwlmgu.cloudfront.net/downloads/Nadav_Hochman_selfiecity.pdf.

Hodara, Susan. 'Liza Lou's Handmade Sea of Sparkling Glass', *The New York Times*, 2 January 2016, http://nyti.ms/1OBekoq.

Hromack, Sarah. 'What is Metahaven?', *frieze* magazine, issue 175, 2015, http://www.frieze.com/issue/article/what-is-metahaven/.

Hui Zhe. 'Pixelate'. *iTunes Store*, September, 2015, https://itunes.apple.com/us/app/id442157795.

Humble Arts Foundation. 'The Artists', *Group Show 42: Occultisms*, http://hafny.org/group-show-42-occultisms-statements-and-bios/.

Hyde, Andrea. 'Metahaven's *Facestate* Social Media and the State', *Walker*, 13 December 2011, http://www.walkerart.org/magazine/2011/metahavens-facestate.

Ikeda, Ryoji. 'supersymmetry', *Ryoji Ikeda*, 2014, http://www.ryojiikeda.com/project/supersymmetry/.

Jayme, Merlee, Gutierrez, Aster, Demata, Eugene and Royong, Biboy. *TXTBKS*, November 2014, https://www.thinkwithgoogle.com/campaigns/smart-communications-txtbks.html.

JCDecaux. 'Old Street EC1', September 2015, http://www.jcdecaux.co.uk/roadside/round-abouts/old-street-ec1.

Jeffries, Adrianne. 'It Will Take Google 22 Days to Find You', *Motherboard*, 2 March 2015, http://motherboard.vice.com/read/it-will-take-google-22-days-to-find-you.

Jobin, Anna. 'Google's autocompletion: algorithms, stereotypes and accountability', *Sociostrategy blog*, 22 October 2013, http://sociostrategy.com/2013/googles-autocompletion-algorithms-stereotypes-accountability/.

Jobson, Christopher. 'The Movement of Air: A New Dance Performance Incorporating Interactive Digital Projection from Adrien M & Claire B', 11 November 2015, *This is Colossal*, http://www.thisiscolossal.com/2015/11/movement-of-air-dance/.

Jobson, Christopher. 'The Rescued Film Project Discovers 31 Rolls of Undeveloped Film Shot by an Unknown WW2 Soldier', *This Is Colossal*, 18 January 2015, http://www.thisiscolossal.com/2015/01/31-rolls-of-ww2-film/.

Jones, Jonathan. 'Should art respond to science? On this evidence, the answer is simple: no way', *The Guardian*, 23 April 2015, http://www.theguardian.com/artanddesign/jonathanjonesblog/2015/apr/23/art-respond-science-cern-ryoji-ikeda-supersymmetry.

Jones, Matt. 'Sensor-Vernacular', *Berg London blog*, 13 May 2011, http://berglondon.com/blog/2011/05/13/sensor-vernacular/.

Juxtapoz. 'The Work of Jean-Pierre Hébert', *Juxtapoz*, May 22 2015, http://www.juxtapoz.com/current/the-work-of-jean-pierre-hebert.

Kant, Immanuel. *Kritik der Urteilskraft*, hrsg. von H.F. Klemme. Mit Sachanmerkungen von P. Giordanetti, Meiner, Hamburg, 2001 (2006).

Kant, Immanuel. *The Critique of Judgment*, trans. Pluhar, Werner, Indianapolis, IN: Hackett, 1987.

Kelion, Leo. 'Apple Maps flaw results in drivers crossing airport runway', *BBC News*, 25 September 2013, http://www.bbc.com/news/technology-24246646.

KentuckyFC, Emerging Technology from the arXiv. 'How to Burst the "Filter Bubble" that Protects Us from Opposing Views', *MIT Technology Review*, 29 November 2013, http://www.technologyreview.com/view/522111/how-to-burst-the-filter-bubble-that-protects-us-from-opposing-views/.

Kër Thiossane. *Villa pour l'art et le multimedia*, http://www.ker-thiossane.org/.

Khaikin, Lital. 'The Radical Capacity of Glitch Art: Expression through an Aesthetic Rooted in Error', *REDEFINE*, 5 February 2014, http://www.redefinemag.com/2014/glitch-art-expression-through-an-aesthetic-rooted-in-error/.

Kleeman Sophie. 'Here Are the Microsoft Twitter Bot's Craziest Racist Rants', *Gizmodo*, 24 March 2016, http://gizmodo.com/here-are-the-microsoft-twitter-bot-s-craziest-racist-ra-1766820160.

Kleinman, Adam. 'Hito Steyerl's "Adorno's Grey"', *art-agenda*, 21 November 2012, http://www.art-agenda.com/reviews/hito-steyerl's-"adorno's-grey"/.

Kohei Nawa, http://kohei-nawa.net/.

Kreines, James. 'The inexplicability of Kant's naturzweck: Kant on teleology, explanation and biology', *Archiv für Geschichte der Philosophie* 87:3, 2005.

Krotevich, Dmitriy. 'PixelDrifter', *Internet Archive*, 11 May 2014, https://archive.org/details/pixeldrifter.

Krotevich, Dmitriy. *Pixel-Drifter*, http://pixeldrifter.tumblr.com/.

Kurutepe, Eugene. 'Face Recognition with OpenCV', *objc.io*, February 2015, https://www.objc.io/issues/21-camera-and-photos/face-recognition-with-opencv/.

Lambirth, Andrew. 'Welcome home, Malcolm Morley', *The Spectator*, 26 October 2013, http://new.spectator.co.uk/2013/10/malcolm-morley-the-last-wild-man-of-modern-art/.

Landy, Michael. 'Home to destruction', *Tate Etc.*, Autumn 2009, http://www.tate.org.uk/context-comment/articles/homage-destruction.

Limer, Eric. 'A Typeface Designed To Thwart Spying Computers', *Gizmodo.com*, 22 June 2013, http://gizmodo.com/a-typeface-designed-to-thwart-sneaky-spying-computers-543341176.

Lofti, Shidan. 'The 'Purposiveness' of Life: Kant's Critique of Natural Teleology', *The Monist*, 93:1, January 2010.

Losh, Elizabeth. 'Beyond Biometrics: Feminist Media Theory Looks at Selfiecity', *Selfiecity*, 2014, http://d25rsf93iwlmgu.cloudfront.net/downloads/Liz_Losh_BeyondBiometrics.pdf.

Lou, Liza. http://lizalou.com/.

Louisgrand-Sylla, Marion. 'Interview: The story of Ker Thiossäne, Villa for Art and Multimedia', 2010, http://www.ker-thiossane.org/spip.php?article10.

Lupton, Ellen. 'The Designer as Producer,' *The Education of a Graphic Designer*, (ed.) Steven Heller, New York: Allworth Press, 1998, http://elupton.com/2010/10/the-designer-as-producer/.

Maigret, Nicolas. *The Pirate Cinema*, http://thepiratecinema.com.

Make a DifferenSe. 'What is Wikileaks? by founder Julian Assange', 11 December 2010, YouTube video, Duration: 14:58, https://youtu.be/DFE7d91vQf4.

Manjoo, Farhad. 'Vertical Video on the Small Screen? Not a Crime', *The New York Times*, 12 August 2015, http://www.nytimes.com/2015/08/13/technology/personaltech/vertical-video-on-the-small-screen-not-a-crime.html?_r=0.

Manovich, Lev. 'Interaction as an aesthetic event', *Receiver*, #17, 2006, http://dm.ncl.ac.uk/courseblog/files/2011/03/Manovich_InteractionAsAestheticEvent.pdf.

Manovich, Lev. *On Broadway*, 2016, http://on-broadway.nyc/.

Manovich, Lev. *Selfiecity*, 2014, http://selfiecity.net/.

Marks, Ben. 'Art in the Infographic Age', 22 August 2014, *Boing Boing*, http://boingboing.net/2014/08/22/art-in-the-infographic-age.html.

Mathis-Lilley, Ben. 'Hacked Confederate Facebook Group Becomes Tribute to LGBT Rights, Obama, Judaism', *Slate.com*, 29 July 2015, http://www.slate.com/blogs/the_slatest/2015/07/29/confederate_flag_pride_facebook_group_hijacked_michelle_obama_and_multi.html.

Mayr, Ernst. 'The Idea of Teleology', *Journal of the History of Ideas*, 53:1, 1992.

McAlone, Nathan. 'The 11 most beautiful apps of the year', *Business Insider*, 31 December 2015, http://www.businessinsider.com/most-beautiful-apps-2015-10.

McQuillian, J. Colin, "Baumgarten on Sensible Perfection" *Philosophica*, 44, Lisboa, 2014, p. 47-64.

Menkman, Rosa. *Glitch Studies Manifesto, Sunshine in My Throat*, 2009/2010, p. 8, 9, 11. http://rosa-menkman.blogspot.com/2010/02/glitch-studies-manifesto.html.

Metahaven (Velden, Daniël van der and Kruk, Vinca). *Black Transparency: The Right to Know in the Age of Mass Surveillance*, Berlin: Sternberg Press, 2015.

Metahaven and The Sprawl (Propaganda About Propaganda). 'THE SPRAWL (PROPAGANDA ABOUT PROPAGANDA) - Official Trailer'. Filmed [2015]. Youtube video, 2:58. Posted January 2016, https://youtu.be/Bs7NFbE2NS8.

Metahaven. http://www.metahaven.net/.

Metahaven. *Metahaven blog*, http://mthvn.tumblr.com/.

Moleskine. 'Afropixel: Using Evernote Notebooks To Spread Knowledge', 2014, http://www.moleskine.com/us/news/afropixel4.

Mondot, Adrien and Bardainne, Claire. *Adrien M / Claire B*, http://www.am-cb.net/.

Morgan, Tiernan and Purje, Lauren. 'An Illustrated Guide to Arthur Danto's "The End of Art"', *Hyperallergic*, 31 March 2015, http://hyperallergic.com/191329/an-illustrated-guide-to-arthur-dantos-the-end-of-art/.

Morinis, Leora. 'Hito Steyerl's HOW NOT TO BE SEEN: A F**king Didactic Educational .MOV File', *Inside/Out, A MoMA/MoMA PS1 Blog*, 18 June 2014, http://www.moma.org/explore/inside_out/2014/06/18/hito-steyerls-how-not-to-be-seen-a-fucking-didactic-educational-mov-file.

Mun, Sang. 'Making Democracy Legible: A Defiant Typeface', *Walker Art Center blog*, 20 June 2013, http://blogs.walkerart.org/design/2013/06/20/sang-mun-defiant-typeface-nsa-privacy/.

Munroe, Randall Patrick. 'Questions', *xkcd.com*, 26 August 2013, http://xkcd.com/1256/.

Murphy James E. 'Found', 2014, http://found.jemurphy.org/.

Murphy, James E. 'Relative Anonymity', 2012, http://jemurphy.org/#df.

Murphy, James E. 'The Politics of Creation', 2013, http://jemurphy.org/#poc.

Murphy, James E. http://jemurphy.org/.

Murray, Ben. 'Artist Q&A: James Bridle', *The Space*, 2015, http://www.thespace.org/news/view/james-bridle-interview.

Museum of Modern Art. 'Dead Drops', Museum of Modern Art Interactive Exhibitions, http://www.moma.org/interactives/exhibitions/2011/talktome/objects/146365/.

Nagy, Attila. 'Fantastic Software Glitch Art Is Better Than the Real World', *Gizmodo*, 10 October 2015, http://gizmodo.com/fantastic-software-glitch-art-is-better-than-the-real-w-1732141946.

Nash, Katherine and Williams, Richard H. 'Computer Program for Artists: ART I', *Leonardo*, Pergamon Press, The MIT Press, 1970.

Newcomb, Ted. 'The Fractal Future: Hybrid reality and the New Aesthetic', *All Things*

Connected blog, 27 June 2012, http://tcnewcomb.com/2012/06/27/the-fractal-future-hybrid-reality-and-the-new-aesthetic/.

Noll, A. Michael. 'Human or Machine: A Subjective Comparison of Piet Mondrian's 'Composition with Lines' and a Computer-Generated Picture,' *The Psychological Record*, Vol. 16. No. 1, January 1966, pp. 1-10.

Noll, A. Michael. http://noll.uscannenberg.org/.

Norges Bank. 'Motifs for the New Banknote Series' (Press Release), 7 October 2014, http://www.norges-bank.no/en/Published/Press-releases/2014/Press-release-7-october-2014/.

Nunes, Mark. (ed.) *Error Glitch, Noise, and Jam in New Media Cultures*, New York and London: Continuum, 2011.

O'Hagan, Sean. 'Exposed: photography's fabulous fakes. Phoney engagements, flying surrealists, faux Instagram celebrities, dubious family portraits ... a short history of performance photography', *The Guardian*, January 31 2016, http://www.theguardian.com/artanddesign/2016/jan/31/exposed-photographys-fabulous-fakes.

Openshaw, Jonathan. *Postdigital Artisans: Craftmanship with a New Aesthetic in Fashion, Art, Design and Architecture*, Amsterdam: Frame Publishers BV, 2015.

Pangburn, DJ. 'Here's What Artificially Intelligent Pixel Bending Looks Like ', *The Creators Project*, 28 July 2014, http://thecreatorsproject.vice.com/blog/heres-what-artificially-intelligent-pixel-bending-looks-like.

Parikka, Jussi. *What is Media Archaeology?*, Cambridge: Polity, 2012.

Pariser, Eli. *The Filter Bubble: How the New Personalized Web Is Changing What We Read and How We Think*, New York: Penguin Books, 2012.

Parker, DeWitt H. 'Introduction', *Schopenhauer Selections*, New York: Scribner, 1928.

Parkin, Simon. 'Desert Bus: The Very Worst Video Game Ever Created', *The New Yorker*, 9 July 2013, http://www.newyorker.com/tech/elements/desert-bus-the-very-worst-video-game-ever-created.

Perez, Sarah. 'iTunes App Store Now Has 1.2 Million Apps, Has Seen 75 Billion Downloads To Date', *TechCrunch*, 2 June, 2014, http://techcrunch.com/2014/06/02/itunes-app-store-now-has-1-2-million-apps-has-seen-75-billion-downloads-to-date/.

Plummer-Fernandez, M. http://www.plummerfernandez.com.

Polymaps, http://polymaps.org/.

Posner, Helaine. 'Liza Lou: Color Field and Solid Grey November 8, 2015 - February 21, 2016', *Neuberger Museum of Art*, https://www.neuberger.org/exhibitions/current/view1/314.html?width=660&height=500.

Poynor, Rick. 'Borderline: Metahaven makes visual proposals that suggest a new role for graphic design in public life', *Eye Magazine*, no. 71 vol. 18, 2009, http://www.eyemagazine.com/feature/article/borderline.

Prosthetic Knowledge blog, http://prostheticknowledge.tumblr.com/.

Quarfood, Marcel. 'Kant on biological teleology: Towards a two-level interpretation', *Studies in History and Philosophy of Biological and Biomedical Sciences*, vol 37, 2006.

Rawsthorn, Alice. 'A Quest for Meaning in a Dystopian Era', *The New York Times*, 16 May 2010, http://nyti.ms/1LyRL8W.

Reynolds, Diana Graham. *Alois Riegl and the Politics of Art History. Intellectual Traditions and Austrian Identity in Fin de Siècle Vienna*, San Diego: University of California, 1997.

Rhodes, Margaret. 'This Glitch Art Is Made of Pixels Powered by Their Own AI', *Wired.com*, 7 August 2014, http://www.wired.com/2014/08/this-glitch-art-is-made-of-pixels-powered-by-their-own-ai/.

Rhodes, Margaret. 'This Glitch Art Is Made Of Pixels Powered By Their Own AI', *Wired.com*, 7 August 2014, http://www.wired.com/2014/08/this-glitch-art-is-made-of-pixels-powered-by-their-own-ai.

Riegl, Alois. *Gesammelte Aufsätze*, Augsburg-Wien: Benno Filser Verlag, 1928.

Rock, Michael. 'The designer as author', *Eye Magazine*, 1996, http://www.eyemagazine.com/feature/article/the-designer-as-author.

Rogers Holly. '"Betwixt and Between" Worlds: Spatial and Temporal Liminality in Video Art-Music' in Richardson, John, et al. (eds), *The Oxford Handbook of New Audiovisual Aesthetics*, Oxford: Oxford University Press, 2013.

Rothenberg, Matthew. *emojitracker: realtime use on twitter*, http://www.emojitracker.com/.

Rothenberg, Matthew. *Matthew Rothenberg Selected Projects*, http://portfolio.mroth.info/.

Rothenberg, Matthew. *Swipe Left: Dating Apps and Drone Strikes*, 2014, https://medium.com/@mroth/swipe-left-dfa947df0355.

Rothstein, Adam. 'New Aesthetics - New Politics', *POSZU blog*, April 2012, http://www.poszu.com/new-aesthetics-new-politics.html.

Rust, Carsten and Buchen, Philip. 'Eingemauert in einer Fassade Bomben-Bauplan auf öffentlichem USB-Stick in der Kölner Südstadt', *Express*, 23 February, 2015, http://www.express.de/koeln/eingemauert-in-einer-fassade-bomben-bauplan-auf-oeffentlichem-usb-stick-in-der-koelner-suedstadt-2031168.

Sandwich: Creative Platform for Contemporary Art. http://sandwich-cpca.net/.

Save The Internet. https://www.savetheinternet.in/.

Sayej, Nadja. 'An Artist Has Made A Primitive Computer Out Of Earth Crystals, And Little Else' *the creators project*, April 2014, http://thecreatorsproject.vice.com/en_uk/blog/an-artist-has-made-a-primitive-computer-out-of-natural-crystals-and-little-else.

Sayej, Nadja. 'Full Screen Is A Group Show Dedicated To Digital Art You Can Wear On Your Wrist', *The Creators Project*, March 12, 2014, http://thecreatorsproject.vice.com/blog/full-screen-is-a-group-show-devoted-to-digital-art-you-can-wear-on-your-wrist.

Schopenhauer, Arthur. *The World as Will and Representation*, trans. E.F.J. Payne. Dover Publications, New York: 1966.

Scott, Damion. 'Functional Analysis and Schopenhauer's Theory of the Will' (*The World as Will and Representation*, Volume I, Sections 17-29), https://www.academia.edu/2576175/Functional_Analysis_and_Schopenhauers_Theory_of_the_Will.

Sierzputowski, Kate. 'The Attention-Sucking Power of Digital Technology Displayed Through

Photography by Antoine Geiger', *Colossal*, 11 November 2015, http://www.thisiscolossal.com/2015/11/cellphone-attention-antoine-geiger/?src=footer.

Silverberg, Michael. 'Google's Street View cameras are touring museums and taking weird selfies by accident', *Quartz*, 3 July 2014, http://qz.com/229852/googles-street-view-cameras-are-touring-museums-and-taking-weird-selfies-by-accident/.

Smith, David. 'NYC is a city that does sleep, a bit', *Revolutions*, 20 March 2015, http://blog.revolutionanalytics.com/2015/03/nyc-is-a-city-that-does-sleep-a-bit.html.

Smits, Helmut. 'Dead Pixel in Google Earth', *helmutsmits.com*, 2010, http://helmutsmits.nl/work/dead-pixel-in-google-earth-2.

Sokol, Zach. 'SelfieCity Might Be The Ultimate Data-Driven Exploration Of The Selfie', *The Creators Project*, 19 February 2014, http://thecreatorsproject.vice.com/blog/selfiecity-might-be-the-ultimate-data-driven-exploration-of-the-selfie.

Sooke, Alastair. 'Is this the first Instagram masterpiece?', *The Telegraph*, January 18th, 2016, http://www.telegraph.co.uk/photography/what-to-see/is-this-the-first-instagram-masterpiece/.

Sterling, Bruce. 'An Essay on the New Aesthetic. Beyond the beyond', *Wired*, April 2012, http://www.wired.com/beyond_the_beyond/2012/04/an-essay-on-the-new-aesthetic/

Steyerl, Hito. 'In Defense of the Poor Image', *e-flux*, November 2009, http://www.e-flux.com/journal/in-defense-of-the-poor-image/.

Steyerl, Hito. 'Zach Blas Future Great 2014', *ArtReview*, March 2014, http://artreview.com/features/2014_futuregreats_zach_blas/.

Stinson, Liz. 'Wonderfully Twisted Photos From a Glitch Art Guru', *Wired.com*, 10 September 2014, http://www.wired.com/2014/10/wonderfully-twisted-photos-glitch-art-guru/#slide-8.

Studio Laviani APFL. http://www.laviani.com/.

Sutherland, Evan E. 'Sketchpad: A Man-Machine Graphical Communication System', in Wardrip-Fruin, Noah and Montfort, Nick (eds). *The New Media Reader*, Cambridge/London: MIT Press, 2003.

SX Schedule 2012. 'The New Aesthetic: Seeing Like Digital Devices', http://schedule.sxsw.com/2012/events/event_IAP11102.

Tate Museums. 'Painting After Technology', March, 2015, http://www.tate.org.uk/whats-on/tate-modern/display/painting-after-technology.

Texas, Virgil. 'How I Infiltrated a White Pride Facebook Group and Turned It into 'LGBT

Southerners for Michelle Obama'', *Vice.com*, 3 August 2015, http://www.vice.com/read/virgil-texas-white-power-facebook-group-troll.

The Rescued Film Project, http://rescuedfilmproject.tumblr.com/.

The Space Commission, *The Sprawl,* October, 2014, http://www.lighthouse.org.uk/pro-gramme/the-space-commission-the-sprawl.

Thoma Foundation, 'There Are Spirals Everywhere,' Says Computer Artist Jean-Pierre Hébert', (Press release), July 25 2015, http://thomafoundation.org/there-are-spirals-everywhere-says-computer-artist-jean-pierre-hebert/.

Thompson, Nicholas. 'The Misappropriation of Teleonomy', in *Perspectives in Ethology,* Bateson, P. Bateosn and P. Klopfer (eds) *Volume 7: Alternatives,* Springer-Verlag, 1987.

Tifentale, Alise .'The Selfie: Making sense of the "Masturbation of Self-Image" and the "Virtual Mini-Me"', *Selfiecity,* 2014, http://d25rsf93iwlmgu.cloudfront.net/downloads/Tifentale_Alise_Selfiecity.pdf.

Tifentale, Alise and Manovich, Lev. 'Selfiecity: Exploring Photography and Self-Fashioning in Social Media' in Berry, David M. and Dieter, Michael (eds) *Postdigital Aesthetics: Art, Computation and Design,* New York: Palgrave MacMillan, 2015.

TNN. 'Students, techies protest Facebook's Free Basics', *The Times of India,* 3 Janu-ary 2016, http://timesofindia.indiatimes.com/city/bengaluru/Students-techies-protest-Facebooks-Free-Basics/articleshow/50424303.cms?utm_source=twitter.com&utm_medium=referral&utm_campaign=TOIBangalore.

Tokumitsu, Miya. 'The Politics of the Curation Craze', *New Republic,* 24 August 2015, http://www.newrepublic.com/article/122589/when-did-we-all-become-curators.

Tom Whalen Illustrations-Design. *Strong Stuff,* http://www.strongstuff.net/about-flatiron/.

Tremblin, Matthieu. Demo De Tous Les Jours, http://demodetouslesjours.free.fr/.

Turner Luke. 'The New Aesthetic's Speculative Promise', *Notes on Metamodernism,* 2 July 2012, http://www.metamodernism.com/2012/07/02/the-new-aesthetics-speculative-promise/.

UN Women, 'UN Women ad series reveals widespread sexism ', 21 October 2013, http://www.unwomen.org/en/news/stories/2013/10/women-should-ads.

Urban FabLab. 'African Fabbers Project', http://www.urbanfablab.it/african-fabber/23-non-categorizzato/projects/53-african-fabbers.html.

Urquhart, Robert. 'An Interview With James Bridle of the New Aesthetic', *The Huffington Post*, 9 May 2012, http://www.huffingtonpost.co.uk/robert-urquhart/james-bridle-the-new-aesthetic_b_1498958.html.

V2_Institute for the Unstable Media. 'Sandbox', http://v2.nl/archive/works/sandbox.

V2_Institute for the Unstable Media. http://v2.nl/.

Valla, Clement. 'The Universal Texture', *Clement Valla*, http://clementvalla.com/work/the-universal-texture-recreated-46423-50n-1202628-59w/.

van den Bommen, Marianne. *Transcoding the Digital: How Metaphors Matter in New Media*, Amsterdam: Institute of Network Cultures, 2014.

Vanhemert, Kyle. 'App Turns Your iPhone Into a Crappy Disposable Camera (And That's a Good Thing)', *Wired.com*, 1 January 2015, http://www.wired.com/2015/01/app-turns-iphone-crappy-disposable-camera-thats-good-thing/.

Vanhemert, Kyle. 'This Is What a Computer Sees When It Watches The Matrix', *Wired.com*, January 2014, http://www.wired.com/2014/01/computer-sees-watches-matrix/.

Vavarella, Emilio. Report a Problem, http://emiliovavarella.com/archive/google-trilogy/report-a-problem/.

Victoria & Albert Museum. 'A History of Computer Art', http://www.vam.ac.uk/content/articles/a/computer-art-history/.

Visconti, Sabato. http://www.sabatobox.com/.

Waelder, Pau. 'Interview with Ralf Baecker', *Telefonica Fundación*, 16 April 2013, https://vida.fundaciontelefonica.com/en/2013/04/16/interview-with-ralf-baecker/.

Wardrip-Fruin, Noah and Montfort, Nick (eds) *The New Media Reader*, Cmbridge/London: MIT Press, 2003.

Weber, Harrison. 'The 15 most beautifully designed apps of 2015', *VentureBeat*, 24 December 2015, http://venturebeat.com/2015/12/24/the-15-most-beautifully-designed-apps-of-2015/.

Westera, Wim. *The Digital Turn: How the Internet Transforms Our Existence*, Bloomington, Indiana: Authorhouse, 2013.

What colour is it?, http://whatcolourisit.scn9a.org/.

WhiteAlbum, https://whitealbumapp.com/.

Wiesenberger, Robert. 'METAHAVEN: Somewhere Near You, Soon', *032c*, Summer, 2014, http://032c.com/2014/metahaven-somewhere-near-you-soon/.

Wikipedia contributors. 'Dazzle camouflage', 23 Feb. 2016, https://en.wikipedia.org/wiki/Dazzle_camouflage, accessed 28 Feb. 2016

Wikipedia contributors. 'Frieder Nake', 26 Feb. 2016, https://en.wikipedia.org/w/index.php?title=Frieder_Nake&oldid=688732078, accessed 23 Mar. 2016.

Wikipedia contributors. 'Multiplan', 18 Sep. 2015, https://en.wikipedia.org/wiki/Multiplan, accessed 23 March 2016.

Wikipedia contributors. 'The School of Athens', 23 February 2016, https://en.wikipedia.org/wiki/The_School_of_Athens, accessed 23 March 2016.

Wiles W. 'The Machine Gaze', *Aeon Magazine*, 17 September 2012, http://aeon.co/magazine/world-views/will-wiles-technology-new-aesthetic/.

Wiles, Will. 'The machine haze', *Aeon*, 17 September 2012, https://aeon.co/essays/what-do-we-uncover-when-we-look-through-digital-eyes.

Worley, Steven. 'My God, It's Full Of Blocks: Population Density Meets The Tile Space', *Data Pointed*, 3 October, 2011, http://www.datapointed.net/2011/10/us-population-density-and-google-maps-tiles/.

Zilber, Emily. *Crafted: Objects in Flux*, Boston: Museum of Fine Arts, 2015.

Žižek, Slavoj. *Welcome to the Desert of the Real!: Five Essays on September 11 and Related Dates*, New York: Verso, 2002.

ZKM Exhibitions. 'Georg Nees – The Great Temptation Early generative computer graphics', August, 2006, *ZKM*, http://on1.zkm.de/zkm/stories/storyReader$5255.

BIOGRAPHIES

Scott Contreras-Koterbay is a professor of contemporary art history and aesthetics at East Tennessee State University in the United States, with a research emphasis on aesthetic ontology and reception theory.

Łukasz Mirocha is Research Project Director in the Faculty of 'Artes Liberales' at the University of Warsaw, Poland, with a research emphasis on digital media studies and software studies. He is also a researcher at the Digital Economy Lab at the University of Warsaw. Beyond the academia, he works as a journalist and consultant covering digital technologies, innovation and emerging trends.

www.ingramcontent.com/pod-product-compliance
Lightning Source LLC
Chambersburg PA
CBHW052309220526
45472CB00001B/41